TEACHER'S GUIDE

GRADE 6

READING AND WRITING Sourcebook

Authors

Robert Pavlik

Richard G. Ramsey

D1567273

Great Source Education Group

a Houghton Mifflin Company
Wilmington, Massachusetts
www.greatsource.com

Authors

Dr. Richard G. Ramsey is currently a national educational consultant for many schools throughout the country and serves as president of Ramsey's Communications. He has been a teacher and a principal for grades 1–12 for 23 years. Dr. Ramsey has also served on the Curriculum Frameworks Committee for the State of Florida. A lifelong teacher and educator and former principal, he is now a nationally known speaker on improving student achievement and motivating students.

Dr. Robert Pavlik taught high school English and reading for seven years. His university assignments in Colorado and Wisconsin have included teaching secondary/content area reading, chairing a reading/language arts department, and directing a reading/learning center. He is an author of several books and articles and serves as director of the School Design and Development Center at Marquette University.

CONSULTANT **Catherine McNary** of Proviso West High School in Illinois is a reading specialist who works with teachers of struggling readers. She has been an invaluable consultant during the development of the *Sourcebook* series. She is currently pursuing a doctorate in reading.

Printed in the United States of America.

International Standard Book Number: 0-669-47633-1

9 10 11 12 13 14 15   1421   14 13 12 11 10
4500232641

Readers and Reviewers

Marsha Besch
Literacy/Secondary Curr. Coordinator ISD #196
Rosemount, Minnesota

Tim McGee
Worland High School
Worland, Wyoming

Mary Grace
Marshall Middle School
Janesville, Wisconsin

Shelly L. Fabozzi
Holmes Middle School
Colorado Springs, Colorado

Jim Burke
Burlingame High School
San Francisco, California

Phyllis Y. Keiley-Tyler
Education Consultant
Seattle, Washington

Jenny Sroka
Learning Enterprise High School
Milwaukee, Wisconsin

Glenda Swirtz
Flint Southwestern Academy
Flint, Michigan

Jeff Wallack
Learning Enterprise High School
Milwaukee, Wisconsin

Jay Amberg
Glenbrook South High School
Glenview, Illinois

Sherry Nielsen
Curriculum and Instruction
Saint Cloud, Minnesota

Deborah Schroeder
Harlan Community Academy
Chicago, Illinois

Richard Stear
Central Office
Rochester, New York

Hilary Zunin
Napa High School
Napa, California

William Weber
Libertyville High School
Libertyville, Illinois

Beverly Washington
Fenger High School
Chicago, Illinois

Lyla Fox
Loy Norrix High School
Kalamazoo, Michigan

Eileen Davis
Banneker Academic High School
Washington, D.C.

Christine Heerlein
Rockwood Summit High School
Fenton, Missouri

Barbara Ellen Pitts
Detroit, Michigan

Kimberly Edgeworth
Palm Beach Lakes High School
West Palm Beach, Florida

Jeffrey Hicks
Whitford Middle School
Beaverton, Oregon

Mark Tavernier
Norfolk, Virginia

Gina La Manna
Southeast Raleigh High School
Raleigh, North Carolina

Jennifer Sharpe-Salter
Southern Nash Sr. High School
Bailey, North Carolina

Elizabeth Dyhouse
Longfellow Middle School
Flint, Michigan

Rose Chatman
Dayton Public Schools
Dayton, Ohio

Gereldine Conaway
Mumford High School
Detroit, Michigan

Barb Evans
Lorain City Schools
Lorain, Ohio

Deborah Gonzalez
Puget Sound Education School District
Burien, Washington

Rosita Graham
Winter Halter Elementary School
Detroit, Michigan

Elaine Hanson
Mounds View School District
Saint Paul, Minnesota

Barbara Heget
Milwaukee, Wisconsin

Patrick Horigan
Milwaukee, Wisconsin

Rose Hunter
Whittier Middle School
Flint, Michigan

Ray Kress
Wilson Middle School
Newark, Ohio

Evelyn McDuffie
Beaubien Middle School
Detroit, Michigan

Robin Milanovich
Jefferson High School
Edgewater, Colorado

Dr. Howard Moon
Kenosha School District
Kenosha, Wisconsin

Jeanette Nassif
Central High School
Flint, Michigan

Dr. Joe Papenfuss
Racine Unified School District
Racine, Wisconsin

Lori Pfeiffer
West Bend School District
West Bend, Wisconsin

Evelyn Price
Milwaukee, Wisconsin

Karen Rano
Educational Consultant
River Forest, Illinois

Karen Ray
Darwin Elementary School
Chicago, Illinois

Renetha Rumph
Flint Southwestern High School
Flint, Michigan

Sarike Simpson
Racine, Wisconsin

Branka Skukan
Chopin School
Chicago, Illinois

Stephanie Thurick
Minneapolis Public Schools
Minneapolis, Minnesota

Gloria Tibbets
Curriculum Institute
Flint, Michigan

Anita Wellman
Northwestern High School
Detroit, Michigan

Barb Whaley
Akron City Schools
Akron, Ohio

Ray Wolpow
Western Washington University
Bellingham, Washington

Robin Gleason
Wilson Elementary School
Wauwatosa, Wisconsin

Kay Briske
Janesville School District
Janesville, Wisconsin

Table of Contents

Table of Contents

Lesson Resources

PUPIL'S EDITION SKILLS AND STRATEGIES

The chart below identifies the strategies for each part of each pupil's edition lesson.

Selection	I. Prereading	II. Response Notes	Comprehension
1. Father (autobiography)	quickwrite	visualize	retell
2. Mother (autobiography)	preview	react and connect	directed reading
3. The Great Whales (nonfiction)	K-W-L Chart	mark or highlight	reciprocal reading
4. Killer Whales (nonfiction)	skim	clarify	graphic organizer
5. Joshua (fiction)	think-pair-and-share	question	story frame
6. The Man (fiction)	story impression	mark or highlight	predict
7. What Happened During the Ice Storm (story)	picture walk	predict	double-entry journal
8. Cheating (fiction)	anticipation guide	react and connect	story frame
9. Egyptian Mummies (nonfiction)	preview	clarify	directed reading
10. Mummies (nonfiction)	K-W-L	question	graphic organizer
11. Summer Berries (fiction)	word web	visualize	graphic organizer
12. Summer Berries (continued)	anticipation guide	predict	directed reading
13. A Better Life (biography)	skim	highlight or mark	directed reading
14. Jackie Robinson's First Game (nonfiction)	walk-through	react and connect	graphic organizer
15. The Strangers Arrive (nonfiction)	picture walk	clarify	reciprocal reading
16. The Great Mocxtezuma (nonfiction)	think-pair-share	question	directed reading
17. I am Miguel (fiction)	quickwrite	visualize	story frame
18. Sangre de Cristo Mountains (nonfiction)	anticipation guide	predict	reciprocal reading
19. Bradley Chalkers (fiction)	word web	react and connect	retell
20. Sam Gribley (fiction)	skim	question	graphic organizer
21. Buffalo Hunt (autobiography)	K-W-L	mark or highlight	directed reading
22. The Sunflower Room (fiction)	picture walk	clarify	reciprocal reading
23. Milo (fiction)	web	predict	double-entry journal
24. Milo (continued)	anticipation guide	react and connect	predict

III. Prewriting	IV. Writing	Grammar/Usage	V. Assessment
narrow a topic	paragraph	sentence	understanding
main idea and details	descriptive paragraph	sentence fragments	meaning
topic sentence	expository paragraph	adjectives/adverbs	ease
supporting a main idea	summary	run-on sentences	enjoyment
web	character sketch	commas	depth
quickwrite	letter	letter-writing form	style
brainstorming	double-entry journal	capitalization	meaning
sequencing	story ending	dialogue	enjoyment
web	descriptive paragraph	verb pairs	understanding
using a graphic organizer	compare and contrast paragraph	subject-verb agreement	ease
organize a paragraph	personal experience paragraph	possessives	style
forming an opinion	review	commas	depth
graphic organizer	speech	capitalization	understanding
character map	biographical paragraph	capitalization	meaning
research	expository paragraph	confusing words	ease
sequence of events	summary	commas	depth
storyboard	narrative paragraph	commas	style
brainstorm	autobiographical paragraph	usage of *two, to, too, affect, effect*	depth
support an opinion	persuasive paragraph	contractions	meaning
using sensory language	descriptive paragraph	usage of *good, well, bad, badly*	understanding
storyboard	personal narrative	comma splices	depth
narrow the topic	reflective paragraph	subject/verb agreement	meaning
forming an opinion	paragraph of opinion	adjectives	enjoyment
supporting an opinion	letter	end punctuation	ease

TEACHER'S GUIDE SKILLS AND STRATEGIES

The chart below identifies the strategies for each part of each teacher's edition lesson.

Selection	Vocabulary	Prereading	Comprehension
1. Father (autobiography)	a) context clues b) prefixes	quickwrite	retell
2. Mother (autobiography)	synonyms	a) preview b) picture walk	directed reading
3. The Great Whales (nonfiction)	word families	a) K-W-L b) quickwrite	a) reciprocal reading b) graphic organizer
4. Killer Whales (nonfiction)	a) context clues b) word analysis	a) skim b) preview	graphic organizers
5. Joshua (fiction)	idioms	think-pair-and-share	a) story frames b) directed reading
6. The Man (fiction)	a) context clues b) homographs	a) story impression b) word web	a) predict b) story frame
7. What Happened During the Ice Storm (story)	a) context clues b) pronunciation	a) picture-walk b) quickwrite	double-entry journal
8. Cheating (fiction)	a) synonyms b) antonyms	anticipation guide	a) story frames b) directed reading
9. Egyptian Mummies (nonfiction)	a) context clues b) irregular verbs	a) preview b) picture walk	directed reading
10. Mummies (nonfiction)	root words	a) K-W-L b) skim	graphic organizers
11. Summer Berries (fiction)	suffixes	word webs	a) graphic organizers b) predict
12. Summer Berries (continued)	compound words and word analysis	anticipation guide	directed reading
13. A Better Life (biography)	idioms	skimming	directed reading
14. Jackie Robinson's First Game (nonfiction)	a) context clues b) Latin roots	a) walk-through b) word web	a) graphic organizers b) reciprocal reading
15. The Strangers Arrive (nonfiction)	a) synonyms b) word analysis	picture walk preview	reciprocal reading
16. The Great Moctezuma (nonfiction)	a) context clues b) pronunciation	a) think-pair-and-share b) read-aloud	directed reading
17. I Am Miguel (fiction)	a) context clues b) heteronyms	quickwrite	a) story frames b) retelling
18. Sangre de Cristo Mountains (fiction)	Mexican Spanish	a) anticipation guide b) picture walk	a) reciprocal reading b) story frame
19. Bradley Chalkers (fiction)	a) context clues b) word families	webs	retell
20. Sam Gribley (fiction)	context clues	skimming	a) graphic organizers b) reciprocal reading
21. Buffalo Hunt (autobiography)	homophones	a) K-W-L b) skim	directed reading
22. The Sunflower Room (fiction)	suffixes	a) picture walk b) read-aloud	reciprocal reading
23. Milo (fiction) comprehension	a) context clues b) negative prefixes	word web	double-entry journal
24. Milo (continued)	prefixes	a) anticipation guide b) think-pair-and-share	predict

Questions	Literary Skill	Prewriting	Assessment
a) comprehension b) critical thinking	sensory language	topic sentence	multiple-choice test
a) comprehension b) critical thinking	tone	a) main idea b) supporting details	multiple-choice test
a) comprehension b) critical thinking	main idea	a) brainstorm b) topic sentence	multiple-choice test
a) comprehension b) critical thinking	details	main idea and details	multiple-choice test
a) comprehension b) critical thinking	inferences	web	multiple-choice test
a) comprehension b) critical thinking	point of view	a) quickwrite b) narrowing a topic	multiple-choice test
a) comprehension b) critical thinking	simile	a) brainstorm topics b) word bank	multiple-choice test
a) comprehension b) critical thinking	plot	a) storyboard b) brainstorming	multiple-choice test
a) comprehension b) critical thinking	nonfiction	word bank	multiple-choice test
a) comprehension b) critical thinking	anecdote	Venn diagram	multiple-choice test
a) comprehension b) critical thinking	characterization	organize a paragraph	multiple-choice test
a) comprehension b) critical thinking	setting	opinion statement	multiple-choice test
a) comprehension b) critical thinking	chronological order	main idea	multiple-choice test
a) comprehension b) critical thinking	inferences	a) character map b) details	multiple-choice test
a) comprehension b) critical thinking	simile	graphic organizer	multiple-choice test
a) comprehension b) critical thinking	mood	main idea and supporting details	multiple-choice test
a) comprehension b) critical thinking	narrator	a) topic sentence b) word bank	multiple-choice test
a) comprehension b) critical thinking	style	a) brainstorm b) narrow the focus	multiple-choice test
a) comprehension b) critical thinking	theme	opinion statement	multiple-choice test
a) comprehension b) critical thinking	sensory language	brainstorm	multiple-choice test
a) comprehension b) critical thinking	climax	a) graphic organizers b) topic sentence	multiple-choice test
a) comprehension b) critical thinking	flashback	narrow the focus	multiple-choice test
a) comprehension b) critical thinking	foreshadowing	web	multiple-choice test
a) comprehension b) critical thinking	style	opinion statement and support	multiple-choice test

CORRELATION TO *WRITE SOURCE 2000*

Like the *Write Source 2000* and *All Write* handbooks, the *Sourcebook* will appeal to teachers who believe that writing is a way of learning or a means of discovery and exploration. Students pursue ideas and interpretations in the *Sourcebook*. They jot notes, create organizers, plan and brainstorm compositions, and write drafts of their work. The *Sourcebook* is one way students clarify in their minds what they have read and how they respond to it. And, in the end, students learn how to write different kinds of compositions—a paragraph, a description, a letter, a character sketch, a persuasive paragraph, or a review.

In the *Sourcebook*, both the kinds of writing and the mini-lessons on grammar, usage, and mechanics afford the best opportunities to use the *Write Source 2000* and *All Write* handbooks as a reference. To make this convenient, both the writing activities and the mini-lessons are correlated below to these two handbooks.

Selection Title	Writing Activity/ Write Source 2000 (pages)	Writers' Mini-Lesson/ Write Source 2000 (pages)
1. "Father"	paragraph 98–105	capitalizing sentences and end punctuation 387.1, 388.3, 398.1, 400.1, 405.1
2. "Mother"	descriptive paragraph 100	sentence fragments 86
3. "The Great Whales"	expository paragraph 102	adjectives/adverbs 393.3, 451.5–453.6, 454.1
4. "Killer Whales"	summary 143, 213–216	run-on sentences 87
5. "Joshua"	character sketch 123	commas 389.1–392.2
6. "The Man"	letter 149–152, 241–250	capitalization in letters 149, 242
7. "What Happened During the Ice Storm"	journal entry 48, 145–148	capitalization 404.1–407.3
8. "Cheating"	story ending 188	dialogue 190–191, 343
9. "Egyptian Mummies"	descriptive paragraph 100	usage of *bring, take leave, let* 422.3, 427.3
10. "Mummies"	compare and contrast paragraph 112–113, 312–313	subject-verb agreement 88–89
11. "Summer Berries"	personal experience paragraph 153–159	possessives 403.1–4
12. "Summer Berries" continued	review 175–181	commas 389.1–393.2
13. "A Better Life"	speech 348–351, 354	capitalization 404.1–407.3
14. "Jackie Robinson's First Game"	biographical paragraph 161–166	capitalization 404.1–407.3
15. "The Strangers Arrive"	expository paragraph 102	Usage of *it's, its their, there, they're* 426.5, 431.7
16. "The Great Moctezuma"	summary 143, 213–216	commas 389.1–393.2
17. "I Am Miguel"	narrative paragraph 101	commas 389.1–393.2
18. "Sangre de Cristo Mountains"	autobiographical paragraph 153–159	usage of *to, too, two affect, effect* 431.9, 419.3
19. "Bradley Chalkers"	persuasive paragraph 103	contractions 402.1
20. "Sam Gribley"	descriptive paragraph 100	usage of *good, well* 425.2
21. "Buffalo Hunt"	personal narrative 154	comma splices 86, 391.1
22. "The Sunflower Room"	reflective paragraph 99–101	subject-verb agreement 88–89
23. "Milo"	paragraph of opinion 121–122	adjectives 451.4–453.6
24. "Milo" continued	letter 149–152, 241–250	end punctuation 387.1, 388.3, 398.1, 400.1

CORRELATION TO *ALL WRITE*

Selection Title	Writing Activity/ All Write Reference (pages)	Writers' Mini-Lesson/ All Write Reference (pages)
1. "Father"	paragraph 59–61, 66–70	capitalizing sentences and end punctuation 311–312, 328–332
2. "Mother"	descriptive paragraph 62	sentence fragments 50
3. "The Great Whales"	expository paragraph 64	adjectives/adverbs 393–395, 396–397
4. "Killer Whales"	summary 104, 179–182	run-on sentences 50
5. "Joshua"	character sketch 132–134	commas 313–318
6. "The Man"	letter 119–123, 143–148	capitalization in letters 143–148, 328–332
7. "What Happened During the Ice Storm"	journal entry 107–110	capitalization 328–332
8. "Cheating"	story ending 35, 170–173	dialogue 24, 109, 110, 116, 274
9. "Egyptian Mummies"	descriptive paragraph 62	Usage of *bring, take leave, let* 347, 353
10. "Mummies"	compare and contrast paragraph 71–85, 236–237, 302	subject-verb agreement 51–52
11. "Summer Berries"	personal experience paragraph 103, 111–118	possessives 325, 326, 378, 381
12. "Summer Berries" continued	review 40–42, 131–136	commas 313–318
13. "A Better Life"	speech 289–296	capitalization 328–332
14. "Jackie Robinson's First Game"	biographical paragraph 125–130, 272	capitalization 328–332
15. "The Strangers Arrive"	expository paragraph 64	usage of *it's, its their, there, they're* 358
16. "The Great Moctezuma"	summary 104, 179–182	commas 313–318
17. "I Am Miguel"	narrative paragraph 63	commas 313–318
18. "Sangre de Cristo Mountains"	autobiographical paragraph 111–118, 125–130, 272	usage of *affect, effect to, too, two* 359
19. "Bradley Chalkers"	persuasive paragraph 65	contractions 325
20. "Sam Gribley"	descriptive paragraph 62	usage of *good, well* 350
21. "Buffalo Hunt"	personal narrative 103, 111–118	comma splices 50, 316
22. "The Sunflower Room"	reflective paragraph 59–70, 80–85	subject-verb agreement 51–52
23. "Milo"	paragraph of opinion 76–79, 223–225	adjectives 393–395
24. "Milo" continued	letter 119–123, 143–148	end punctuation 311–312

OVERVIEW

The *Sourcebook* is directed to struggling readers. These students seldom receive adequate help, partly because they need so much. They need to be motivated. They need quality literature that they can actually read. They need good instruction in strategies that will help them learn how to transform a mass of words and lines into a comprehensible text. They need help with getting ready to write; with grammar, usage, and mechanics; and with writing different kinds of texts themselves—letters, journal entries, summaries, and so forth.

A Comprehensive Approach

Because of the multitude and enormity of their needs, struggling readers all too often are subjected to a barrage of different remedies. It is all too easy simply to say "This doesn't work" and turn to yet another text or strategy. The *Sourcebook* takes a holistic approach, not a piecemeal one. Through a five-part lesson plan, each *Sourcebook* lesson walks the student through the steps needed to read actively and to write well about literature.

The five-part lesson plan is:

I. **BEFORE YOU READ** (prereading)

II. **READ** (active reading and responding to literature)

III. **GATHER YOUR THOUGHTS** (prewriting)

IV. **WRITE** (writing, revising, grammar, usage, and mechanics)

V. **WRAP-UP** (reflecting and self-assessment)

Through a comprehensive, structured approach, students can see the whole process of reading and writing. By following a consistent pattern, students can internalize the steps in the process, and they can move forward and experience success along the way, on a number of different fronts at once. See also the book and lesson organization on pages 18–22.

A Strategy-intensive Approach

The *Sourcebook* also is a strategy-intensive approach. Each *Sourcebook* builds students' repertoire of reading strategies in at least three areas.

1. To build motivation and background, prereading strategies are used to get students ready to read and to help them see the prior knowledge they already bring to their reading experiences.

2. To build active readers, each *Sourcebook* begins with an overview of interactive reading strategies (called response strategies), explicitly showing students six ways to mark up texts. Then, at least one of these strategies is used in each lesson.

3. To build comprehension, each *Sourcebook* uses six to nine different comprehension strategies, such as prediction, reciprocal reading, retelling, and using graphic organizers. By embedding these strategies in the literature, the *Sourcebook* shows students exactly which strategies to use and when to use them, building the habits of good readers.

A Literature-based Approach

Above all, the *Sourcebook* takes a literature-based approach. It presents 24 selections of quality literature of various genres by a wide range of authors. Some selections focus on literature; others are cross-curricular in emphasis, taking up a subject from history or geography; and others focus on issues of importance and relevance to today's students.

An Interactive Approach

The *Sourcebook* is, in addition, an interactive tool. It is intended to be a journal for students, where they can write out their ideas about texts, plan and write out compositions, and record their progress throughout the year. Students should "own" their *Sourcebooks*, carrying them, reading in them, marking in them, and writing in them. They should become a record of their progress and accomplishments.

Lesson Planning

A *Sourcebook* lesson can be taught in approximately 10 class periods, whether that is over two, three, or even four weeks.

DAY 1 Build background and discuss unit theme. Introduce selection.

DAY 2 Read introduction. Start prereading activity.

DAY 3 Continue prereading activity. Discuss activity.

DAY 4 Introduce selection. Discuss response strategy and example. Read.

DAY 5 Finish reading and do comprehension activities in selection.

DAY 6 Start prewriting activities.

DAY 7 Continue with prewriting activities.

DAY 8 Begin writing activity.

DAY 9 Talk about mini-lesson and revise writing.

DAY 10 Reflect on selection and what was learned.

Assessment

The *Sourcebook* includes a multiple-choice test for assessment, as well as a more holistic self-assessment in the pupil's book in Part V. Either of these are useful gauges of student progress. Teachers would, of course, like to demonstrate the progress their students have made—the number of grade levels students have progressed throughout the year. In point of fact, that progress is enormously difficult to demonstrate with any degree of reliability. The best measure of student progress will most likely be a student's marked-up *Sourcebook* and the greater confidence and fluency with which students will be reading by the end of the year.

On a day-to-day basis when teaching each lesson, teachers and students should use the Readers' Checklist for assessment. Asking a different combination of 2–3 questions from the Readers' Checklist will help students become increasingly clear about why and how they are reading.

UNDERSTANDING Did you understand the reading?

Was the message or point clear?

Can you restate what the reading is about?

On a monthly basis, one of the best measures of student progress will be a student's marked-up *Sourcebook*. Teacher-student conferences can use the following questions to reflect on the quality of a student's written responses among lessons:

a. In what ways has the content of your written responses improved?
   (e.g., accuracy, clarity, amount of comprehension)

b. In what ways has the structure of your written responses improved?
   (e.g., organization, coherence, neatness, spelling, punctuation)

c. In what ways is your reading improving?

d. What new reading habits are you finding useful? Why?

WHO IS THIS BOOK FOR?

Struggling Learners

Frequently, high schools have classes specifically designed for students who consistently rank in the lower 50 percent of the class. Instead of the usual focus on literary masterworks, these classes focus on improving reading and writing skills and often are labeled with anonymous-sounding names such as English I, Applied Communication, or Fundamentals of Reading and Writing. The *Sourcebook* was designed with such courses in mind. It offers a comprehensive program of student-appropriate literature, strategy building, writing, and revising. Quite often teachers in these classes pull an exercise from one text on the shelf, a reading from another, and a blackline master activity from still another. The materials are a patchwork, with the teachers making the best of the meager offerings available.

Each *Sourcebook* has a comprehensive network of skills (see pages 6–9) that brings together the appropriate literature, reading strategies for that literature, and prewriting, writing, and revising activities. Students who work through even two or three entire selections will benefit greatly by seeing the whole picture of reading actively and writing about the text. They will also benefit from the sense of accomplishment that comes through completion of a whole task and that results in creative, original work of their own—perhaps some of the first they have accomplished.

Reading Classes

Students who clearly are reading two or more levels below grade often are put into "special reading" courses. Quite often these classes feature a great number of blackline masters on discrete skills, such as "main idea and details," "analogies," and the like. Such classes are ideal for the *Sourcebook*. Instead of covering one discrete skill, each *Sourcebook* selection offers students reading strategies that they can use on any text, and it offers them high-quality literature. All too often students in reading classes are given "high-interest" materials. The materials have regulated vocabulary and short sentences and are on topics that range from natural disasters to biographies of rock divas. The *Sourcebook* focuses on high-quality literature that is also high interest because it addresses questions and issues of significance to students.

With the *Sourcebook*, a better choice exists. The literature was chosen specifically with struggling readers in mind. It offers compelling subjects, such as the Holocaust and prejudice, and offers a worthy challenge for students.

ESL Classes

Students for whom English is a second language can also benefit from the *Sourcebook*, even though the *Sourcebook* is not an ESL program. The literature selections in the *Sourcebook* vary in difficulty level. The level for each selection is given on the first page of the *Teacher's Guide* lesson. But the subjects of the literature—immigrants, being an outsider, understanding different cultures—are ones that will naturally appeal to ESL students.

In addition, summaries of each selection appear in Spanish in the *Teacher's Guide*, along with additional help with vocabulary and comprehension. So, while not explicitly for ESL students, the program offers good support for them and may be more appropriate than some of the other materials they are currently using.

Alternative Settings

Many school systems also have whole schools or classes that are called "alternative" for students who, for a variety of reasons, are not mainstreamed. The *Sourcebook* is appropriate for these students as well, if only because of its literature selections, which focus on themes of identity, prejudice, and separateness about which many alternative students will have a natural interest.

Summary

The *Sourcebook* cannot reach every struggling student. It is not a panacea. It will be helpful with struggling readers, especially those who are reading a grade level or two below their academic grade. The challenges struggling readers face, especially those reading more than two grades below their academic grade level, ought not to be underestimated or minimized. Reading and writing deficits are hard, almost intractable problems for high school students and require a great amount of effort—on the part of the teacher and the student—to make any real improvement. The *Sourcebook* is one further tool in helping create better readers and writers.

FREQUENTLY ASKED QUESTIONS

Because the *Sourcebooks* were extensively reviewed by teachers, a number of commonly asked questions have surfaced already, and the answers to them might be helpful in using the program.

1. Why is it called a *Sourcebook*?

The word *Sourcebook* captures a number of connotations and associations that seemed just right. For one, it is published by Great Source Education Group. The word *source* also had the right connotation of "the place to go for a real, complete solution," as opposed to other products that help in only a limited area, such as "main idea" or "analogies." And, lastly, the term *Sourcebook* fits nicely alongside *Daybook*, another series also published by Great Source that targets better readers and writers who need help in fluency and critical reading, as opposed to this series, which targets struggling readers.

2. Can students write in the *Sourcebook*?

Absolutely. Only by physically marking the text will students become truly active readers. To interact with a text and truly read as an active reader, students *must* write in the *Sourcebook*. The immediacy of reading and responding right there on the page is integral to the whole idea of the *Sourcebook*. By writing in the text, students build a sense of ownership about their work that is impossible to match through worksheets handed out week after week. The *Sourcebook* also serves, in a sense, as the student's portfolio and can become one of the most tangible ways of demonstrating a student's progress throughout the year.

3. Can I photocopy these lessons?

No, you cannot. Each page of the pupil's book carries a notice that explicitly states "copying is prohibited." To copy them illegally infringes on the rights of the authors of the selections and the publishers of the book. Writers such as Paul Fleischman, John Christopher, Maya Angelou, and others have granted permission to use their work in the *Sourcebook*, but have not granted the right to copy it.

You can, however, copy the blackline masters in this *Teacher's Guide.* These pages are intended for teachers to photocopy and use in the classroom.

4. Can I skip around in the *Sourcebook*?

Teachers will naturally wish to adjust the *Sourcebook* to their curriculum. But a logical— that is, the optimum—order of the book is laid out in the table of contents. The difficulty of the literary selection, the kind and difficulty of writing assignments, the amount of scaffolding provided for a specific reading strategy—all are predicated on where they occur in the text. Easier assignments and selections, naturally, tend to cluster near the beginning of the *Sourcebook*; in the back half of the book, both the assignments and selections challenge students with more rigorous demands.

5. Where did the strategies used throughout the book come from?

Most of the reading strategies used are commonplace in elementary classrooms throughout the country. They are commonly described in the standard reading education textbooks, as well as at workshops, conferences, and in-services. What is unusual in the *Sourcebook* is the way these strategies have been applied to high school–appropriate literature.

6. Why did you label the strategies with names such as "stop and think" when they are really just directed reading or some other reading technique?

The pupil's edition of the *Sourcebook* uses student-friendly terms, such as "stop and think," "retell," or "stop and record." Throughout, an attempt was made to motivate students, not hammer them with pedagogical terms. Leaden-sounding names for reading strategies (for example, directed reading strategy or reciprocal reading) seemed counterproductive for students, even while being perfectly descriptive to teachers. The same logic explains why such student-friendly titles as "Before You Read" were used instead of "Prereading." In the *Teacher's Guide*, reference is frequently made to the more formal pedagogical term (directed reading) alongside the friendlier student term (stop and think).

7. Has anyone told you that the *Sourcebook* doesn't follow the textbook definition of a number of strategies?

Yes, absolutely. Teachers who reviewed the *Sourcebooks* were quick to mention that "textbook" definitions and application of strategies were not followed. One clear example is reciprocal reading. It is an intervention strategy in which a reading partner or teacher works with a student to clarify, question, predict, and summarize; but the *Sourcebook* is a text, not a walking-and-breathing reading tutor. As a result, the questioning strategy of reciprocal reading is employed in the *Sourcebook*, with full knowledge that the technique cannot be perfectly replicated using a book. Yet the force of these strategies seemed too potent simply to discard, so, like any good teacher, the *Sourcebook* authors adapted a strategy to fit their particular needs.

8. How were the selections chosen and what is their readability?

The decision to use "real" or "quality" literature by well-known authors was, in fact, made by teachers. They selected the authors they wanted to use with their students. They insisted that the quality and force of the literature itself—not its readability—become the primary selection criteria for the literature. Especially when a selection would become the focal point of an extended lesson, the literature had to be primary. "If my students are going to spend several days on a lesson, the literature needs to be worth spending time and attention on it," one early reviewer said.

Plus, they insisted that their struggling readers be challenged. Among teachers of struggling readers, a consistent appeal was that the literature challenge their students, yet also give them lots of support. Challenge and support were the watchwords that guided the development of the *Sourcebook* program. Choosing high-quality literature was the first consideration; secondarily, the syntactical difficulty, sentence length, and vocabulary level were also considered.

9. How can I know if my students can read this literature?

Teachers have a number of ways to know how well their students can read the selections. For one, they can simply try out a lesson or two.

Second, teachers can also use a 20- or 30-word vocabulary pretest as a quick indicator. For each selection, randomly select 20 words from a selection. Ask students to circle the ones they know and underline the ones they don't know. If students know only one to five or six to nine words, then the selection will probably be frustrating for them. Spend some time preteaching the key vocabulary.

10. What if my students need even more help than what's in the book?

This *Teacher's Guide* has been designed as the next level of support. Extra activities and blackline masters on vocabulary, comprehension, prewriting, and assessment are included here so that they can be used at the teacher's discretion. Parts of each lesson could have been scaffolded for five to ten more pages, but at a certain point more worksheets and more explanation become counterproductive. Teachers advised the authors again and again to give students worthwhile literature and activities and let the students work at them. Students' work will not be perfect, but, with the right tools, students will make progress.

ORGANIZATION

Book Organization

Each **Sourcebook** has 24 selections organized into three general categories:

1. Contemporary Issues

2. Cross-curricular Subjects

3. Literature

The purpose of this organization is to provide selections that are relevant and purposeful in students' lives. By pairing selections students can take the time to build extended background on a topic or idea (for example, identity, the Holocaust), building upon knowledge they gained in earlier selections. Each of the 12 units in the **Sourcebook** is introduced by an opener that helps teachers build background on the subject. Ways to teach and introduce each opener are included in the **Teacher's Guide**.

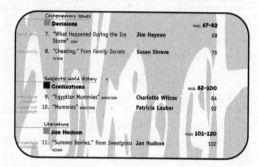

Lesson Organization

Each lesson in the **Sourcebook** has five parts:

I. Before You Read

- Each lesson begins with **I. Before You Read** to emphasize to students how important prereading is. The lesson starts with an introductory statement that draws students into the lesson, often by asking a provocative question or making a strong statement.

- The prereading step—the critical first step—builds background and helps students access prior knowledge. Among the prereading strategies (see page 6) included in Part I of this **Sourcebook** are:

- Think-Pair-and-Share

- K-W-L

- Anticipation Guide

- Preview or Walk-through

- Skimming

- Picture Walk

- Quickwrite

- Word Web

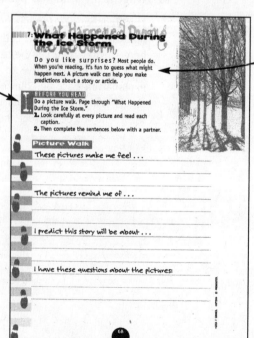

II. Read

- The reading step, called **II. Read,** begins with an invitation to read and suggestions for how to respond to the literature and mark up the text. An example is provided.

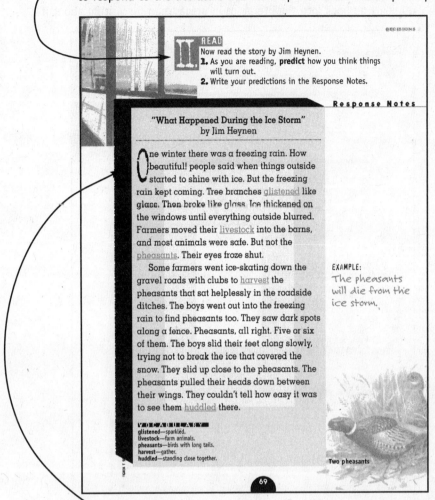

- The selection follows, with the difficult vocabulary highlighted throughout the selection and defined at the bottom of the page.

- Then, within the selection, a powerful comprehension strategy is embedded to help build in students the habits of good readers. Among the comprehension strategies included (see also page 50 in Part II of this *Sourcebook*) are these:

- Predict

- Stop and Think (directed reading)

- Stop and Clarify, Question, Predict (reciprocal reading)

- Storyboard (using graphic organizers)

- Double-entry Journal

- Retelling

- Story Frame

III. Gather Your Thoughts

- The prewriting step is called **III. Gather Your Thoughts**. It starts with the literature selection. Through two or three carefully sequenced activities, the prewriting step helps students go back into the literature in preparation for writing about it.

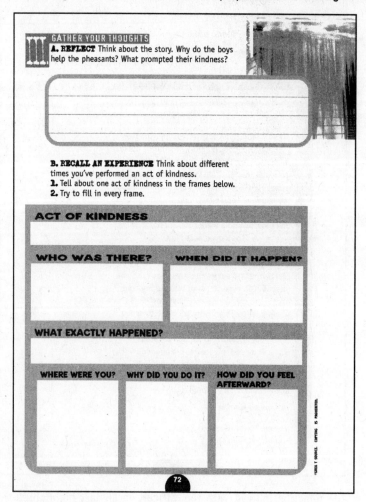

Among the more common prewriting activities are these:

- Character Map
- Main Idea and Supporting Details
- Brainstorming
- Building a Topic Sentence
- Forming an Opinion
- Supporting a Main Idea

IV. Write

- The writing step begins with step-by-step instructions for building a writing assignment. Taken together, these instructions form the writing rubric for students to use in building the assignment. Among the writing assignments students are asked to write are these:

- Paragraph with topic sentence and supporting details

- Narrative paragraph

- Expository paragraph

- Compare and contrast paragraph

- Paragraph of reflection

- Autobiographical paragraph

- Journal entry

- Story

- Character sketch

See page 7 for a full list.

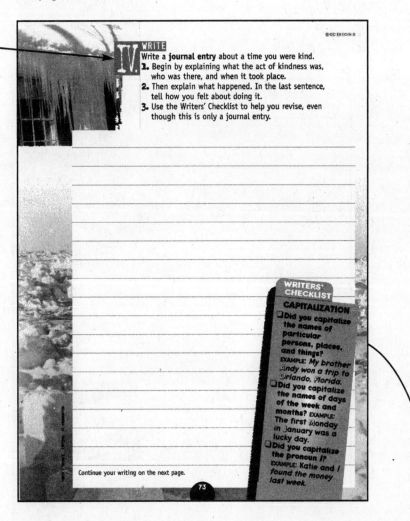

DECISIONS

WRITE

Write a **journal entry** about a time you were kind.

1. Begin by explaining what the act of kindness was, who was there, and when it took place.
2. Then explain what happened. In the last sentence, tell how you felt about doing it.
3. Use the Writers' Checklist to help you revise, even though this is only a journal entry.

Continue your writing on the next page.

73

WRITERS' CHECKLIST

CAPITALIZATION

❏ Did you capitalize the names of particular persons, places, and things? EXAMPLE: *My brother Andy won a trip to Orlando, Florida.*

❏ Did you capitalize the names of days of the week and months? EXAMPLE: *The first Monday in January was a lucky day.*

❏ Did you capitalize the pronoun *I*? EXAMPLE: *Katie and I found the money last week.*

- Each **IV. Write** also includes a **Writers' Checklist**. Each one is a brief mini-lesson on a relevant aspect of grammar, usage, or mechanics. The intent of the **Writers' Checklist** is to ask of the students appropriate questions after they write, instilling the habit of going back to revise, edit, and proof their work. The **Writers' Checklist** also affords teachers the opportunity to teach relevant grammar, usage, and mechanics skills at a teachable moment.

V. Wrap-up

- The last step of each lesson is to reflect. Students are asked a question about their reading and writing experience from the **Readers' Checklist**. This "looking back" is intended to help students see what they learned in the lesson. They are intentionally asked more than simply, "Did you understand?"

- For good readers, reading is much, much more than "Did you get it?" Good readers read for pleasure, for information, for the pure enjoyment of reading artfully written material, for personal curiosity, for a desire to learn more, and countless other reasons. So that students will begin to see that reading is worthwhile to them, they need to believe the payoff is more than "Did you get it?" on a five-question multiple-choice test.

- The **Sourcebook** attempts with **V. Wrap-up** to help students ask the questions good readers ask of themselves when they read. It attempts to broaden the reasons for reading by asking students to consider six reasons for reading:

- Meaning

- Enjoyment

- Understanding

- Style

- Ease

- Depth

Continue your writing from the previous page.

WRAP-UP

What did you learn from reading "What Happened During the Ice Storm"?

READERS' CHECKLIST

MEANING

❑ Did you learn something from the reading?

❑ Did it affect you or make an impression?

74

Organization

TEACHER'S LESSON PLANS

Each lesson plan for the teacher of the *Sourcebook* has eight pages:

PAGE 1 Overview and Background

- The chart at the beginning of each lesson plan gives an "at-a-glance" view of the skills and strategies, plus the difficulty level of the reading and five key vocabulary words.
- Background on the author and selection and a graphic are included.

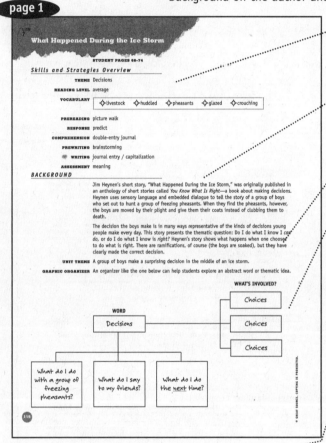

page 1

What Happened During the Ice Storm

STUDENT PAGES 68–74

Skills and Strategies Overview

THEME Decisions

READING LEVEL average

VOCABULARY ◈livestock ◈huddled ◈pheasants ◈glazed ◈crouching

PREREADING picture walk

RESPONSE predict

COMPREHENSION double-entry journal

PREWRITING brainstorming

WRITING journal entry / capitalization

ASSESSMENT meaning

BACKGROUND

Jim Heynen's short story, "What Happened During the Ice Storm," was originally published in an anthology of short stories called *You Know What Is Right*—a book about making decisions. Heynen uses sensory language and embedded dialogue to tell the story of a group of boys who set out to hunt a group of freezing pheasants. When they find the pheasants, however, the boys are moved by their plight and give them their coats instead of clubbing them to death.

The decision the boys make is in many ways representative of the kinds of decisions young people make every day. This story presents the thematic question: Do I do what I know I *can* do, or do I do what I know is *right*? Heynen's story shows what happens when one chooses to do what is right. There are ramifications, of course (the boys are soaked), but they have clearly made the correct decision.

UNIT THEME A group of boys make a surprising decision in the middle of an ice storm.

GRAPHIC ORGANIZER An organizer like the one below can help students explore an abstract word or thematic idea.

WHAT'S INVOLVED?

WORD
Decisions

Choices
Choices
Choices

What do I do with a group of freezing pheasants?
What do I say to my friends?
What do I do the next time?

overview chart

additional background

tie-in to theme

model graphic organizer

page 2

WHAT HAPPENED DURING THE ICE STORM : STUDENT PAGES 68–74

BEFORE YOU READ

Read through the introduction to the lesson (page 68) with students. The purpose of this opening paragraph is to motivate and focus students, as well as to forge an initial connection between the reading and the student's own life. Then introduce the prereading activity, a **picture walk**. (Refer to the **Strategy Handbook** on page 40 for more help.)

Motivation Strategy

ENGAGING STUDENTS In "What Happened During the Ice Storm," a group of boys have to choose between doing what's right and doing what's "cool." Ask students to think of a time they had to make this kind of choice. What decision did they make, and why? A short discussion on this topic will help students connect the theme of the selection to their own lives.

Vocabulary Building

Discuss with students the key vocabulary words for this selection: *livestock, huddled pheasants, glazed,* and *crouching*. Have them circle these words in the text and then encourage them to define the words in context before checking the footnote definition. Students will benefit from the additional work with using **context clues**.

STRATEGY LESSON: PRONUNCIATION Knowing the pronunciation of a word is as important as knowing its correct meaning. Write the following words from the selection and their pronunciations on the board. Ask students to practice saying the words: *pounce* (POWNS), *glistened* (GLISS nd), and *pheasants* (FEZ nts).

For additional practice on this strategy, see the **Vocabulary** blackline master on page 120.

Prereading Strategies

As a prereading activity, students are asked to take a **picture walk** of the selection. Explain that during a picture walk, the reader looks only at the art, photographs, and captions. In many instances, these elements can give valuable clues about the plot, characters, and author's message. When they have finished their picture walks of "What Happened During the Ice Storm," students might work together to explain how the photographs made them feel. In addition, they should use the pictures to make predictions about the topic. After they have read the story, you might have students return to the pictures and explain the connections they see between the photographs and the mood of Heynen's writing. Do you think the art matches the mood? Why or why not? What pictures would students have chosen to accompany this story if they were the designers of the book?

QUICKWRITE As an alternate prereading strategy, ask students to think about a time they had to make an important decision. Ask them to write for one minute about the decision and how it made them feel. Remind the class that quickwriting means jotting down whatever words, phrases, and images come to mind about a topic. Sentence structure and grammar are not as important as getting some ideas down on paper. This quick activity will help students connect the theme of the selection and unit to their own lives. In addition, it may give them ideas for the writing activity they are asked to complete on page 73.

Spanish-speaking Students

En "Lo que sucedió durante la tormenta de hielo," dos chicos intentan salvar a unos faisanes que se están muriendo. Hace mucho frío y todo está cubierto de hielo. Los faisanes no pueden volar ni ver porque sus ojos se han cogelado. Los chicos, sin embargo, están determinados a calentar los pájaros y ayudarlos por el resto de la tormenta.

how to teach the pupil's page "at-a-glance"

additional strategies

cross-reference to blackline master

selection summary in Spanish

PAGE 2 Before You Read

- The first page of the teacher's plan begins with a motivation strategy and a suggestion for vocabulary building. Additional prereading strategies are suggested, along with a summary of the selection in Spanish.

Each lesson plan in the *Sourcebook Teacher's Guide* follows the pupil's lesson step-by-step.

PAGE 3 Read

- The response strategy gives students one way to interact with the text as they read.

- Additional comprehension strategies are suggested, along with a **Comprehension** blackline master found later in the lesson.

- The discussion questions cover both literal and interpretative levels of thinking.

- A literary skill is suggested for each selection, allowing teachers to build literary appreciation as they provide basic support with reading comprehension.

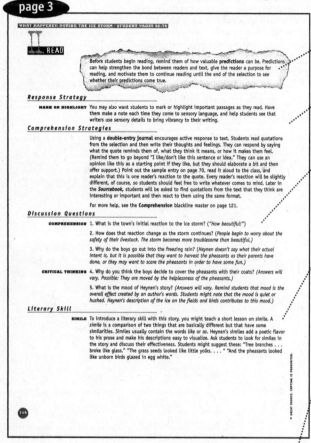

how to teach the pupil's page "at-a-glance"

interactive reading (or response) strategy

additional help with comprehension

discussion questions and literary skill

how to teach the pupil's page "at-a-glance"

additional prewriting strategies

mini-lesson on grammar, usage, and mechanics

two forms of assessment—Readers' Checklist and test

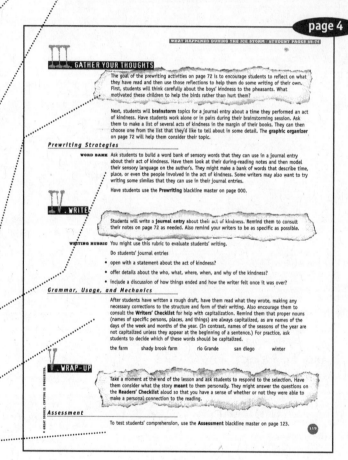

PAGE 4 Gather Your Thoughts, Write, Wrap-up

- The page begins with additional help with prewriting and references another blackline master that offers additional support.

- Next, the students write and are directed to the **Writers' Checklist** in the pupil's book, which gives the grammar, usage, and mechanics mini-lesson.

- The writing rubric gives teachers a way to evaluate students' writing.

- The lesson ends with reference to the **Readers' Checklist** in the pupil's book, encourages students to reflect on what they have read, and cross-references the **Assessment** blackline master.

Each lesson plan in the *Sourcebook Teacher's Guide* has four blackline masters for additional levels of support for key skill areas.

PAGE 5 Vocabulary

- Each **Vocabulary** blackline master helps students learn the meanings of five words from the literature selection and focuses on an important vocabulary strategy, such as understanding prefixes, root words, and word families.

page 5

WHAT HAPPENED DURING THE ICE STORM / STUDENT PAGES 67-74

Name _____

VOCABULARY
Words from the Selection

DIRECTIONS Using context clues, fill in each blank with the most appropriate word from the box.

◇livestock ◇huddled ◇pheasants ◇glazed ◇crouching

1. The animals _____ together to keep warm during the ice storm.

2. We herded all the _____ into the barn to get them out of the rain.

3. Because their eyes were frozen shut, the _____ couldn't see us.

4. We were _____ behind the bush to surprise the birds.

5. The branches of the trees were _____ with a thin coat of ice.

Strategy Lesson: Pronunciation

DIRECTIONS Each sentence below contains the pronunciation of a word in parentheses. From the list on the right, choose the word that is pronounced. Write that word on the blank.

6. The farmers had to (POWNS) _____ on the pheasant so he didn't get away.

7. I used (JEL uh tin) _____ to make my dessert.

8. The ice on the trees (GLISS nd) _____ in the sunlight.

9. Summer is the season in which we (HAR vest) _____ the corn.

10. The boys saw five (FEZ nts) _____ sitting on a fence.

glistened

pheasants

harvest

pounce

gelatin

129

© GREAT SOURCE. PERMISSION IS GRANTED TO COPY THIS PAGE.

meanings from five words from the selection are taught

important vocabulary strategy introduced and practiced

page 6

WHAT HAPPENED DURING THE ICE STORM / STUDENT PAGES 67-74

Name _____

COMPREHENSION
Graphic Organizer

Directions Use this story pyramid to show what you know about Heynen's story.

1. _____
   Name of story

2. _____
   Two words about the character

3. _____
   Three words about the setting

4. _____
   Four words about the problem

5. _____
   Five words about the solution

Word Bank

DIRECTIONS Now think of words that you might use to describe your act of kindness. Try to think of words that appeal to the five senses.

WORD BANK

121

© GREAT SOURCE. PERMISSION IS GRANTED TO COPY THIS PAGE.

additional support for understanding every selection

different strategy from the one used in the pupil's book

PAGE 6 Comprehension

- Each **Comprehension** blackline master affords teachers still another way to build students' understanding of the selection, using a different strategy from the one found in the *Sourcebook*.

PAGE 7 Prewriting

- Occasionally students will need even more scaffolding than appears in the pupil's lesson as they prepare for the writing assignment.

- The "extra step" in preparing to write is the focus of the **Prewriting** blackline master.

PAGE 8 Assessment

- Each lesson in the *Sourcebook* ends with the opportunity for students to reflect on their reading with the **Readers' Checklist**. This self-assessment is an informal inventory of what they learned from the reading.

- The **Assessment** blackline master gives a multiple-choice test on the selection and suggests a short-essay question for a more formal assessment.

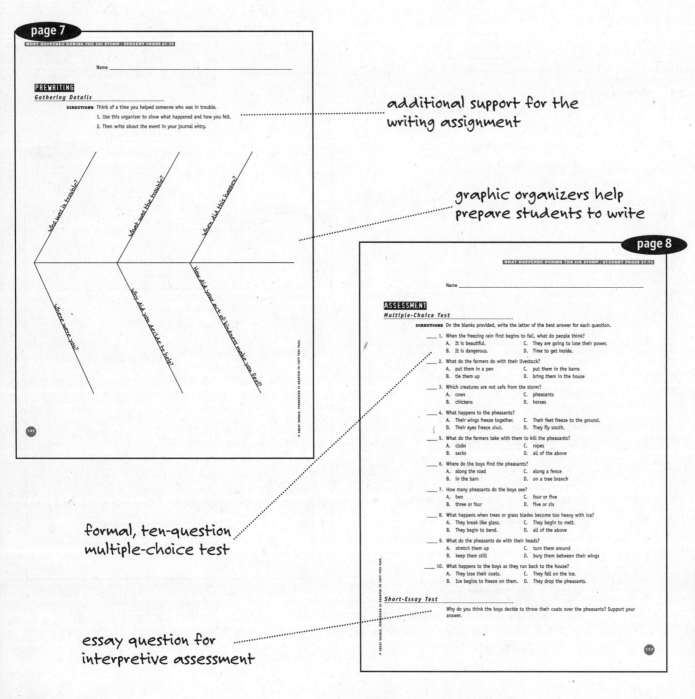

additional support for the writing assignment

graphic organizers help prepare students to write

formal, ten-question multiple-choice test

essay question for interpretive assessment

Teaching Struggling Readers

BY DR. RICHARD G. RAMSEY

What It Means to Teach

I enjoy being an educator. . . . We have the best job in the world, because we touch the future every day. We are in the business of making dreams come true for children. . . . And every day that I get up I'm excited about just going to work because now I know I have an opportunity to touch another life. . . . We have so many kids right now in our country coming to us from all walks of life, walking through our school doors every single day. When they walk through those doors, they're looking for one thing: they have open eyes, open minds, and open hearts seeking your validation. . . . The last thing children need to have done to them when they walk into your classroom is to be discouraged. They need hope, they need to be inspired by you every single day. . . .

The names of those who practice our profession read like a hall of fame for humanity: Booker T. Washington, Buddha, Confucius, Ralph Waldo Emerson, Leo Buscaglia, and many, many others. . . . Through and through the course of being a teacher, I've been called upon to be an actor, a nurse, a doctor, a coach, a finder of lost articles, a money lender, a taxicab driver, and also a keeper of the faith. I'm a paradox and I speak loudest when I listen the most to my students. I, as a teacher, am the most fortunate person who labors. A doctor is allowed to bring life into the world in one magic moment, but I, as a teacher, I am allowed to see that life is reborn each and every day with new questions, ideas, and friendship. I'm a warrior doing battle every single day against peer pressure, negativity, fear, conformity, and prejudice. . . .

Elements of Teaching

ATTITUDE But there are three things I always say that a teacher has to have to be able to survive: The first thing you have to have is the proper attitude. . . . I say attitudes are contagious, is yours worth catching? . . . Our attitude plays a big role when we're dealing with children and I tell myself to come to school smiling every day, be happy. . . . Children are looking for you to be that positive example for them. . . . Every day we have two choices. . . . You can complain about your job every day and let children fail or you can begin to love what you do every single day and make sure that every child has the opportunity to be successful. . . .

Life is a challenge. We are challenged with diverse populations that we're not accustomed to working with. Life is a gift. Teach our children that you only go around one time and it's not a practice run. Respect the gift of life. Life is an adventure. . . . Life is also a saga . . . and teach our kids that there will be a better tomorrow if they just hold on and don't quit. Life is also a tragedy; unfortunately we are going to lose kids to homicide, drug abuse, and all kinds of dreadful diseases. And I say, hold on to those that we have because they are our future. Life is also a duty; you have a duty as a teacher to teach every child the way you would want somebody to teach yours, and if you do that, you've done your duty for that day. Life is also a game; be the best player so you can help children. Life is an opportunity; take advantage of it and make sure that the children understand that opportunities in life only come one time. Life is also a struggle; fight it with every ounce of energy that you have to do the best with children. Life is also a goal; set goals for yourself, set goals for the children. But more importantly, make sure that you work with them so they can achieve the goals they've set. Finally, life is a puzzle; but if all of us today take back what we have and work together as a team, we can solve that puzzle and make sure that children are successful in life. To teach is to heal, to teach is to love, to teach is to care, to teach is to set high expectations. You are a teacher. There are many kids waiting for you and looking in your eyes every day and saying, "I need your help, I need your motivation." But remember,

27

you don't motivate with fear, you may get compliance, but you certainly won't get commitment.

CARE Good teaching, as I tell my teachers all the time, does not come from behind the desk, it comes from behind the heart. . . . And kids know whether you care about them, and kids can be successful because excellence can be obtained if you just care more than other people think is wise, risk more than others think is safe, dream more than others think is practical, and expect out of your students more than others think is possible. An unspoken belief can teach young minds what they should be. You as a teacher can make that difference. . . . Remember, good teachers explain, superior teachers demonstrate. The great teachers, they inspire their students every single day. And if a kid can be inspired by you, he's going to want to come to your class every day, he's going to give you his best or her best every single day. . . .

COMMITMENT I'm going to tell a little story to you called, "Three Letters of Teddy."

"Teddy's letter came today and now that I've read it, I will place it in my cedar chest with the other things that are important in my life. I, as a teacher, had not seen Teddy Starlin since he was a student in my fifth-grade class fifteen years ago. It was early in my career and I had only been teaching for two years. From the first day he stepped into my class, I disliked him. Teachers are not supposed to dislike any child, but I did and I showed my dislike to this young boy."

Any teacher would tell you it's more of a pleasure to teach a bright child. It's definitely more rewarding to one's ego with any teacher, with their credentials, a challenge working with a bright child and keeping them challenged and learning while they spend a major effort for those students who need help. Any teacher can do this, most teachers do, but she said she didn't, not that year. In fact, she concentrated on her best students and let the others follow along the best they could. Ashamed as she is to admit it, she took pleasure in using her red pen. And every time she came to Teddy's paper, the cross marks, and they were many, were always a little larger and a little redder than necessary. While she didn't actually ridicule the boy, her attitude, ladies and gentlemen, was obvious and quite apparent to the whole class for he quickly became the class goat, the outcast, the unlovable and the unloved child in that classroom. He didn't know why she didn't like him, nor did she know why she had such an intent dislike for this boy. All he wanted was somebody just to care about him, and she made no effort on his behalf. . . .

She knew that Teddy would never catch up in time to be promoted to the sixth-grade level. She said he would be a repeater. And to justify herself, she went to his folder from time to time. He had very low grades for the first four years but not failures. How he had made it, she said, she didn't know. But she closed her mind to all of the personal remarks in Teddy's folder. It said: first grade—Teddy shows promise by working attitude but has poor home situation. Second grade—Teddy could do better but his mother is terminally ill and he receives no help at home. Third grade—Teddy's a pleasant boy, helpful but too serious, slow learner. His mother, she passed away at the end of the year. Fourth grade—very slow but well behaved. His father shows no interest at all. She said, well, they passed him four times but he would certainly repeat the fifth grade, she said, it would do him good.

And then the last day before the holidays arrived, the little tree on the reading table supported paper and popcorn chains and many gifts were underneath the tree awaiting a big moment. Teachers always get several gifts at Christmas, she said, but hers that year were more elaborate than ever. Every child had brought her a gift and each unwrapping brought squeals of delight and the proud giver received profusive thank yous. His gift wasn't the last one she picked up; in fact, it was in the middle of the pile. Its wrapping was a brown paper bag and he had colored Christmas trees and red bells all over it and it was stuck together with masking tape. And it read "For Ms. Thompson, from Teddy, I love you." The group was completely silent, and for the first time she felt very embarrassed because all of the students stood there watching her unwrap that gift. And as she removed the last bit of masking tape, two items fell to her desk, a gaudy rhinestone bracelet with several stones missing and a small bottle of dime store cologne half empty. She heard the snickers and the whispers from the students and she wasn't even sure that she could hold her head up and look at Teddy, but she said, "Isn't this lovely." And she asked Teddy to come up to help her fasten the clasp. He smiled as he fixed the clasp on her arm and then there were finally a few hesitant oohs and ahs from the students. But as she dabbed the cologne behind her ears, all the little girls got up to get a dab behind theirs. She continued to open the gifts until she reached the bottom of the pile. They ate their refreshments and the bell rang. The children filed out and shouted, "See you next year, Merry Christmas," but Teddy, he waited at his desk. When they all had left, he walked toward her clutching his books and his gift to his chest with tears streaming down his face and he said to her, you smell just like my mom, her bracelet looks real pretty on you, too. I'm glad you like it. He left quickly. She got up and locked the door, sat at her desk, and wept resolvedly to make Teddy what she had deprived him of, to be a teacher who cared.

She stayed every afternoon with Teddy until the last day of school. Slowly but surely, he caught up with the rest of the class. Gradually, there was a definite upward curve in his grades. He didn't have to repeat the fifth grade; in fact, his average was among the highest in the class. Even though he was moving next year with his father, she wasn't worried because Teddy had reached a level that would serve him anywhere, because her teaching training had taught her that success deals success. She didn't hear from Teddy until seven years later when his first letter appeared in the mailbox. It said, "Dear Ms. Thompson, I want you to be the first to know that I'll be graduating second in my class next month, very truly yours, Teddy Starlin." She sent him a congratulatory card, wondering what he would do after graduation. Four years later she received another letter. It said, "Dear Ms. Thompson, I want you to be the first to know that I was just informed that I will be graduating first in my class. The university hasn't been easy; however, I liked it." She sent him silver monogrammed cufflinks and a card, so proud of him that she could burst. The final note came from him. It said, "Dear Ms. Thompson, I want you to be the first to know that as of today I am Theodore J. Starlin, M.D., how about that?" He said, "I'm going to be married in July, to be exact, and I want to ask you if you would come and do me a big favor, I would like you to come to my wedding and sit where my mom would have been if she was alive. I have no family now because my dad died last year. Ms. Thompson, you are all I have left, please come to my wedding, very truly yours, Teddy Starlin." She said, "I'm not sure what kind of gift one sends to a doctor on completion of medical school and state board; maybe I'll just wait and take a wedding gift," but she said, "my note cannot wait." It said, "Dear Ted, congratulations, you made it, you did it yourself. In spite of those like me and not because of us, this day has come for you. God bless you and I'll be at your wedding with bells on."

You have a lot of students like that in your classroom right now; all they need is a push. These kids are coming to us and they're looking for that special person to be there for them. . . .

RESPONSIBILITY We have a responsibility to touch the lives of children. But the question is: "Are we walking away from the children who need us, or are we coming to them and picking them up when they fall down? Children are not responsible for their parents, they are not responsible for where they live, they're only trying to make it with the conditions that they have. . . . Don't quit on children. Let them know they can be somebody. . . .

NOTE The article above is a transcript adapted from a lecture.

Building Expert Readers and Writers

BY DR. ROBERT PAVLIK

REFLECTIONS • What was one of your most valuable learning experiences that involved reading and writing?

• What made the learning experience so valuable? So memorable?

Defining Expert Readers and Writers

Experts in various professions have extensive content knowledge and efficient skills:

> . . . experts have acquired extensive knowledge that affects what they notice and how they organize, represent, and interpret information in their environments. This, in turn, affects their abilities to remember, reason, and solve problems. (Bransford, Brown, and Cocking, 1999)

Novices, in contrast, lacking extensive content knowledge and efficient skills, tend to make confusing interpretations, record and retrieve information laboriously, and solve problems inaccurately.

The overall goal of the *Sourcebook* is to build expert readers and writers, learners who develop extensive content knowledge and efficient skills for using reading and writing to meet their needs within and beyond school. Expert readers and writers also develop their own "voices" for interacting within and among families, fellow learners, and community members. Far too many middle school students, especially those at the lower end of the academic spectrum, lack extensive content knowledge or efficient skills. As a result, they can become confused, confusing, inefficient, and ineffective when attempting to use reading and writing to meet their needs. In addition, far too many middle school students do not develop their own "voices."

REFLECTIONS • For which school subjects were you a novice or an expert reader? A novice or expert writer? How did you know?

• How would you describe your "voice" in middle school? today?

• Which of your recent/current students would you describe as novice or expert readers? As novice or expert writers? How do you know?

• How would you describe the "voices" of your students?

Using Culturally Diverse Literature

Rapidly changing national demographics require us to reconsider what fiction and nonfiction literature we include in our curricula. In essence, to what extent do we study the literature from and about people who helped shape the United States, and to what extent do we study the literature from and about people who shape the United States today and are shaping the future of the United States?

The *Sourcebook* provides fiction and nonfiction selections that represent current demographics of middle school students. Approximately 60 percent of the selections represent traditional ideas and values, while the remaining 40 percent represent the ideas and values of several other cultures. This range of culturally diverse literature provides optional selections for meeting students' needs to

• understand themselves.

• understand the worldviews and culture of the United States.

• understand others.

• understand the worldviews and cultures of other countries.

For students, this range of culturally diverse literature provides meaningful, authentic opportunities to read and write and to learn new and familiar vocabulary in a variety of contexts. In addition, the breadth and depth of the selections can inspire further student reading, student-teacher discussions, and student-student discussions.

REFLECTIONS

- How culturally diverse was the fiction you studied as a middle school student? The nonfiction?

- How valuable was the literature you studied in middle school for the four needs cited above?

- What are the demographics of your students?

- What cultures and "voices" must your literature selections address?

Using an Interactive Instructional Approach

Current approaches for improving the reading and writing of middle school students range

- from telling students to "practice, practice, practice" their reading and writing. In essence, teachers tell students to read a lot to become better readers and write a lot to become better writers.

- to identifying a student's level of skill mastery for reading and writing and, then, organizing students into groups for appropriate reading and writing skills instruction.

- to inviting students to discover their own strategies through teacher-guided discussions.

- to creating stimulating environments and meaningful projects around significant themes that motivate students to build and refine their uses of reading, writing, speaking, listening, and viewing.

All of these approaches to instruction have proven effective in recent decades, especially with populations of similar students. However, increasing numbers of middle school students represent diverse cultures, perform well below their potential, speak English only in school, and attend school irregularly.

Vygotsky's thinking (1978) inspires and informs much of our approach to instruction. We believe that today's middle school students can become expert readers and writers despite the challenges confronting them. To do so, students need

- meaningful, authentic fiction and nonfiction.

- an approach to instruction that respects how they are trying to learn within their fragmented, often chaotic lives.

- teachers and materials that direct and guide them to form, state, and test strategies for reading with peers and adults.

Therefore, our overall instructional approach involves modeling what expert readers and writers do as they negotiate with fiction and nonfiction and, then, inviting students to adapt what they learn from the modeling to their own reading and writing strategies. In the process, students can build and refine their thinking with others in order to apply the strategies on their own as needed.

For example, the *Sourcebook* opens with a feature entitled **"Responding to Literature"** that directs and invites students to

- see examples of written responses to ideas in a short selection from an expert reader-writer.

- engage a strategy sheet for making similar responses.

- make similar responses to a short selection on their own.

We apply this overall instructional approach throughout the *Sourcebook*.

REFLECTIONS
- What instructional approaches did your teachers apply to improve your reading and writing?

- Which approaches did you as a middle school student find valuable? Not valuable?

- As a teacher, what instructional approaches have you found effective and why? Ineffective and why?

Teaching Meaning-making Strategies

Research studies on expert readers and writers reveal two important insights:

- Expert readers and writers will use a variety of strategies automatically when they encounter new and difficult tasks—strategies that novice readers and writers would not use.

- A number of reading and writing strategies have been developed and can be taught (Paris, Wasik, and Turner, 1991; Dahl and Farnan, 1998).

Within our five-part lesson framework for each piece of fiction and nonfiction, students apply several meaning-making strategies to become expert readers and writers.

Part I. Before You Read

Struggling novice readers tend to avoid most types of reading in and outside of school. Even some expert readers often choose to spend only a few minutes each day reading in and outside of school, on either assigned or independent reading. The reasons why middle school students choose not to read range from having poor reading skills to responding to peer pressure and even gender expectations.

The *Sourcebook* addresses these avoidance behaviors by presenting two prereading strategies per selection and guiding students to apply the strategies successfully. We assign specific strategies for each selection to get students doing something before they read, e.g., asking their opinions, engaging with a sample from the selection to read, or responding to a quick survey about their expectations. Our prereading strategies applied among the selections include these:

- Walking through a selection
- Using an anticipation guide
- Using K-W-L
- Using word webs
- Using a read-aloud
- Using a think-pair-and-share
- Previewing
- Skimming and scanning

Initially, engaging students in the prereading strategies motivates them to "get into" any selection. Eventually, students apply these prereading strategies to build background, activate prior knowledge, or raise questions that become part of the purpose for reading. With consistent practice, coaching, and guided reflection over the use of prereading strategies, students can build and refine their own lifetime prereading strategies.

Part II. Read

Novice readers usually do not choose to read with pencil in hand and mark up the text. Their reasons range from fearing to write in the text to not having a personal system of symbols for their responses, to fearing to make their "thinking tracks" public, to not having accurate language for describing the author's content and structure in annotations. Expert readers typically mark up a text, though not always. They will often mark up texts in which they find new or difficult information. They will rarely mark up texts in which they find familiar, easy-to-access or easy-to-remember information.

The *Sourcebook* addresses these varying comfort levels by presenting one or more interactive reading strategies per selection and guiding students to apply the strategies successfully. Our goal is to get students actually to write in their texts. The interactive reading strategies include these:

- Marking and highlighting

- Questioning

- Clarifying

- Visualizing

- Predicting

- Reading and connecting

The major purposes of these interactive reading strategies are to help students learn how and when to mark up texts and how to focus on specific content or structures of texts. Later, as their abilities develop for describing, labeling, commenting on, and reorganizing the information they read, students may find that these strategies slow down rather than accelerate their reading—a behavior indicating that they are becoming more expert readers.

Struggling novice readers often find themselves reading with no understanding or, even worse, reading with their eyes closed and imagining they are making sense of a piece of fiction or nonfiction. Expert readers develop new levels of understanding each time they read whole texts or parts of texts. They have learned where to pause and reread and how to apply any of several strategies to help understand what they read.

The comprehension strategies applied in the *Sourcebook* include these:

- Directed reading

- Predicting

- Using graphic organizers

- Using reciprocal reading questions

- Retelling

- Making double-entry journals

We assign one of these tried-and-true strategies to the appropriate types of fiction and nonfiction. Our goal is to model how expert readers come to understand a text. Ultimately, after students experiment with a variety of comprehension strategies, they will modify the strategies for their purposes until the strategies are no longer recognizable as they are developed in the *Sourcebook*—another indication of an expert reader in the making.

Part III. Gather Your Thoughts

Struggling novice writers usually do not choose to engage in any prewriting activities when they have a choice. Expert writers, while they vary widely in the breadth and depth of their prewriting strategies, view prewriting activities as the time when personally significant learning takes place. Prewriting activities provide the time and the means for engaging in critical and creative thinking.

Part III of the *Sourcebook* presents one or more prewriting strategies per selection. Students receive step-by-step guidance for applying each strategy successfully. The prereading strategies we apply among the selections include these:

- Discussing in pairs and small groups

- Clustering details

- Drawing a place

- Brainstorming

- Quickwriting

- Using anecdotes

- Comparing and contrasting

- Using a graphic organizer

- Using storyboards

Most of these prewriting activities involve two or more persons. Most thinking is social, according to Vygotsky; group interactions following various learning experiences, including reading and before writing, provide students with valuable opportunities to develop, refine, and internalize their purposes and plans for writing.

Part IV. Write

Struggling novice writers often think of completing a writing assignment as involving a two-step, one-time process—just sit down and write. They often postpone completing writing assignments, thinking that once they sit down and write, they can complete the assignment in one work session. Expert writers think of completing a writing assignment as involving several steps, e.g., narrowing the topic, planning, gathering data, drafting, revising one or more times, sharing and publishing; personalizing ways to complete each of the steps; and involving more than one work session.

The *Sourcebook* invites students to engage in several small writing tasks. Note the types of writing listed in the Table of Contents to the left of each selection title. The writing tasks become increasingly larger so that students come to view the writing process as a series of recursive, interlocking steps. When students present and reflect on their best writing samples, they come to understand how the writing process varies among types of writing and among students—another indication of an expert writer.

Part V. Wrap-up

Being able to answer such reflection questions as these indicates how well readers and writers understand the fiction and nonfiction selections they study:

1. UNDERSTANDING Did I understand? How do I know?

Is the message or point clear?

Can I restate what it was about?

2. EASE Was it easy to read?

Was I able to read it smoothly and without difficulty?

3. MEANING Did I learn something or take away something from it?

Did it affect me or make an impression?

4. STYLE Did I find it well written?

Was the writing well crafted, the sentences well constructed, the words well chosen?

Does it show me how to be a better writer?

5. DEPTH Did it make me think about things?

Did it set off thoughts beyond the surface topic?

What are the immediate implications for me? Others?

What are the long-term implications for me? Others?

6. ENJOYMENT Did I like it?

Was the experience pleasurable?

Would I want to reread it or recommend it to someone?

Answering such questions as these honestly and consistently for a wide variety of texts and purposes indicates that a learner is becoming an expert reader.

REFLECTIONS
- What strategies do you find personally valuable

 for prereading?

 for reading?

 for gathering your thoughts?

 for writing?

 for reflecting on your reading and writing?

- What are your roles when using the *Sourcebook* to build expert readers and writers? How might your roles change during this school year?

- How can you create the most significant learning experiences when your students use reading and writing?

REFERENCES Bransford, J. D., A. L. Brown, and R. R. Cocking, eds. *How People Learn: Brain, Mind, Experience and School.* Washington, D.C.: National Academy Press, 1999.

Cawelti, G., ed. *Handbook of Research on Improving Student Achievement.* 2nd ed. Arlington, Va.: Educational Research Service, 1999.

Graves, M., and B. Graves. *Scaffolding Reading Experiences: Designs for Student Success.* Norwood, Mass.: Christopher-Gordon Publishers, 1994.

BY CATHERINE McNARY

The Situation in Middle School

In middle school, strategic reading is an essential learning tool. Two primary learning mediums are used to disseminate information—classroom lecture and textbook reading. The middle school student must develop sufficient vocabulary, background knowledge, metacognitive strategies, and motivation to translate textbook print into usable, applicable information.

For some students, the expectations are realistic. For many, they are not. (The 1998 NAEP assessment stated that 31 percent of fourth graders, 33 percent of eighth-graders, and 40 percent of twelfth graders attained a proficient level of reading [Donahue, Voelkl, Campbell, & Mazzeo, 1999].) What happens with the 67 percent of students in eighth grade and the 60 percent of students in twelfth grade who are not proficient readers? What strategies and teaching methods have been proven to provide this group with the best possible instruction in reading so that they, like their more able peers, may keep pace with the middle school curriculum?

In the literature, five traits have been identified that provide readers with the cognitive tools to learn from text: general cognitive capacity, reader strategies and metacognition, inferential and reasoning abilities, background knowledge, and basic reading skills (Van Den Broek & Kremer, 2000). Most middle school students, even those reading two years below grade level, have adequate basic skills, and general cognitive capacity is beyond the purview of the middle school. However, the remaining abilities are integral to an instructional program at the middle school level and include these:

- Reader strategies and metacognition

- Inferential and reasoning ability

- Background knowledge.

Best Practices to Use with High-Risk Students

Dr. Norman Stahl has suggested ten recommendations for programs from research for teaching high-risk college students (Stahl, Simpson, and Hayes, 1994). Dr. Stahl's list can be consolidated into four components that are relevant to middle school reading programs and that match the five traits for success outlined by Taylor and others.

Best practices for a middle school reading program should reflect instruction in these four components:

1. develop background knowledge

2. model metacognitive strategies and promote their independent usage

3. incorporate writing into the curriculum

4. develop vocabulary

Develop Background Knowledge

The importance of developing background knowledge has been emphasized by several researchers (Alvermann and Moore, 1996). Because reading is thought to be a construction of meaning in which the reader not only absorbs information from the text but also combines that information with his or her own prior knowledge, background is essential. The reader cannot interact with the text without prior understanding of the content. He or she would ·have no groundwork upon which to build.

Teachers use several strategies to build background before reading. These include field trips, films, guest speakers, discussions, short articles, library research and projects, anticipation guides, K-W-L, brainstorming, quickwrites, DRTA, simulations, questionnaires, structured overviews, and advance organizers.

The *Sourcebook* is organized with a prereading activity at the beginning of each selection. These prereading activities include quickwrites, K-W-L, anticipation guides, previews, and other sound activities. Not only do these lessons serve as models for prereading strategies, they also provide strategic practice for students.

Other important prereading practices that go hand-in-hand with background building are setting purpose and previewing. Just as a reader must have background information to interact with text, a reader must also have a clear understanding of why he or she is reading a selection. Purpose can be set by teacher direction. Instead of suggesting, "Read Chapter Five for a quiz on Tuesday," the teacher should probably say, "Read Chapter Five to find three reasons why or how a problem was solved. Concentrate on the sequence of the solution." This small change gives a concrete purpose to the reading and helps students to focus on the main idea.

Previewing is another strategy that directs a student to discover the main idea of the text. Previewing activities include looking at titles, subheadings, chapter questions, photos, and captions. The information gathered acts as a director for how the student approaches the information.

These strategies are not new to teachers. The challenge is the number of times students must practice the strategy before it is internalized, until it can be done independently. The *Sourcebook* provides numerous opportunities for practicing each strategy. Repeated practice helps the student make the strategy automatic. The *Sourcebook* also provides the student with a written record of his or her strategy development. This record allows the student to monitor his or her own progress.

Model Metacognitive Strategies

It is clear from the literature that strategic readers comprehend print more efficiently (Paris, Wasik, and Turner, 1996) than those readers without strategies. Typically, the less-able reader has no plan for attacking print—he or she just reads every word, each with the same emphasis. He or she skips problematic words or passages or rereads them in exactly the same manner—with no strategies for monitoring the effectiveness of his or her comprehension. The goals of strategic reading instruction are to model a variety of strategies to students (both teacher- and student- generated), to give students sufficient guided and independent practice to incorporate the strategies into his or her own portfolio, and to observe the student using these strategies in his or her own independent reading. This instruction will then allow students to monitor the effectiveness of their own reading—and adjust if the reading has not been sufficient.

For many middle school readers, self-monitoring of comprehension is a new concept. Explicit instruction and practice are necessary for these students to develop self-monitoring techniques. Several strategies are available. While a student reads, he or she should mark up the text, underlining and highlighting information. In addition, note-taking of text during reading is also suggested. Students should be taught to write down the questions that come up while reading; write down issues that need clarification or that they wish to discuss; draw pictures of characters they need to visualize; note any parts or quotes within the selection that provoke a reaction; and graph any process or sequence that seems important. The *Sourcebook* is excellent for modeling and providing students with the opportunity to practice student-generated during-reading strategies.

In the space called **"Response Notes,"** students record questions, clarifications, pictures, and graphic representations. Highlighting and underlining are also modeled. In addition, students can write in their books. Reading teachers are often at a disadvantage in teaching self-monitoring because students do not own the books and cannot write in the books they are reading. Consequently, these strategies are ignored or modified beyond recognition. With the *Sourcebook,* these activities can be practiced as they are meant to be—in the book. This is an opportunity for both teacher monitoring and self-monitoring of strategy acquisition.

Many of the during-reading strategies are teacher-generated. These include K-W-L, DRTA, and study guides. Two of the teacher-generated strategies the *Sourcebook* encourages during reading are **stop and think** questions and the **double-entry journal**. **Stop and think** (directed reading) activities function like a within-text study guide. Text is broken, at a strategic place, with a question box. Students are expected to stop and answer the question and then continue reading.

The location of the **stop and think**, within text, is of great value. This proximity helps to keep students connected to text to evaluate both their response and the place in text that referenced it. The repeated usage of **stop and think** in the *Sourcebook* permits students the practice to make the connection from text to response, as well as to establish a habit of questioning to check for understanding while reading.

The **double-entry journal** also appears within text. The student is required to stop reading and respond to a quote. This strategy not only emphasizes the importance of closely attending to text but also brings the student's experience and prior knowledge into the reading process. The strategy is quite useful in helping students learn how to interpret text, especially when they later write about it.

Many activities are used to assess knowledge of a selection after reading. These include dramatizations, debates, tests, and group and individual projects. These culminating activities reflect the use of many strategies but are not a single strategy themselves. Any unit in the *Sourcebook* lends itself to the development of a culminating activity. For example, after reading "The Sunflower Room," a culminating activity might be for groups in the class to choose an aspect about Native Americans on which to present. After-reading strategies that reflect the reader's process of organizing and applying his thoughts about the selection can be exemplified by content mapping, summarizing, discussion, and guided writing.

The *Sourcebook* uses the strategies of content mapping and summarizing, as well as journaling and webbing, to encourage student reflection. The content mapping, which is text structure sensitive, is a particularly good way for students to "gather their thoughts" after reading. In this manner, graphic organizers are modeled and made available for practice.

One of the most powerful strategies for showing an understanding of main idea and subsequent detail is the ability to summarize. Summarization is not an easy task. Several activities that include mapping main idea and detail, both graphically and in prose, accompany summary writing activities in the *Sourcebook*. Graphic and prose organizers are explained in a step-by-step fashion. Repeated practice, paired with these several instructional models, is a valuable practice.

Incorporate Writing into the Curriculum

In reviewing the literature on writing, one statement summarizes the current thinking:

> We believe strongly that in our society, at this point in history, reading and writing, to be understood and appreciated fully, should be viewed together, learned together, and used together. (Tierney and Shanahan, 1996)

Writing and reading complement each other. Each can be used as a strategy to strengthen the other. **Quickwrites** at the beginning of a selection can bring up background and focus purpose for reading. During reading, note-taking and questioning can increase metacognitive awareness and enhance comprehension. After reading, summarizing, journaling, and paragraph and theme writing can extend thought and enhance higher-order thinking.

The *Sourcebook* is an excellent resource for presenting reading and writing in tandem. Writing is integrated into before-, during-, and after- reading instruction. Journal responses, paragraph and theme writing, summarization, quickwrites, and the graphic organizers are integrated seamlessly with the reading, creating a complete, fully integrated lesson.

Develop Vocabulary

Several researchers have shown that direct instruction in vocabulary does enhance comprehension (Beck and McKeown, 1996). It is known that effective vocabulary instruction connects prior knowledge to new words (Lenski, Wham, and Johns, 1999) and provides instructional strategies that promote the active processing of words (Beck and McKeown, 1996). Examples of strategies that do this are list-group-label, concept mapping, semantic feature analysis, synonym clustering, semantic mapping, and word sorts. Each of these strategies is involved in mapping word relationships. For example, a synonym cluster begins with a word and attaches three synonyms to that word. Attached to those three synonyms are three more synonyms, and so on.

All the above strategies can be used independently with a word journal or a word box, in pairs or small groups with a word box or a word journal, or as a whole-class activity with a word box or a word wall. It is most effective if new vocabulary is highly visible and used.

The *Sourcebook* best enhances vocabulary instruction by making the student aware of the need for growth in vocabulary. Each selection has difficult vocabulary words highlighted in the text and defined at the bottom of the page. In addition, the *Teacher's Guide* includes practice on selected words from the lesson and introduces students to a vocabulary strategy.

Conclusion

The teaching of secondary reading is not an easy endeavor. Pressures by other teachers, students, and administrators are apparent daily. Not only is the reading teacher faced with the classroom challenges of students with diverse and serious issues but also with unrealistic expectations and goals from other teachers and administrators.

Because students in the classroom are diverse in their educational needs, the secondary reading teacher is constantly juggling curriculum and time to focus on the individual needs of his or her students. Each reading teacher is his or her own research assistant, constantly reviewing the literature for best practices and strategies, through that to motivate and engage the reluctant reader. He or she is forever combing the teacher store for materials that are relevant, strategic, and appropriate.

The *Sourcebooks* are a fine resource. Not only do they model strategies at the cutting edge of research, they are also made up of good-quality, highly motivating literature, both narrative and expository. Selections from authors such as Gary Soto, Walter Dean Myers, Shelley Tanaka, and Luther Standing Bear reflect the populations of our classes and their multicultural nature.

Here is a quick guide to the main prereading, comprehension, and reflecting strategies used in the *Sourcebooks*. In order to help students internalize these strategies, the number and use of them were limited so that students could encounter them repeatedly throughout the book.

Overview

PREREADING STRATEGIES
Picture Walk

What It Is

A picture walk is a prereading activity in which students look at the images from a selection to get a sense of what the selection will be about. Other strategies may be more powerful, but a picture walk is a necessary strategy for all students to have in their repertoire. Once they become more skilled readers, they will most likely use it in conjunction with other prereading strategies—for example, skimming.

How to Introduce It

Have students page through the selection and look at the images.

Ask them questions such as the ones below to help them reflect on the images.

- How do the images make you feel?

- Based on the images, what do you think the selection will be about? Why?

Read the selection.

Encourage students to generate other questions of their own.

After reading, invite students to return to the images to discuss the accuracy of their predictions.

Example

THE PHOTO OF ...	TELLS ME ...

THE PHOTO OF ...	REMINDS ME OF ...

I think this story will be about . . .

PICTURE WALK

Why It Works

Picture walks get students, especially visual learners, actively involved in the prereading process. Questions about the images spark students' interest, activate prior knowledge, and encourage prediction.

Comments and Cautions

As an extension to the activity, invite students to add a new image, either before reading (to illustrate their prediction) or after.

Picture walks work well with both fiction and nonfiction material. You can also use a modified version for selections involving graphic sources, such as maps and diagrams.

What It Is

K-W-L is a pre- and post-reading strategy designed to facilitate students' interest in and activate their prior knowledge of a topic before reading nonfiction material. The letters *K, W,* and *L* stand for "What I **K**now," What I **W**ant to Know," and "What I **L**earned."

Look at the example of a K-W-L chart from Lesson 4, "The President's Been Shot."

Example

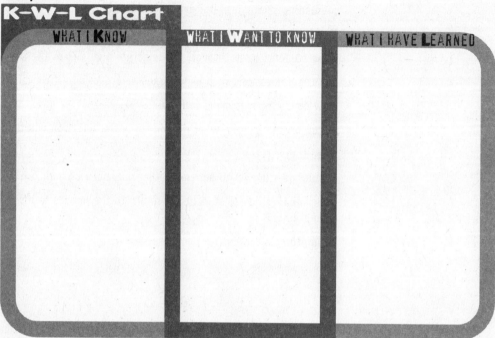

How to Introduce It

For students unfamiliar with the strategy, you might try to introduce K-W-L as a whole-class activity. Once students are familiar with the strategy, they can complete the charts on their own.

Ask students what they know about the topic. List their answers in the *K* column.

Discuss what students hope to learn about the topic from reading the selection. Write their questions in the *W* column.

Read the selection.

Return to the chart and list what students learned in the *L* column.

Why It Works

Brainstorming (the *K* part) activates prior knowledge. What sets K-W-L apart from other prereading strategies is that K-W-L also encourages students to ask questions (the *W* component), thereby setting meaningful purposes for their reading. Returning to the chart (the *L* component) brings closure to the activity and demonstrates the purposefulness of the task.

Comments and Cautions

Don't worry about the accuracy of the answers under the *K* column; this is a brainstorming activity; students can correct any errors later during the *L* part of the activity.

After brainstorming, have students categorize their lists into three or four general groups.

You might add a fourth column, "What I Still Need to Learn," for questions that aren't answered in the text or that arise after reading the material.

Anticipation Guide

What It Is

An anticipation guide is a series of statements to which students respond, first individually and then as a group, before reading a selection. For example, in Lesson 12, students are asked to circle the number that best represents their opinion about each statement.

Example

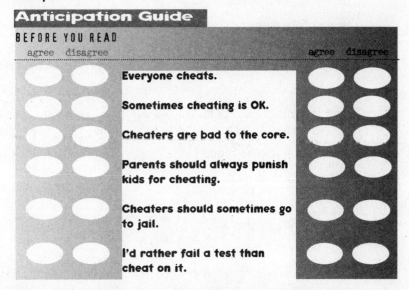

Anticipation Guide

BEFORE YOU READ

agree disagree

Everyone cheats.

Sometimes cheating is OK.

Cheaters are bad to the core.

Parents should always punish kids for cheating.

Cheaters should sometimes go to jail.

I'd rather fail a test than cheat on it.

agree disagree

How to Introduce It

Have students read the statements. (When making your own guides, keep the number of statements to fewer than 10. More than that makes it difficult to discuss in detail.)

Discuss the students' responses. This is the point of an anticipation guide—to discuss. Build the prior knowledge of one student by adding to it the prior knowledge of other students, which can be done through discussion. The discussion of anticipation guide statements can also be a powerful motivator, because once students have answered the statements, they have a stake in seeing if they are "right."

Encourage students to make predictions about what the selection will be about based on the statements.

Then read the selection.

After reading the selection, have students return to their guides and reevaluate their responses based on what they learned from the selection.

Why It Works

Anticipation guides are useful tools for eliciting predictions before reading both fiction and nonfiction. By encouraging students to think critically about a series of statements, anticipation guides raise expectations and create anticipation about the selection.

Comments and Cautions

This is a motivational activity. Try not to allow the class discussion to become divisive or judgmental; the teacher's role is that of a facilitator, encouraging students to examine and reexamine their responses. The bigger stake students have in an opinion, the more they will be motivated to read about the issue.

The focus of the guides should not be whether students' responses are "correct" or not but rather the discussion that ensues after completing the guides individually.

Anticipation guides can help students learn to express their opinions about major topics, as in lesson 12.

You can turn the entire anticipation guide process into a whole-group activity by having students respond with either "thumbs up" or "thumbs down."

Preview or Walk-through

What It Is

Previewing is a prereading strategy in which students read the title and first paragraph or two of a selection and then reflect on a few key questions. It asks the students to "sample" the selection before they begin reading and functions very much like the preview to a movie. Occasionally it is simply referred to as a *walk-through* and is a less formal variation of skimming and scanning.

How to Introduce It

Previewing can be done as an individual or group activity. You might introduce it to the group and in later lessons encourage students to work on their own.

Read aloud, or have students read to themselves, the first paragraph or two of a selection.

Have students respond to four or five questions about the selection. Their responses will be predictions based on their initial sampling of the piece. Questions might include these:

- What is the selection about?
- When does it take place?
- Who is in it?
- How will the selection end?

Read the rest of the selection.

Return to the questions and discuss the accuracy of students' predictions. Were they surprised at how the selection turned out based on their initial preview? Why or why not?

Example

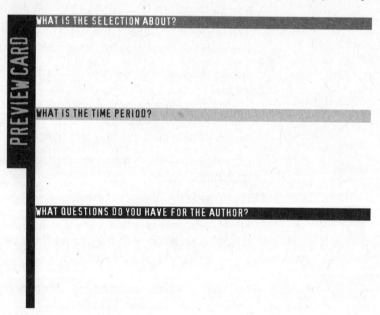

PREVIEW CARD

WHAT IS THE SELECTION ABOUT?

WHAT IS THE TIME PERIOD?

WHAT QUESTIONS DO YOU HAVE FOR THE AUTHOR?

Why It Works

Previews work because they provide a frame of reference in which to understand new material. Previews build context, particularly when students read about unfamiliar topics. Discussing the questions and predicting before reading help students set purposes for reading and create interest in the subject matter.

Comments and Cautions

Previews work best with more difficult reading selections, especially texts with difficult vocabulary. Previewing helps students to understand a context for a selection—what's the subject? Where's the story located? Who's involved?

Once students are familiar with previews, you might ask them to generate their own list of questions and have a partner respond to them.

Quickwrite

What It Is

A quickwrite is just what the name implies, a short, one- to ten-minute activity in which students write down their thoughts about a topic. Quickwriting is impromptu writing, without concern for spelling and grammatical conventions. It is intended to help students articulate some of the prior knowledge they have on a subject.

How to Introduce It

Provide students with a topic on which to focus.

Invite students to write about whatever comes to mind regarding the topic.

Encourage students to share their quickwrites in a small group. Discuss their similarities and differences.

Ask students to predict what they think the selection will be about based on their quickwrites.

Read the selection.

Discuss the connections between students' quickwrites and the selection.

Example

BEFORE YOU READ
Do a 1-minute quickwrite.
1. Write about what you want and need. Is there any difference between the two?
2. When you've finished, look over what you wrote.
3. Circle your most important ideas and share them with a partner.

1-MINUTE QUICKWRITE

Why It Works

Quickwriting works as a prereading strategy on a number of levels. For one, the very process of writing without regard to writing conventions frees up students to write from a deeper level of understanding. Quickwriting encourages students to make connections between their own lives and the reading material, activates prior knowledge, and sparks interest. Quickwriting can also help correct misconceptions about a topic.

Comments and Cautions

As an extension to the activity, have students quickwrite again after reading the selection and compare their two quickwrites to see what they've learned from reading the material.

Skimming

What It Is

Skimming is a prereading strategy in which students look over the entire selection to get a sense of what it will be about. It is one of the best prereading strategies and best known. Much of the time, however, students never learn how to skim effectively and what to look for.

How to Introduce It

Skimming is a useful tool, both for prereading and content area reading, but one that many students have difficulty mastering. Therefore, introduce skimming as a whole-group activity; teacher modeling might work best for the initial activity. Skimming involves these activities:

- Examining the table of contents
- Reading the first and last paragraph
- Checking the selection's length and reading difficulty
- Reading any captions
- Looking over illustrations
- Noting section headings, diagrams, and other graphic sources

Example

Skimming Notes

THIS SELECTION IS FICTION/NONFICTION BECAUSE:

WHAT 4–5 KEY WORDS AND PHRASES DID YOU NOTICE?

WHAT IS THE TOPIC OF THE FIRST PARAGRAPH?

WHAT IS THE LAST PARAGRAPH ABOUT?

To help students master the technique of skimming, provide them with a series of questions to answer about the selection, as in the example above. Questions such as these provide a clear purpose for skimming and help students focus their attention on the key parts of the selection.

Why It Works

Skimming is an excellent tool for setting purposes and activating prior knowledge before reading nonfiction material. Like a picture walk, skimming draws students into a selection.

Comments and Cautions

Skimming works best when students have a clear purpose for going through a selection. Direct students, for example, to underline one to two words in each line of the first and last paragraph, or to circle names or words that appear a number of times.

Teach a clear method for skimming and try not to assume students will know what it means.

Think-Pair-and-Share

What It Is

Think-pair-and-share is a prereading strategy that encourages group discussion and prediction about what students will read. Students work in pairs to discuss sentences selected from the text.

How to Introduce It

Break students into groups of two or three. Present three to six sentences from the selection. Ask group members to read the sentences and discuss what they mean and in what order they appear in the text.

Encourage groups to make predictions and generate questions about the reading.

Then read the selection.

Have groups discuss the selection and the accuracy of their think-pair-and-share sentences. How many were able to correctly predict the order in which they appeared? How many could predict what the selection was about?

Example

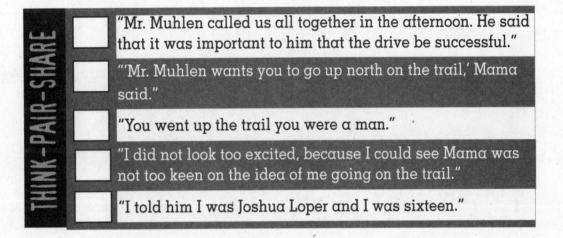

THINK-PAIR-SHARE

- "Mr. Muhlen called us all together in the afternoon. He said that it was important to him that the drive be successful."
- "'Mr. Muhlen wants you to go up north on the trail,' Mama said."
- "You went up the trail you were a man."
- "I did not look too excited, because I could see Mama was not too keen on the idea of me going on the trail."
- "I told him I was Joshua Loper and I was sixteen."

Why It Works

Think-pair-and-share can be a powerful tool for getting students motivated to read. Small-group work such as this gives students the chance to discover that they don't always have to come up with all the answers themselves; sometimes two or three heads *are* better than one. Working in groups also provides reluctant readers with the understanding that all readers bring different skills and schema to the reading task. The activity also begins the critical process of "constructing meaning" of the text.

Comments and Cautions

Enlist students in building the think-pair-and-share activity. Have each group member write one sentence from the text on a file card. Then ask groups to exchange file cards—one group pieces together the sentences of another group.

The active, social nature of this activity stimulates students, which can be highly motivational and beneficial if properly channeled into purposeful activity.

Word Web

What It Is

A word web is a prereading activity in which students brainstorm and make connections to a key concept from the reading material.

Example

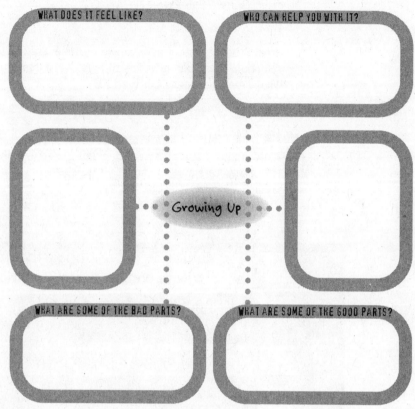

How to Introduce It

Word webs can be done independently or as a whole-group activity. You might want to do the initial word webs with the whole group and assign later word webs for independent learning.

Write a key concept in a circle. For example, in Lesson 10, "Hera," students are to describe Hera or Zeus.

Have students brainstorm words related to the concept on spokes coming out of the circle.

Discuss with students how the key word is connected to the reading material.

Read the selection.

Return to the word web and add any new ideas brought about by reading the selection.

Why It Works

Word webs are excellent tools for developing students' conceptual knowledge. They tap into students' prior knowledge and help students make connections between what they know and what they will learn.

Comments and Cautions

Even though this is a brainstorming activity, do challenge incorrect assumptions about the concept, particularly when using the word web with a whole group. You want to be sure that students go into the reading assignment with an accurate impression of the concept.

If students get "stuck," encourage them to write down words, phrases, examples, or images they associate with the concept.

RESPONSE STRATEGIES

The response strategies are introduced at the beginning of each *Sourcebook* (pages 8–10). They are the heart of the interactive reading students are asked to do throughout the book. In Part II of each lesson, one or two response strategies are suggested to help teach students how to mark up a text and become active readers.

Struggling readers do not naturally know how to interact with a text, so these strategies are designed to help them get started. Examples are also provided in each lesson to model the strategy. The intent is to build the habit of reading with a pen in hand and marking up the text until it becomes a natural way to read.

Response Strategies

1. Mark or highlight
2. Question
3. Clarify
4. Visualize
5. Predict
6. React and connect

Example

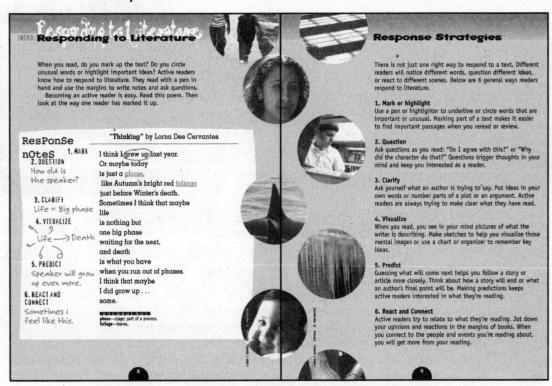

The purpose of these response strategies in each lesson is to

1. help students learn how to mark up a text
2. help students focus on specific aspects of a text and find the information they need
3. build lifelong habits for students by repeating good reading practices

COMPREHENSION STRATEGIES
Directed Reading

What It Is

Directed reading is a structured activity designed to guide students through a reading selection. Directed reading is composed of a series of steps, including readiness, directed silent reading, comprehension check and discuss, oral rereading, and follow-up activities. In the *Sourcebook*, students gain readiness in Part I, read silently in Part II, and then encounter questions that check their comprehension throughout the selection. Teachers are encouraged to have students go back through selections with this strategy and read the selection a second time. Repeated reading of a selection often increases reading fluency, which in itself often increases comprehension.

How to Introduce It

First, help students get ready to read by activating their prior knowledge, creating interest, and setting purposes. The prereading strategies described in Part I of the lesson offer suggestions for activities that promote reading readiness.

Next, have students read the selection silently. Guide them as they read by providing stopping points, such as the stop and think sections in the *Sourcebook*. Encourage them to focus on the purpose for reading that they established in Part I.

Example

STOP AND THINK

How long ago did the Egyptians start making mummies?

After students have read the selection, take a moment to engage them in a discussion about what they read.

During or directly after the discussion, have students orally reread the selection to answer any remaining questions or clear up any confusion about the reading material.

During the discussion and oral rereading stages, you can get a sense of what kind of difficulties students are having with the material. Use follow-up activities to work on these areas of weakness and to extend students' understanding of the material, or use the additional comprehension activities included in each *Teacher's Guide* lesson. Follow-up activities range from direct skill instruction designed for individual or small-group work to response activities, such as those found in the *Sourcebook*.

Why It Works

Directed reading enhances students' ability to think critically and reflectively about the reading material. It helps them ask the questions good readers ask themselves as they read. The structured format ensures that students of all reading levels will be asking the right kinds of questions needed to comprehend the text.

Comments and Cautions

As with any comprehension strategy, directed reading needs to be modified to fit the needs of individual students.

Directed reading can be overly prescriptive, and overuse can contribute to passive reading, if it is relied on exclusively. Including activities that require student speculation and higher-level thinking will foster more active reading.

Prediction

What It Is

Prediction is both a comprehension strategy and a prereading strategy, but in the *Sourcebooks* it is formally used mostly as a comprehension strategy. Nearly all of the prereading strategies used in the *Sourcebooks* involve some level of prediction, but prediction is categorized as a comprehension strategy. When students predict during reading, they rely on information they have already read in the selection.

How to Introduce It

Break the selection into three or four parts.

Have students read to the first stopping point and then ask them to predict what they think will happen. Predictive questions include these:

- What will happen to the character?
- How do you think the problem will be resolved?
- How do you think the selection will end?

Example

stop+predict
What do you think Milo will do with the tollbooth?

As students read on, encourage them to reflect on their predictions and modify them as further information is provided.

After reading, discuss the accuracy of students' predictions, not to determine if the predictions were "correct" but to provide closure to the activity and validate students' responses. Reflecting on the predictions will also help students see the information they might have used from the selection to predict but did not.

Why It Works

Because of the students' assertions about "what will happen," predicting gives students a stake in what they read. Their opinion is on the line, and this helps students set purposes for reading.

Comments and Cautions

Look for natural stopping points in texts; obvious spots to stop and predict what will happen next usually occur before episodes, or events, that occur in the story.

Prediction is best used with fiction, although it can also be applied to nonfiction with readers skilled at making predictions.

Graphic Organizer

What It Is

A graphic organizer is a visual representation of the key information for a reading selection. Graphic organizers can be as simple as a two-column chart or as complicated as a multi-dimensional diagram. They come in many sizes and shapes, such as plot charts, cause-effect charts, and character maps.

How to Introduce It

Begin by explaining the purpose of the graphic and the kind of information students should put into each of its parts.

Invite students to fill in the graphic organizer as they read, and then review it and make any modifications after completing the selection. For example, on page 207 in "Alaskan Bears," students use the graphic organizer to keep track of the details about grizzly bears in Alaska. As they read, they write the name of an animal in each column and describe how it adapts to the desert.

Examples

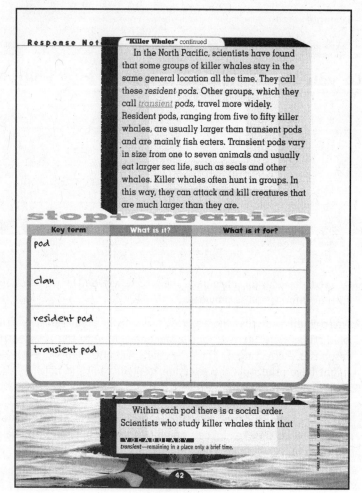

Examples

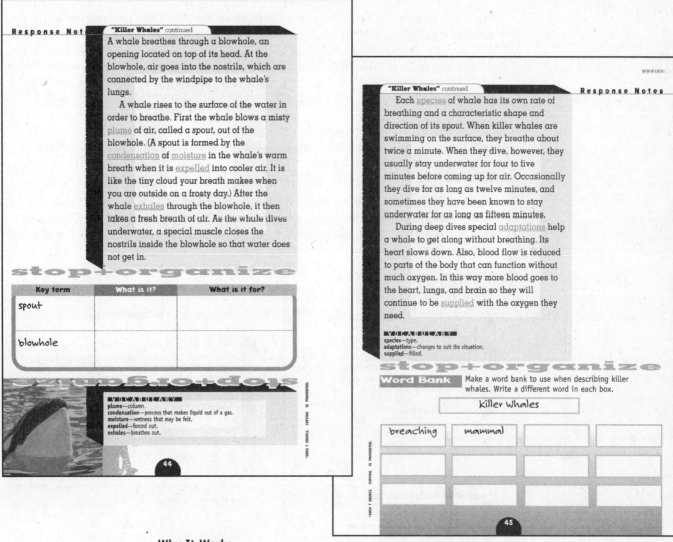

Why It Works

A graphic organizer is a useful tool for helping students to structure what they understand from their reading. It also helps students make connections between ideas, especially in flow charts or cause-effect charts.

Comments and Cautions

Some of the more common graphic organizers are these:

- Venn diagram for showing comparison and contrast

- Cause-and-effect chart for demonstrating causal relationships

- Sequence map for keeping track of a series of events

- Problem-solution map for identifying the problem and its solution(s)

- Word web for representing information about a particular concept

Graphic organizers are excellent tools for all students but are especially helpful for visual learners.

Reciprocal Reading

What It Is

Reciprocal reading is a small-group activity in which students take turns reading aloud to each other or with a tutor. It is such a powerful reading strategy that it has been modified for use in the *Sourcebooks*. The power of the questions generated does not diminish when reciprocal reading is taken out of the group work or tutor/pupil setting and transferred to a pupil-and-text relationship. The strategy is characterized by asking students to ask questions, clarify, predict, and summarize.

How to Introduce It

Take a moment to introduce the strategy to the whole class. Explain that this strategy involves working with a partner or reading tutor and asking four kinds of questions: clarifying ones, predicting ones, exploratory ones, and summarizing ones.

Invite one student to read the title and opening paragraphs aloud. At the first question point, ask for a volunteer to answer the question. Work through the entire selection with students as a group. Then, ask students to reread the selection again in pairs, taking turns asking and then answering the questions.

Example

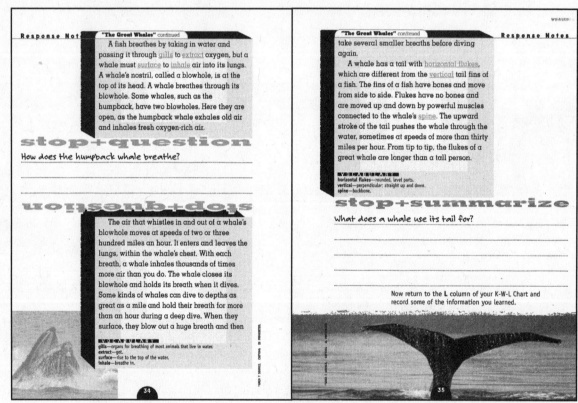

Why It Works

Reciprocal reading can be an excellent tool for both reinforcing listening skills (an often-overlooked skill) and improving reading fluency. It structures the work of students working with a reading partner and naturally helps them ask useful questions—the kinds good readers automatically ask—about a text.

Comments and Cautions

To ensure that the activity doesn't turn into a word-attack session, go over unfamiliar vocabulary before reading.

For reciprocal reading to be successful, it is important to introduce the idea to the whole class before turning students loose with a reading partner. Taking the time to walk through the process will prove beneficial later on when students are asked to work with their reading partners because they will have a structured routine to fall back on.

Double-Entry Journal

What It Is

A double-entry journal is an adaptation of the more familiar response journal. Typically, the left column includes quotes or facts from a selection, while the right column offers students the opportunity to respond to the quotation or idea. It is a very good strategy to build students' ability to comprehend and interpret a text.

How to Introduce It

Begin by having students list quotations from the selection that interest them, or you can pull out some quotations yourself, as is done in the *Sourcebook*. The benefits of selecting the quotations for students are that the focus is then on interpreting passages of the text and that the task is simplified, making it easier for students to succeed.

Invite students to reflect on the meaning of each quotation and write their thoughts in the right column.

Example

Double-entry Journal

Read this quote from the story. Then write how it makes you feel.

Quote	My thoughts
"And worst of all . . . there's nothing for me to do, nowhere I'd care to go, and hardly anything worth seeing."	

Why It Works

Double-entry journals encourage students to become more engaged in what they are reading by focusing on just one part of the text at a time. With this kind of journal, students naturally make connections between the literature and their own lives. Double-entry journals expand on students' understanding of the material and build an initial interpretive response. By beginning the interpretation of literature, students will find writing about a text easier if they focus on the quotations they (or you) selected and their interpretations of them.

Comments and Cautions

Even if you structure the activity by selecting quotations, invite students to add those that have particular meaning to themselves as well.

Encourage students to use double-entry journals in other reading situations, including content-area reading.

What It Is

Retelling is a comprehension strategy and assessment tool in which students retell a selection. It works best with chronological selections as a means of checking whether students followed the sequence of events.

How to Introduce It

Before reading the selection, let students know that they will be asked to retell or summarize their reading in their own words.

Either at the end of the selection or at certain stopping points within the selection (as done in the *Sourcebook*), have students retell what they have read as if they are telling it to a friend who has never heard it before.

Have students compare their retellings to examine each other's interpretations of the reading material.

Why It Works

Because retelling allows students to respond in their own words to what they've read, it increases both the quality and quantity of what is comprehended. Retelling also helps students make the text more personally meaningful and provides a deeper understanding of the reading material.

Comments and Cautions

You might have students tape-record the retellings and let students listen and assess their own work.

For fictional selections, try having students retell the story from another character's point of view to provide a different perspective to the tale.

A student's retelling offers a window into the student's thinking and is, therefore, a valuable assessment tool as well.

Example

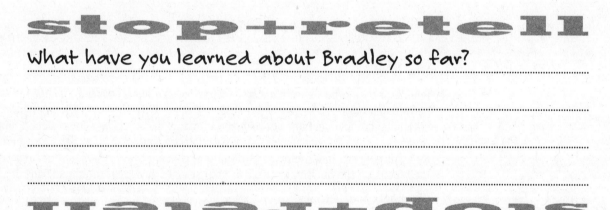

stop+retell

What have you learned about Bradley so far?

....

....

....

....

Story Frame

What It Is

A story frame is a visual representation of one or more of the key elements of a story: character, setting, plot, and theme. It helps students graphically construct the main elements of a story.

How to Introduce It

First, explain the idea of a story frame and its elements: plot, setting, characters, and themes. Be sure students understand that story frames can organize events, too. Just as there are many kinds of stories, students need to understand that there are many kinds of story frames.

Example

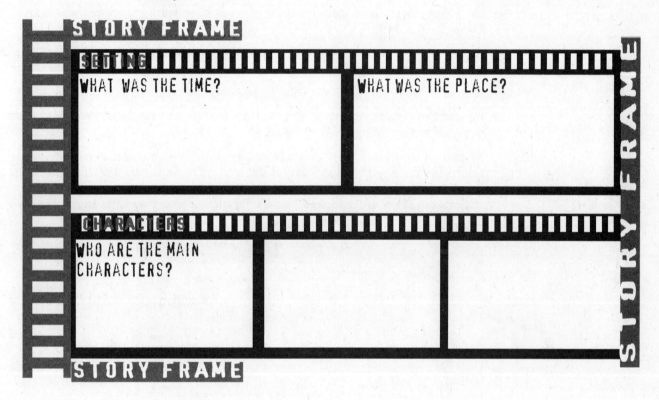

STORY FRAME

SETTING

WHAT WAS THE TIME?

WHAT WAS THE PLACE?

CHARACTERS

WHO ARE THE MAIN CHARACTERS?

STORY FRAME

After completing the frame, have students use it as the basis for discussion about the selection or to help in their written responses.

Comments and Cautions

Story frames come in all shapes and sizes. Modify the frame to fit the needs of the students and the focus of the material. For instance, in "Thank You, Ma'am," the story frame focuses on plot, characters, and setting; others focus on character development throughout a story. Other frames might focus on theme or other story elements.

For students who need more guidance filling in their frames, provide them with question prompts, such as "What happened first?" "What happened next?" "Who did it happen to?" Let students know this is a strategy they are free to experiment with and use in whatever way they find is most helpful.

REFLECTIVE READING STRATEGIES

The reflective reading strategies occur in **Part V** of each lesson. They help students take away more from what they read. All too often students are asked, "Did you get it?" Reading seems like a code they have been asked to decipher but cannot. They feel stupid and think they have failed.

How can we turn around struggling readers if the only payoff for reading is "getting it"? Good readers read for a variety of reasons: to entertain themselves, to expand their understanding of a subject or develop their thinking in an area, or simply because they have to read. Yet good readers naturally take away more from what they read. For example:

- We read novels by Nobel Prize winners because of their writing **style**.

- We read sports pages because they are **enjoyable**.

- We read philosophy or religious meditations to add more **depth** to how we think about things.

- We read about such topics as Lamaze childbearing techniques or natural foods because they are personally **meaningful** to us.

- We read cartoons and *People* magazine because they are **easy** to browse through.

- We read directions about setting up a computer because we **have to**; we need to have that particular understanding.

We read, in other words, for a variety of reasons. As teachers, we need to help struggling readers see that—and not just that they did not "get it" on the multiple-choice test. So, **Part V** of each lesson in the *Sourcebook* is a "reflective" assessment, a looking back, so students can see what they *gained* from the lesson, not what they failed to understand.

Example

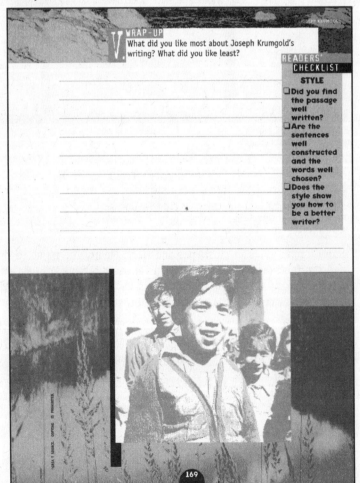

V WRAP-UP
What did you like most about Joseph Krumgold's writing? What did you like least?

READERS' CHECKLIST

STYLE
☐ Did you find the passage well written?
☐ Are the sentences well constructed and the words well chosen?
☐ Does the style show you how to be a better writer?

169

The purposes of the **Readers' Checklist** in each lesson are to:

1. model for students the questions good readers ask of themselves after reading.

2. expand the reasons for which students want to read.

3. build lifelong habits for students by repeating best reading practices.

Reflective Assessment

1. **Understanding**

   Did you understand the reading?

   Was the message or point clear?

   Can you restate what the reading is about?

2. **Ease**

   Was the passage easy to read?

   Were you able to read it smoothly and without difficulty?

3. **Meaning**

   Did you learn something from the reading?

   Did it affect you or make an impression?

4. **Style**

   Did you find the passage well written?

   Are the sentences well constructed and the words well chosen?

   Does the style show you how to be a better writer?

5. **Depth**

   Did the reading make you think about things?

   Did it set off thoughts beyond the surface topic?

6. **Enjoyment**

   Did you like the reading?

   Was the reading experience pleasurable?

   Would you want to reread the piece or recommend it to someone?

   Invite students regularly to provide examples and reasons for their answers to these questions.

Family Matters

Unit Background   FAMILY MATTERS (pages 11–30)

Two excerpts from autobiographies are included in this unit: "Father" from Gary Soto's *Living Up the Street: Narrative Recollections* and "Mother" from *The Seventh Child: A Lucky Life* by Freddie Mae Baxter.

Gary Soto was born in Fresno, California, in 1952 and graduated magna cum laude from California State University in 1974. He received an M.F.A. in creative writing from the University of California in 1976 and began teaching at Berkeley in 1977. He received a Guggenheim fellowship in 1979 and a Levinson Award from *Poetry* in 1984. His books include *Baseball in April and Other Stories* (1990), *Who Will Know Us?* (1990), and *New and Selected Poems* (1995). He is known primarily as a poet and as a writer for young adults. *Living Up the Street* won the American Book Award in 1985.

Freddie Mae Baxter grew up in Denmark, South Carolina, one of five girls and three boys and the youngest in the family. Her father left the family when she was a child, and her mother died in 1940 when Freddie Mae was 16. When she was 17, she moved to New Jersey to live with an aunt and found a job cooking for a family. She then moved to Harlem, where she has worked and lived ever since. The excerpt in the *Sourcebook* is from the first chapter of the book about her life, which she told to Gloria Bley Miller, who taped Baxter's reminiscences and prepared them for publication.

Teaching the Introduction

Photos on this page show a coach holding a bat, a large family at dinner, and a pensive young boy.

Families deal with all sorts of matters. They celebrate the births of children and mourn the deaths of relatives. When tragedy strikes or when good fortune shines down, it's comforting to have your family by your side.

1. Read the unit introduction with students, and ask them to think about a time when a family, a parent, or a grandparent was a comfort. If some students would like to tell about such a time, encourage them to do so. (If there are students in your class who lack family or for some reason may find discussion about their own families painful, provide alternate activities involving their ideas about how families are depicted on television and in movies.)

2. Ask students to make a list of things they like best about their family. They might think about customs, family activities, food, or special family members. After students have completed their list, they might compose a poem using what they have written on the list.

3. Tell students that the first selection in this unit is about a boy whose father died and the second selection is about a mother who, despite poverty, was successful in instilling love and compassion in her large family. Ask students to brainstorm about why they think it might be hard to be a parent and what they think parents most want for their children.

Opening Activity

Have students talk about what they think children, of all ages, owe their parents. Ask how the responsibilities of children can contribute to harmony in a family.

Father

Skills and Strategies Overview

THEME	Family Matters
READING LEVEL	easy
VOCABULARY	◇flecked ◇imply ◇coiled ◇sorrow ◇gleamed
PREREADING	quickwrite
RESPONSE	visualize
COMPREHENSION	retell
PREWRITING	narrowing a topic
WRITING	paragraph / sentences
ASSESSMENT	understanding

BACKGROUND

Gary Soto is a poet, short story writer, and essayist who focuses much of his writing on his experiences growing up in the barrio of Fresno, California. The short story "Father" is taken from his 1985 memoir, *Living Up the Street: Narrative Recollections*, which won an American Book Award. The story concerns the accidental death of young Soto's father shortly after the family has moved into a new home, the circumstances surrounding his funeral, and the aftermath of the funeral. Soto describes his reactions at the time—conspicuousness in the midst of grieving relatives, discomfort from his tight clothes and the heat, fear, and embarrassment.

UNIT THEME Gary Soto explores themes of death, grief, and family relationships in this memoir.

GRAPHIC ORGANIZER A chart like the one below can help readers keep track of the sensory language Soto uses in his writing. Your students may be able to find twice as many words as listed here.

Sensory Language in "Father"

sight words	sound words	taste words	touch words
showed silver	hissing	iced tea	leveled
water-stained	slammed	candies	dragged
flecked	shouting	doughnut	combed
nickel-colored	banged		late summer heat
trigger-like	clatter		pinched
lined			punched
harsh afternoon light			coiled
moist-looking			pressing
gleamed			itchy
twisted from crying			

BEFORE YOU READ

Read through the introduction to the lesson (page 12) with students. Help them begin thinking about the theme of family matters. Then introduce the prereading activity, a **one-minute quickwrite**. (Refer to the **Strategy Handbook** on page 40 for more help.)

Motivation Strategy

If possible, borrow a copy of *Living Up the Street* or *A Summer Life* (1991), both of which are autobiographical accounts of Soto's boyhood in Fresno, California, during the 1950s and 1960s. Read aloud a page or two from each book to give students a sense of the author's writing style. Point out the imagery in Soto's writing.

ENGAGING STUDENTS Explain that "Father" is an autobiographical essay about a painful childhood memory. Ask students to think about something painful or difficult that happened to them when they were children. Have them make a note of the experience in the margins of the book. Keeping this memory in mind as they read Soto's reminiscences will help them understand some of the feelings and events he describes.

Vocabulary Building

Help students use **context clues** as they read to figure out the meanings of difficult words, especially the key vocabulary for this lesson: *flecked, imply, coiled, sorrow,* and *gleamed*. Have students circle these words in the text. Although the footnotes define these words, you'll still want to be sure students are making some attempt to define in context. Model using context and then checking your ideas against the footnote: "I don't know the word *gleamed*. I see, though, that it describes shiny things. Could *gleamed* mean 'shine'? I can check the footnote to see if my guess is correct." For additional practice with these words, see page 66.

STRATEGY LESSON: PREFIXES As students read, point out words with prefixes, such as *depressed, recall,* and *unfurnished*. Model for students how to separate a prefix from the root word (un + furnished). Remind the class that when a prefix is added to a word, the meaning of the word changes. Also help them become familiar with the definitions of these three prefixes: (*de-* = from, down), (*re-* = back, again), and (*un-* = not).

For additional practice on this strategy, see the **Vocabulary** blackline master on page 66.

Prereading strategies

The purpose of a **quickwrite** is to get students writing almost before they know it. To avoid the problem of students staring at a blank sheet of paper, always suggest a topic for a class quickwrite. In this case, students should write everything that comes to mind when they hear the word *father*. Remind students that during a quickwrite, ideas are more important than sentence structure and grammar. They should feel free to jot down impressions, ideas, thoughts, and feelings in any form. When students have finished, you might have them read what they have written and circle words or phrases that they like. They may be able to use some of these details later in their own writing.

Spanish-speaking Students

"Papá" viene de la autobiografía de Gary Soto. En esta selección, describe la relación fuerte con su padre. Dependía de él por guía y le consideraba una figura muy importante en su vida. Cuando el padre se muere inesperadamente, Soto está triste e incrédulo. Le cuesta trabajo expresar las muchas emociones que provocó la muerte.

II. READ

Gary Soto uses a great deal of sensory language in his writing. Students should have no trouble **visualizing** the people, places, and events that he describes. Ask students to keep track of what they "see" by making sketches in the **Response Notes**. Their sketches might be fairly detailed, like the example on page 13, or very simple and quick.

Response Strategy

HIGHLIGHT AND MARK As an alternate or additional response strategy, have students highlight or mark words and phrases that they think are interesting, important, confusing, or surprising. Ask them to watch carefully for clues about Soto's personality and emotions. Each time they find a new clue, they should underline or circle it. Students can use these notes to help them answer the **stop and think** questions that interrupt the text.

Comprehension Strategies

Be sure students understand that as they are reading, they will stop occasionally in order to **retell** the events described. Retelling can help readers make connections between events and ideas and clarify what exactly has occurred. Remind the class that when they retell, they'll need to be thorough but brief. Each time they come to a **stop and retell**, they should think of one or two sentences to write that summarize the events up to that point.

For more help, see the **Comprehension** blackline master on page 67.

Discussion Questions

COMPREHENSION 1. What are Gary and his father doing at the beginning of the selection? *(watering the ground in anticipation of a new lawn)*

2. What happens to Gary's father? *(He has an accident at work and dies as a result.)*

CRITICAL THINKING 3. What inferences can you make about the relationship between Gary's parents? *(They obviously care about each other. They are affectionate and playful.)*

4. What emotions does Gary feel at his father's funeral? *(Answers will vary. Possible: confusion, embarrassment, shyness, uncertainty.)*

5. What is the significance of the last line of "Father"? *(Ask students to reread the final sentence on page 18. Students might suggest that it shows the depth of Soto's grief. The clatter of the marbles in the empty room symbolizes the clatter and confusion he feels in his heart.)*

Literary Skill

SENSORY LANGUAGE To introduce a literary skill with this selection, you might teach a short lesson on sensory language. Remind the class that sensory language appeals to the five senses and brings freshness and immediacy to a narrative. For practice with this skill, ask the class to skim the story again. Have them circle words and phrases that appeal to the senses. (You might have them keep track of the images they find on a chart similar to the one on page 62 of the teacher's guide.) Discuss the effect this imagery has upon the text as a whole.

III. GATHER YOUR THOUGHTS

The prewriting activities on page 19 will help prepare students to write a **paragraph** about a family event or experience. After they choose a topic, students **narrow the focus** of their writing.

They can plan their **paragraphs** at the bottom of page 19. Remind them not to skimp on details at the planning stage. When they start to write, they can pick and choose the details they like best.

Prewriting Strategies

TOPIC SENTENCE After students narrow their focus and plan their paragraphs, you may want to help them write topic sentence for their paragraph. This simple formula can help students write their topic sentences:(A specific topic) + (a specific feeling) = a good topic sentence.

IV. WRITE

Explain to students that their **paragraphs** should begin with their topic sentence. They will use the body of the paragraph to support the first sentence. (Have them use the details they wrote on the organizer on page 19 as support for their topic sentences.). Ask them to try to use one or two sensory details in their writing.

After students have written a first draft, have them exchange papers with a partner. Partners should check that the paragraph opens with a clear topic sentence and contains adequate supporting details.

WRITING RUBRIC You might show students this rubric to help them with their assignment:

Do students' paragraphs

- begin with a topic sentence that names the experience and how they felt about it?

- include information about who was there, what happened, where it happened, and why it happened?

- contain at least two sensory details?

Grammar, Usage, and Mechanics

When they are ready to proofread their work, refer students to the **Writers' Checklist**. Remind the class that every sentence must begin with a capital letter, end with a punctuation mark, and express a complete thought. For example:

Incomplete thought: My father, who drove us across the country the summer I was eight years old.

Complete thought: My father, who drove us across the country the summer I was eight years old, was the kindest man I've ever known.

V. WRAP-UP

Ask students to use the **Readers' Checklist** to help them think about the message of the writing. The questions will help them reflect on their **understanding** of the reading.

Assessment

To test students' comprehension, use the **Assessment** blackline master on page 69.

Name _____

VOCABULARY

Words from the Selection

DIRECTIONS Circle the word or words in each sentence that give you context clues about the meaning of the underlined words. Then write what the words mean. The underlined words are from the story.

1. Mother laughed when she saw how spotted Father's shirt was. It was <u>flecked</u> with mud.

_____

2. Mother held up the pitcher of iced tea and pointed to it, as if to <u>imply</u> that Father should sit down and rest.

_____

3. Father had showed me how he wound the hose in a spiral, so I always <u>coiled</u> it the same way after watering the yard.

_____

4. I wasn't exactly happy, but neither did I feel any <u>sorrow</u> at first.

_____

5. Father gave me a big smile, and his teeth <u>gleamed</u> in the light of the lamp.

_____

Strategy Lesson: Prefixes

DIRECTIONS Look at the meanings of the prefixes in the box below. Then write the word from the list that fits each sentence.

Prefixes

de- = from, down
re- = back, again
un- = not

6. There was a lot of space in our house because most of the rooms were _____.

7. We need to fill in the _____ areas of the yard with dirt.

depressed

8. I can't _____ exactly where we planted the morning glory seeds.

uncertain

9. I am also _____ about where we buried the gold.

unfurnished

10. My sister will _____ soon and straighten everything out.

return

recall

Name _____

COMPREHENSION
Graphic Organizer _____

DIRECTIONS Use this web to show what you know about "Father."

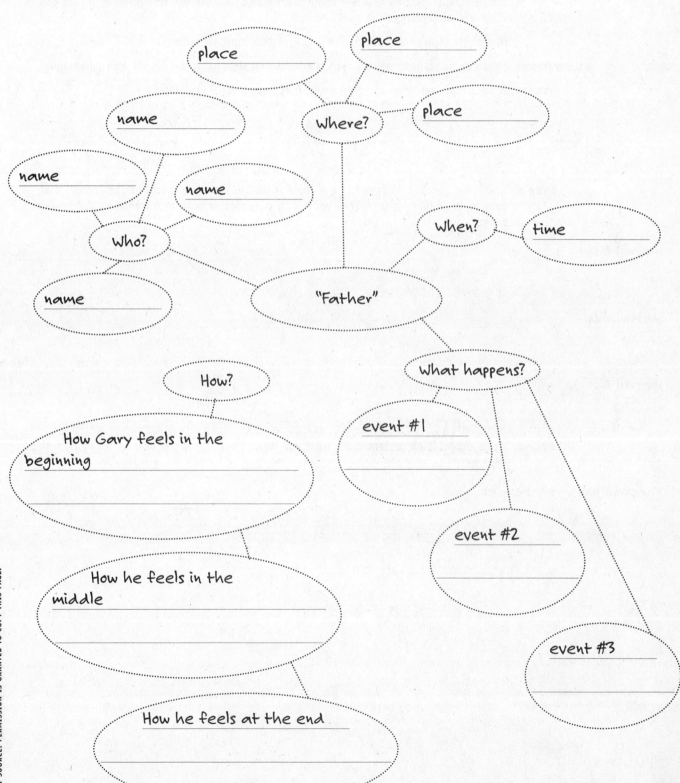

Name _____

PREWRITING
Writing a Topic Sentence and Details

Every paragraph you write must have a topic sentence. A topic sentence tells the subject of the paragraph and how you feel about the subject. You can use this formula to help you write a topic sentence:

(A specific topic) + (a specific feeling) = a good topic sentence.

DIRECTIONS Follow these steps to write a topic sentence and supporting details for your paragraph.

STEP 1. Write a topic sentence about an event that happened to your family.

	+		=	
(event)		(how it made me feel)		your topic sentence

STEP 2. Next, plan details that support your topic sentence. Your details will be the "proof" that your topic sentence is true. They will also give readers important information about your topic.

detail #1: _____

_____

detail #2: _____

_____

detail #3: _____

_____

STEP 3. Write a concluding sentence. Tell what you learned about yourself or your family from this experience.

My concluding sentence: _____

_____

_____

_____

Name _____

ASSESSMENT
Multiple-Choice Test

DIRECTIONS On the blanks provided, write the letter of the best answer for each question.

_____ 1. In the beginning of the story, what are the men preparing the ground for?
   A. a tree   C. a pool
   B. a garden   D. a new lawn

_____ 2. What are the men talking about planting?
   A. fruit trees   C. a flower garden
   B. a vegetable garden   D. A. and B.

_____ 3. What does Gary's father show him how to do?
   A. plant a garden   C. plant a tree
   B. use the hose to water D. level the yard

_____ 4. Who sits with Dad?
   A. Gary's mother   C. the neighbor
   B. Gary   D. no one

_____ 5. What is one thing Gary's parents do not discuss?
   A. their new home   C. their jobs
   B. their neighbors   D. the playground

_____ 6. How do Gary and his parents feel after their long day of work?
   A. happy   C. tired
   B. unsure   D. A. and C.

_____ 7. How does Gary try to please his father?
   A. He waters the patch of dirt.   C. He cleans up the tools.
   B. He plants a garden.   D. He helps level the yard.

_____ 8. After he learns his father has died, how does Gary feel?
   A. sad   C. empty
   B. conspicuous   D. numb

_____ 9. How does Gary feel as he views his father in the casket?
   A. sad   C. scared
   B. surprised   D. B. and C.

_____ 10. What do the relatives help to finish after Mr. Soto has died?
   A. a sidewalk   C. a fence
   B. a garage   D. a garden

Short-Essay Test

What does Soto mean when he says that the clatter of the marbles hitting the wall stopped him from hearing "the things in my heart"?

Skills and Strategies Overview

THEME	Family Matters
READING LEVEL	average
VOCABULARY	◇married ◇starch ◇leftovers ◇grace ◇shared
PREREADING	preview
RESPONSE	react and connect
COMPREHENSION	directed reading
PREWRITING	main idea and details
WRITING	descriptive paragraph / sentence fragments
ASSESSMENT	meaning

BACKGROUND

"Mother" is an excerpt from Freddie Mae Baxter's critically acclaimed autobiography, *Seventh Child: A Lucky Life*. Baxter was born in 1923 in rural South Carolina. Her family was so poor, she says, that she spent all of her childhood in a house with no running water. The family's situation worsened when Freddie Mae's father abandoned them, although Freddie Mae's mother refused to spend time lamenting her situation. Instead, she picked herself up and in so doing instilled in her children a self-help philosophy for which Baxter is eternally grateful.

Baxter tells her story in a voice that provides clues about her personality. Her straightforward, no-nonsense view of family teaches a valuable lesson about appreciating what you have and patiently waiting for what you don't.

UNIT THEME Freddie Mae Baxter describes her hardworking, optimistic mother and the lessons this woman was able to teach her eight children.

GRAPHIC ORGANIZER A word web can help students keep track of descriptive words in a narrative. After they finish reading, show students the web below. What words would they like to add?

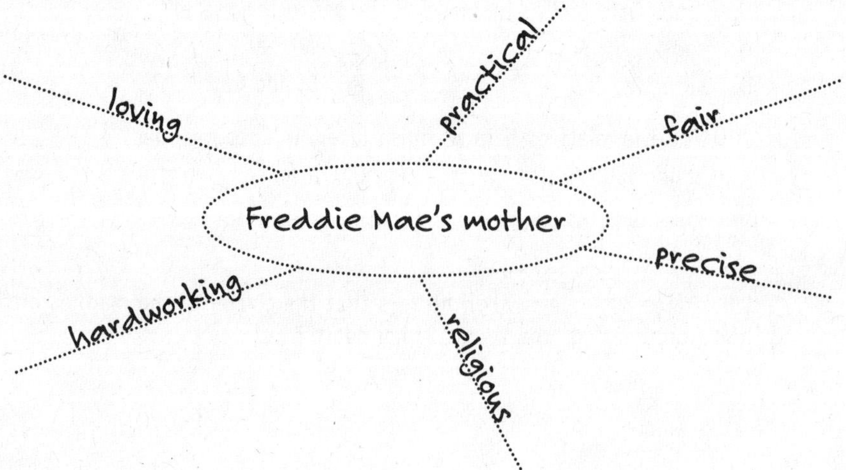

loving   practical   fair

Freddie Mae's mother

hardworking   religious   precise

BEFORE YOU READ

Read through the introduction to the lesson with students and tell them that this selection is from an autobiography. The purpose of the opening of the lesson is to motivate and focus students. Then introduce the prereading activity, a **preview**. (Refer to the **Strategy Handbook** on page 40 for more help.)

Motivation Strategy

Read aloud the first few sentences of "Mother" to familiarize students with Baxter's chatty style. Then ask students what they can infer about the author.

ENGAGING STUDENTS In "Mother," Freddie Mae Baxter describes life in a big family. Ask students to say how many children they'd like to have when they grow up. Would they consider having eight, as Baxter's mother did? Why or why not? Students might enjoy speculating about the future and pondering some of the difficulties a mother with eight children might face.

Vocabulary Building

Draw attention to key vocabulary words for this selection: *married, starch, leftovers, grace,* and *shared*. (Only *starch* and *grace* are footnoted.) Have students circle these words in their texts. Help students learn the new words and reinforce their understanding of the words they already know. For practice work, turn to the **Vocabulary** blackline master on page 74.

STRATEGY LESSON: SYNONYMS As an alternate vocabulary strategy, teach a short lesson on synonyms. Explain that sometimes it is easier to memorize the synonym for a word than its full dictionary definition. Show students a list of words from the selection. What synonyms can they come up with? If one or more words cause problems, have students consult a dictionary or thesaurus. You might include these words from the selection on your list: *job, poor,* and *produce*.

For additional practice on this strategy, see the **Vocabulary** blackline master on page 74.

Prereading Strategies

Before they read, students will do a **preview** of "Mother." A preview is a helpful prereading strategy because it gives readers a glimpse of what is to come. Thumbing through the pages they are about to read can help students learn about the subject and anticipate any comprehension problems they might have. Have them glance at the **stop and think** questions that interrupt the text. Students' quick previews of these items will give them an idea of what they can expect on their close readings.

PICTURE WALK As an alternate prereading strategy, ask students to do a picture walk of the selection. Have them tell you what the pictures remind them of. Based on what they have seen, what do they predict the selection will be about? When they have finished reading, they might return to the pictures and explain the connections they see between the photos and the selection.

Spanish-speaking Students

Freddie Mae Baxter describe su juventud en "Madre," parte de su autobiografía, *The Seventh Child*. A pesar de ser muy pobre, su familia era feliz. Los hijos ayudaban en la casa, cocinando la cena, limpiando, y cuidando uno a otro. La madre le preocupaba mucho por el bien estar y éxito de sus hijos, y les enseñaban unos valores muy importantes.

Before students begin their close readings, be sure they understand that they are to **react and connect** to the story Baxter tells. Each time they meet a character who seems familiar or come to an event that reminds them of their own life, they should make a note of it. This response strategy helps readers become actively involved in reading.

Response Strategy

VISUALIZE As an alternate or additional response strategy, have students sketch what they read about. Each time they "see" something new, they should make a drawing of it in the **Response Notes** column.

Comprehension Strategies

Directed reading can help reluctant or low-level readers better comprehend what they are reading. In a directed reading, you guide the reading by posing open-ended questions designed to elicit factual and inferential responses or by using the stop and think questions in the text. If you like, ask students to read the selection silently. Have them stop and look up each time they come to an interrupter question. Read the question aloud to the class and then ask for responses. Students can use written responses to help them with the graphic organizer at the top of page 27.

For more help, see the **Comprehension** blackline master on page 75.

Discussion Questions

COMPREHENSION 1. Who is the narrator of "Mother"? *(Freddie Mae Baxter)*

2. What qualities did Baxter's mother believe were most important? *(cleanliness, sharing, kindness, and so on)*

3. Judging from the selection, what was most difficult about Baxter's childhood? *(There was not enough food or money.)*

CRITICAL THINKING 4. How did Baxter feel about her mother? *(Answers will vary. Possible: She admired her and appreciated the lessons she taught her children.)*

5. How would you describe Baxter's outlook on life? *(Answers will vary. Possible: She is upbeat and optimistic.)*

6. What is your opinion of the fact that there were no boy jobs or girl jobs? *(Answers will vary.)*

Literary Skill

TONE To introduce a literary skill with this lesson, you might discuss tone with students. Remind the class that *tone* is the author's attitude toward his or her subject or the audience. Tone can be serious, mock-serious, humorous, melodic, and so on. Ask students to think carefully about Baxter's tone. Have them notice the conversational, confiding effect created by her word choices and sentence structures. Phrases such as "Now I always say" and "Them boys" make for a chatty, casual tone that invites the reader into the narrative. There's nothing intimidating about Baxter's writing. She has a simple story to tell, and she tells it as simply as she can. This is a part of the charm of her autobiography.

III. GATHER YOUR THOUGHTS

Prewriting Strategies

The purpose of the prewriting activities on pages 27 and 28 is to prepare students to write a **descriptive paragraph** about a person who is special to them. Before they begin, students will briefly tell what they know about Freddie Mae Baxter's mother. If you like, work together as a class to brainstorm writing ideas. Then have students list their reasons for thinking their person is special. Finish the prewriting session by having students complete the **main idea/supporting details** organizer on page 28. Encourage students to list details that will help readers visualize the person they want to describe.

Have students use the **Prewriting** blackline master on page 76.

IV. WRITE

Read aloud the directions on page 29 to be sure that students understand the assignment. Remind them that their **descriptive paragraphs** should begin with a topic sentence that names the person to be described and how they feel about this person (or the qualities that make him or her special). Before students begin, you might want to review the characteristics of a descriptive paragraph. Explain the sentences must work together to present a single, clear picture (description) of a person, place, or thing.

WRITING RUBRIC Use this writing rubric to help students focus on the assignment requirements.

Do students' descriptive paragraphs

- begin with a topic sentence that identifies the person and reveals how the reader feels about him or her?
- include details about the person?
- stay focused on this one person throughout?

Grammar, Usage, and Mechanics

When students are ready to proofread, refer them to the **Writers' Checklist.** Remind the class that every sentence should have a subject and a verb. If it does not, it is a fragment. For practice, ask students to say which of these sentences is a fragment. (Point out that students shouldn't be misled by the number of words in a sentence or fragment. A complete sentence can be quite short, and a sentence fragment can be quite long.)

Fragment: When I was growing up in a poor town in South Carolina.

Complete: I lived there.

V. WRAP-UP

Take a moment at the end of this unit for students to reflect on the literature and the theme of family matters. Point out the **Readers' Checklist** at the top of page 30. Ask students to discuss what Baxter's article **meant** to them personally. What connections were they able to make to her writing? Was there anything about Baxter's childhood that reminded them of their own lives?

Assessment

To test students' comprehension, use the **Assessment** blackline master on page 77.

Name _____

VOCABULARY

Words from the Selection

DIRECTIONS To build vocabulary, answer these questions about five words from the selection.

1. If a woman is <u>married</u>, does she live alone or with a husband?

    _____

2. If clothes have <u>starch</u> in them, are they stiff or limp?

    _____

3. If you have <u>leftovers</u> after a meal, did you have too much food or not enough?

    _____

4. Is <u>grace</u> commonly said before or after a meal? _____

5. If a man <u>shared</u> his food, did he eat it all himself or give some to another person?

    _____

Strategy Lesson: Synonyms

DIRECTIONS Substitute a synonym from the word box for the underlined word or words.

> ✧job ✧angry ✧produce ✧poor ✧enough

6. When we grew up, we had at least one <u>chore</u> to do every day.

    _____

7. My parents always made sure we had <u>plenty</u> of food.

    _____

8. I was <u>upset</u> when my sister broke my favorite bracelet.

    _____

9. It was true that our family was <u>needy</u>. _____

10. We didn't have a lot, but mother could always <u>supply</u> something for the table.

    _____

Name _____

COMPREHENSION
Directed Reading

DIRECTIONS Work through the answers to these questions with a partner. Check details in your book if you need to.

1. What do you know about Freddie Mae Baxter from reading "Mother"?

_____

_____

2. How does Baxter feel about her mother? Support your answer.

_____

_____

_____

My support: _____

_____

3. What were the most difficult parts of Baxter's childhood?

_____

_____

_____

_____

4. What were the best parts? _____

_____

_____

5. What would you say is Baxter's main idea in "Mother"?

_____

_____

_____

MOTHER / STUDENT PAGES 22–30

Name _____

PREWRITING
Writing a Topic Sentence and Details

The first sentence of a paragraph should set the stage for what you want to tell readers. The first sentence is your topic sentence.

DIRECTIONS Follow these steps to write a topic sentence and supporting details for your descriptive paragraph.

STEP 1. List six qualities or characteristics about the person you want to describe. Don't worry about writing complete sentences—just list words that you think describe this person.

quality #1: _____   quality #2: _____

quality #3: _____   quality #4: _____

quality #5: _____   quality #6: _____

STEP 2. Now look at your list.

    a. Circle the three words that you think best describe your person.

    b. Then write them below.

Three words: _____ _____ _____

STEP 3: Write a topic sentence using these words.

My topic sentence: _____ is _____ ,

           (person's name)   quality #1

_____ , and _____ .

      quality #2   quality #3

STEP 4. Now plan the rest of your paragraph. Write one piece of "proof" for each quality. Your proof will convince readers that what you say is true.

proof #1: _____

_____

proof #2: _____

_____

proof #3: _____

_____

Name _____

ASSESSMENT
Multiple-Choice Test

DIRECTIONS On the blanks provided, write the letter of the item that best answers each question or completes each statement.

_____ 1 What could all of the children in the Baxter family do?
- A. cook
- B. sew
- C. wash clothes
- D. all of the above

_____ 2. Why did Mother say her children didn't have to get married?
- A. Mother would take care of them.
- B. They could take care of themselves.
- C. They could take care of each other.
- D. all of the above

_____ 3. Mother's advice was to make sure that anything you had was . . .
- A. useful.
- B. big.
- C. clean.
- D. expensive.

_____ 4. What makes the Baxter angry?
- A. to see people who are poor
- B. to see people who are dirty
- C. to see people who are cruel
- D. to see people who are homeless

_____ 5. According to Baxter, what was the best time of the week?
- A. Saturday nights
- B. Friday nights
- C. Saturday mornings
- D. Sunday mornings

_____ 6. What would the boys do on the weekend?
- A. wash, starch, and iron shirts
- B. do the shopping
- C. play kickball
- D. visit other family members

_____ 7. What was always said at dinner?
- A. please
- B. thank you
- C. grace
- D. a funny story

_____ 8. What did Mother sometimes bring home from work?
- A. clothes
- B. leftover food
- C. toys
- D. books

_____ 9. What did the siblings fight about?
- A. food
- B. chores
- C. playtime
- D. nothing

_____ 10. What did Baxter's family have a lot of?
- A. toys
- B. money
- C. love
- D. food

Short-Essay Test

Explain Baxter's statement, "We were poor but we didn't have a bad life. You know you can have and not be happy and you cannot have and be happy."

Whales

Unit Background   WHALES (pages 31–48)

Two excerpts about whales make up this unit: "The Great Whales" from *Whales* by Seymour Simon and an excerpt from *Killer Whale* by Caroline Arnold.

Seymour Simon has written more than 100 science books for young readers, including *Icebergs and Glaciers,* which was named Best Children's Science Book of the year by the New York Academy of Sciences in 1987. Simon was born in 1931 in New York.

Caroline Arnold was born in Pittsburgh in 1944. She received a B.A. degree from Grinnell College in 1966 and an M.S. degree from the University of Iowa in 1968. She has also attended Hunter College and studied at the Art Students League of New York. She has been a freelance writer, art instructor, and lab technician, has exhibited her paintings and drawings in many juried shows, and won numerous awards for her science books. *Saving the Peregrine Falcon* (1985) was named a Best Book by the *School Library Journal*, and *Dinosaur Mountain: Graveyard of the Past* (1989) was named a Notable Book by the American Library Association. Her other books include *The Ancient Cliff Dwellers of Mesa Verde* (1992) and *Stories in Stone: Rock Art Pictures by Early Americans* (1996).

Teaching the Introduction

Photos of whales appear on page 31.

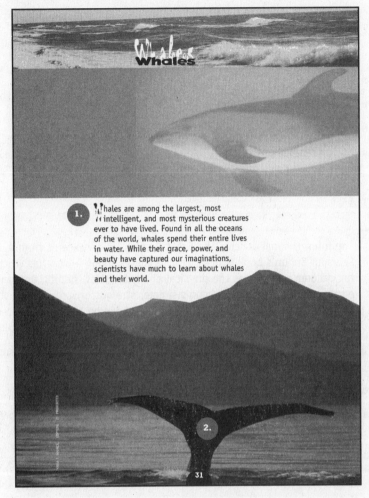

1. Ask a student to read the unit introduction aloud, and then ask the class what they know about whales. Ask how many students have seen a whale or heard the sounds a whale makes.

2. Tell students that some whales are 65 feet long. Ask students to measure 65 feet, perhaps in the school hallway. The author of the first selection says that "the tongue of a blue whale weighs as much as an elephant." Ask students to find out how much an adult elephant weighs.

Opening Activity

Have students find out how many different types of whales there are. Then divide the class into small groups and ask each group to research and give a report, with visuals if possible, on one type of whale.

The Great Whales

Skills and Strategies Overview

THEME Whales

READING LEVEL challenging

VOCABULARY

◆ breaching   ◆ surface   ◆ inhale   ◆ vertical   ◆ spine

PREREADING K-W-L

RESPONSE mark or highlight

COMPREHENSION reciprocal reading

PREWRITING topic sentence

WRITING expository paragraph / adjectives and adverbs

ASSESSMENT ease

BACKGROUND

The informational article "The Great Whales" is an excerpt from award-winning author Seymour Simon's book *Whales*. In this book, Simon—who has written many nonfiction books for children—examines the physical characteristics, habits, and environment of some of the earth's largest mammals. Simon's simple, straightforward writing style makes the broad subject of whales immediately accessible to young or inexperienced readers.

In this excerpt, Simon explores the mysterious world of whales in general: why they breach, what they eat, where they live, and how they have managed to survive in the oceans of the world for thousands and thousands of years.

UNIT THEME Seymour Simon explores the characteristics and habitat of whales.

GRAPHIC ORGANIZER A topic net such as the one below can help readers and writers break large topics into smaller, more manageable chunks.

Topic Net: Whales

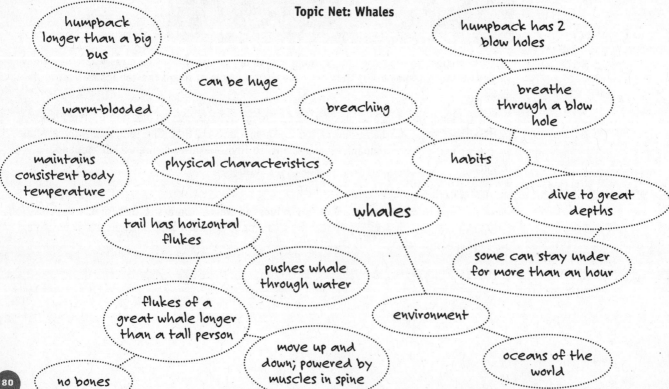

BEFORE YOU READ

Read aloud the introduction to the lesson with students. Explain that students are about to read two nonfiction articles about whales. Have them pause for a moment and consider what they know about this topic. Then ask the class to complete the prereading activity, a **K-W-L**. (Refer to the **Strategy Handbook** on page 40 for more help.)

Motivation Strategy

Seymour Simon's *Whales* is a visual feast for students who are eager for information about these amazing mammals. If possible, borrow a copy of this book from the library and do a walk-through of the 20 or more amazing photographs. All of the photos show whales in their natural habitat, and some provide a glimpse of whales not often seen in science photography. Use your walk-through as a warm-up to the topic of "The Great Whales."

ENGAGING STUDENTS Ask students to think about movies or TV shows they've seen about whales. Or have them tell about an aquarium they've visited or ocean theme park that has a whale exhibit. What do they know about these creatures? What would they like to learn?

Vocabulary Building

Draw attention to the key vocabulary words for this lesson: *breaching, surface, inhale, vertical,* and *spine*. Have students circle these words in the text. Help students pronounce and define each word. Students should add some new words to their vocabulary each time they read. For additional practice, see the **Vocabulary** blackline master on page 84.

STRATEGY LESSON: WORD FAMILIES English words that share the same roots are said to be in the same word families. Common English roots include *–tract–* ("pull" or "drag") and *–cide* ("kill" or "cut down"). Ask students to build families using these two roots. They might suggest *extract, tractor, attract, subtract, traction, suicide, homicide, pesticide, insecticide* and *decide* ("cut off uncertainty").

For additional practice on this strategy, see the **Vocabulary** blackline master on page 84.

Prereading Strategies

A **K-W-L** can be helpful to those students who have trouble settling down to read and write. In addition to assisting with organization, a K-W-L gives students the chance to activate prior knowledge about a subject. After recording what they already know, they can think carefully about gaps in their knowledge. This way, *they* (as opposed to *you*) decide what they need to learn.

QUICKWRITE As an alternate prereading strategy, ask students to do a quickwrite that relates to the theme of the unit. Assign a topic from the list below and have students write for one minute about this topic without stopping. Encourage students to include sensory details in their writing. Later, they may want to use some of their images in their expository paragraphs (see Part IV on page 38). Possible topics for a quickwrite include these:

• whales I've seen up close;

• fictional stories about whales;

• why I would/would not want to be an oceanographer.

Spanish-speaking Students

En esta selección, Seymour Simon explica el modo de vivir de las ballenas grandes. Describe que aunque vivan en agua, las ballenas son mamíferas. Son de sangre caliente como los seres humanos, pero gracias a su capacidad de guardar mucho oxígeno, logran sobrevivir por mucho tiempo bajo el agua. Simon también explica que las ballenas muevan más de treinta miles a la hora.

II. READ

Before students begin their close readings, ask them to review the directions at the top of page 33. Since this is the first expository nonfiction selection in the *Sourcebook*, be sure that students understand how important it is for them to **mark** the text as they are reading. They should underline, circle, or **highlight** things that they find interesting, important, confusing, or surprising. They should also make notes in the margins about details they want to remember.

Response Strategy

QUESTION As an alternate or additional response strategy, ask students to keep track of questions that occur to them as they are reading. Each time they think of a question, they should make a note of it in the **Response Notes.** Students may find that Simon answers some of their questions later in the article. Any remaining questions can be discussed as a group after everyone has finished reading.

Comprehension Strategies

Students will do a **reciprocal reading** of "The Great Whales." During a reciprocal reading, students read the selection aloud in pairs or small groups, switching readers after every page or so. As students read, they stop and work together to answer questions that help them: 1. clarify information; 2. make predictions about details; 3. raise questions about the topic; and 4. summarize what they have learned. Encourage students to pause as often as they like during their oral readings to make comments or ask questions of each other.

GRAPHIC ORGANIZER As an alternate or additional comprehension strategy, ask student to fill in a graphic organizer as they read. Create an organizer that will help them keep track of facts and details of the reading. A graphic organizer such as the one on page 85 is an excellent strategy to use because it can help students remember information they might normally forget as soon as they've closed the book. Writing the fact or detail reinforces understanding and increases the chances that the fact will be committed to memory.

For more help, see the **Comprehension** blackline master on page 85.

Discussion Questions

COMPREHENSION 1. What kind of writing is "The Great Whales"? *(informational article; nonfiction)*

2. How do whales breathe? *(They take air in through their blowholes.)*

3. How do they move? *(Whales have tails with horizontal flukes that move up and down. The flukes are powered by muscles connected to the whale's spine.)*

CRITICAL THINKING 4. What are some similarities and differences between fish and whales? *(Answers will vary. Remind students to use details from the reading to support what they say.)*

5. What do you find most interesting or surprising about whales? *(Answers will vary. Ask students to fully explain their response.)*

Literary Skill

MAIN IDEA To introduce a literary skill with this lesson, you might discuss main idea. Simon includes many facts or details in his article about whales that all seem to point to one central idea—that whales are amazing creatures. Have students discuss this main idea and then point to the details that seem to support it. What other ideas would they say are of importance in the article?

III. GATHER YOUR THOUGHTS

Prewriting Strategies

The goal of the prewriting activities on pages 36 and 37 is to get students to the point that they feel comfortable writing their own **expository paragraph** about a bird, animal, or insect. To begin, students will **brainstorm** a short list of possible topics. Then they'll circle the one topic that they feel they know the most about. (If you plan to give students time to research information on the topic, then they should feel free to circle the topic that they find most interesting.)

Next, students will write a **topic sentence** for their paragraph. If students are unsure of themselves, they should use the formula printed at the bottom of page 36. Students will finish the prewriting session by completing a main idea/supporting details graphic organizer.

Have students use the **Prewriting** blackline master on page 86.

IV. WRITE

Be sure students understand the assignment. They are to write an **expository paragraph** about a bird, insect, or animal. To narrow the focus a bit, you might have them write about one aspect of their topic, such as physical characteristics, habits, or environment.

Remind the class that an expository paragraph is one that presents facts, gives directions, or defines terms. Also remind the class that their expository paragraphs should open with a topic sentence, include support for the topic sentence in the body of the paragraph, and then end with a concluding sentence that ties up any loose ends and acts as a restatement of the topic sentence.

WRITING RUBRIC You might use this rubric to help students focus on the assignment requirements and to assist with a quick assessment of their writing.

Do the students' expository paragraphs

- begin with a topic sentence and contain three or more details as support??
- stay focused on the topic throughout?

Grammar, Usage, and Mechanics

When students are ready to proofread their work, refer them to the **Writers' Checklist.** At this point, you may want to teach a brief lesson on using *good/well* and *bad/badly*. For practice, ask students to correct problems with this sentence.

I felt ~~badly~~ that the zookeeper didn't speak as ~~good~~ as she could have.
  bad   well

V. WRAP-UP

Take a moment at the end of the lesson for students to reflect on whether they found the reading **easy** or difficult using the **Readers' Checklist.** If Simon's article was difficult for students to read, the questions may help them figure out why. Use their responses to help you plan strategies for "Killer Whales," which they'll be reading next.

Assessment

To test students' comprehension, use the **Assessment** blackline master on page 87.

Name _____

VOCABULARY

Words from the Selection

DIRECTIONS Use context clues to figure out the meaning of the underlined words. On the blanks, write your best guess about the meaning of the words.

"This humpback whale is breaching—jumping almost clear out of the water and then crashing down in a huge spray of foam."

1. Breaching probably means _____

"A fish breathes by taking in water and passing it through gills to extract oxygen, but a whale must surface to inhale air into its lungs."

2. Surface probably means _____

3. Inhale probably means _____

"A whale has a tail with horizontal flukes, which are different from the vertical tail fins of a fish."

4. Vertical probably means _____

"Flukes have no bones and are moved up and down by powerful muscles connected to the whale's spine."

5. Spine probably means _____

Strategy Lesson: Word Families

DIRECTIONS The root word -tract- means "pull or drag." The words in the box all contain this same root. Choose the word that correctly fits in each sentence, and write it in the blank.

extract = get or take from	tractor = a machine used to pull
attract = to pull something toward you	subtract = to take something away
traction = a pulling force	

6. Whales _____ oxygen from air so they can breathe.

7. My bag was too heavy to carry, so I had to _____ something from it.

8. The farmer used the _____ to move the wagon.

9. We use honey to _____ bees to the hive.

10. They put the patient with the broken back in _____ so that she would not move.

Name _____

COMPREHENSION
Graphic Organizer

DIRECTIONS Use this topic net to show what you know about whales.

1. Include information from the article and what you know from outside reading.

2. Add circles if you need to.

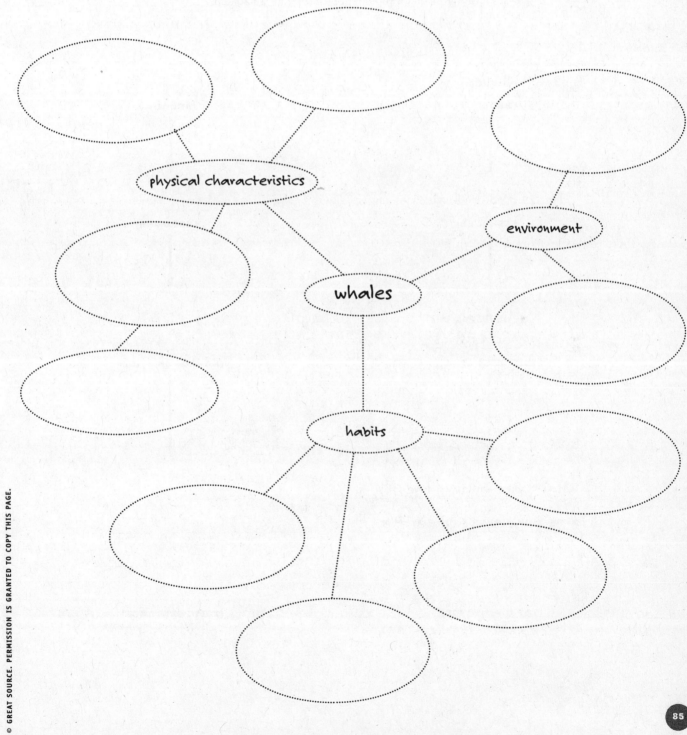

Name _____

PREWRITING
Narrowing a Topic

Before you begin your paragraph, be sure your topic is narrow enough to write about.

DIRECTIONS Use this organizer to narrow your topic.

1. Read the example on the left.
2. Then narrow your own topic.
3. Finish by writing a topic sentence for your paragraph.

EXAMPLE

_____Whales_____
(BROAD)

↓

_____Facts about Whales_____
(NARROWER)

↓

_____Physical characteristics_____
(NARROWER STILL)

↓

_____Whales are among the_____
_____largest mammals on earth_____
_____
_____
(TOPIC SENTENCE)

_____
(BROAD)

↓

_____
(NARROWER)

↓

_____
(NARROWER STILL)

↓

_____
_____
_____
(TOPIC SENTENCE)

Name _____

ASSESSMENT

Multiple-Choice Test

DIRECTIONS On the blanks provided, write the letter of the item that best answers each question or completes each statement.

_____ 1. The humpback whale is longer than a . . .
   A. dump truck.   C. house.
   B. big bus.   D. city block.

_____ 2. The tongue of a blue whale weighs as much as . . .
   A. a big dog.   C. an elephant.
   B. a car.   D. a ship.

_____ 3. Whales are . . .
   A. mammals.   C. fish.
   B. reptiles.   D. birds.

_____ 4. What stays the same with whales even when water temperature changes?
   A. their size   C. their body temperature
   B. their appetite   D. their breathing

_____ 5. What must a whale do to breathe?
   A. surface   C. take in water
   B. use gills   D. all of the above

_____ 6. What part of its body does a whale use to breathe?
   A. its gills   C. its fins
   B. its eyes   D. its blowhole

_____ 7. What does a whale do when it dives?
   A. It breathes deeply.   C. It exhales.
   B. It holds its breath.   D. none of the above

_____ 8. How deep can some whales dive?
   A. 1 mile   C. 2 miles
   B. 1/2 mile   D. 100 meters

_____ 9. What does a whale rely on to move its flukes?
   A. water flow   C. muscles
   B. air   D. all of the above

_____ 10. How fast can a whale move?
   A. 5 miles per hour   C. 20 miles per hour
   B. 10 miles per hour   D. 30 miles per hour

Short-Essay Test

What is the most interesting fact you learned from this article, and why do you think so?

Killer Whales

Skills and Strategies Overview

THEME	Whales
READING LEVEL	challenging
VOCABULARY	◇offspring ◇transient ◇display ◇assert ◇irritate
PREREADING	skim
RESPONSE	clarify
COMPREHENSION	graphic organizer
PREWRITING	supporting a main idea
WRITING	summary / run-on sentences
ASSESSMENT	enjoyment

BACKGROUND

Caroline Arnold's book *Killer Whale* is filled with information about Baby Shamu of Sea World and killer whales in general. Arnold offers information about physical characteristics, habits, and the environment of the killer whale and also tries to dispel some myths surrounding this "ferocious" predator.

"Killer Whales," a short excerpt from Arnold's book, focuses on the habits of killer whales, their instinct to live in pods, and the physical adaptations that allow killer whales to dive deeply and stay under the waves for relatively long periods.

UNIT THEME Caroline Arnold presents the world of the killer whale.

GRAPHIC ORGANIZER Students' word banks on page 45 might look something like this.

breaching	mammal	travelers	clans
resident pods	transient pods	attack	dominant
	blowhole	adaptations	

BEFORE YOU READ

Read aloud the introduction to the lesson on page 40. Remind students of the theme of the unit (whales) and ask a volunteer to summarize the information in Seymour Simon's article, "The Great Whales." Then ask the class to turn to the prereading activity, a **skim**. (Refer to the **Strategy Handbook** on page 40 for more help.)

Motivation Strategy

Borrow a video on killer whales from your library. (Many public libraries have excellent wildlife video collections.) Show the video before students read the article. Give your class the chance to see killer whales in action before they begin reading about them.

Vocabulary Building

Help students use **context clues** as they read to figure out the meanings of difficult or unknown words. Ask them to pay particular attention to the key vocabulary words for this lesson: *offspring, transient, display, assert,* and *irritate*. Have students circle these words in the text. Although the footnotes define these words, you'll want to model using context clues and then checking your ideas against the footnote: "I'm not sure of the word *irritate*. I notice that the word is used to describe the tiny parasites that cling to the whales' skin. I also see that the whales breach in order to knock off these creatures. I wonder if *irritate* means 'bother.' I can look at the footnote to see if my guess is correct." For additional practice, see the **Vocabulary** blackline master on page 92.

STRATEGY LESSON: WORD ANALYSIS Students are learning a number of strategies for defining new words, including using context clues, word families, prefixes, and synonyms. To help students review some of these strategies, assign the **Vocabulary** blackline master on page 92.

Prereading Strategies

During a **skim**, students glance through the selection quickly, looking for words and phrases that can reveal information about the topic. Skimming gives readers an idea of what they can expect during their close readings and can alert them to words, phrases, or concepts that might cause difficulty. This may be particularly important for those students who feel intimidated by nonfiction. Remind the class that when they skim, they don't look at every word. They let their eyes roam back and forth and down the page, watching for things that pop out at them. Work through the skimming questions on page 40 as a group. This can help students see that everyone skims differently. Not everyone will catch every detail.

PREVIEW As an alternate prereading strategy, ask students to preview the selection. This activity also will help familiarize them with the topic of "Killer Whales." Have students look at art, headlines, vocabulary words (in boldface), and interrupter questions. Then ask: "What is the topic of this selection?" and "What do you think the most challenging part(s) of the selection will be?"

Spanish-speaking Students

Esta selección describe en detalle las ballenas asesinas. Caroline Arnold explica que hay dos tipos de ballenas asesinas, las que se quedan en al mismo área, y los que viajan. Algunas ballenas comen peces, mientras otras comen focas y otras ballenas. Arnold también escribe las razones de por qué las ballenas a veces sueltan del agua.

II. READ

When students are ready to begin their close readings, remind them how important it will be for them to make notes that **clarify** the characteristics of killer whales. These notes will be especially useful later, when students are asked to think about the main idea and summarize the information that Arnold presents. Also encourage students to jot down their questions in the **Response Notes**. You may want to pause after the reading is over to answer any remaining questions.

Response Strategy

VISUALIZE Arnold offers a highly detailed explanation of the habits and physical characteristics of whales. As an alternate response strategy, have students sketch in the **Response Notes** what they "see." Again, students' notes and drawings may come in handy later, when they summarize Arnold's article.

Comprehension Strategies

Graphic organizers keep students organized and on task as they read. For this selection, students will complete three small key term organizers (pages 42, 43, and 44) and a word bank (page 45). These organizers will help them work their way through the challenging vocabulary in the selection. In addition, students will be able to pull words from the organizer and word banks when they summarize Arnold's article.

For more help, see the **Comprehension** blackline master on page 93.

Discussion Questions

COMPREHENSION 1. Where would you be most likely to see a killer whale? *(in the ocean, within 500 miles of land)*

2. Why do killer whales usually hunt in groups? *(It makes it easier to attack and kill creatures that are larger than they are.)*

3. What is the difference between a resident pod and a transient pod? *(A resident pod describes a group of whales that stay in the same general location for their whole lives. Transient pods travel more widely.)*

CRITICAL THINKING 4. Would you say that killer whales are social creatures? Explain. *(They are considered social because they live in pods.)*

Literary Skill

DETAILS Because they will write a summary paragraph in Part IV, students might benefit from a quick lesson on details. Most writers use either personal (sensory, memory, or reflective) details, details from other sources, or a combination of the two. Caroline Arnold relies heavily on details from experts (she mentions scientists) and perhaps details from written sources. Details from other sources can come from a variety of locations, including other people (people who have information about the topic), an expert (someone who is knowledgeable about the topic), written sources (books, magazines, library resources, and so on), and the computer (Internet searches, information archives, and so on).

III. GATHER YOUR THOUGHTS

Prewriting Strategies

The prewriting activities on page 46 will help students reflect carefully on the information in Arnold's article. Students' purpose is to sort through what they have learned so that they can write a detailed, accurate **summary** of "Killer Whales." Ask the class to begin by figuring out the **main idea** of the article. Have them work in pairs or alone on this activity.

Next students will list on an organizer the **details** that Arnold uses to support the main idea. When they've finished writing their main idea sentence and details, students will write a closing sentence about what the author says about the whales.

Have students use the **Prewriting** blackline master on page 94.

IV. WRITE

Set aside plenty of time for students to write their **summaries,** as Arnold's article is highly detailed. Remind them to consult their topic sentence/supporting details organizer as they write and to use words from the word bank they created on page 45.

WRITING RUBRIC Use this rubric to help students focus on the assignment requirements and for assistance with a quick assessment of their writing.

Do students' summaries

• clearly state Arnold's main idea?

• contain at least four details in support of the main idea?

• include the most important information from the article, including facts about the physical characteristics, habits, and environment of killer whales?

Grammar, Usage, and Mechanics

After students have written a first draft, have them review the information on the **Writer's Checklist.** Consider teaching a brief lesson on run-on sentences. Explain that a run-on sentence is two complete sentences joined without adequate punctuation or a connecting word. A run-on can be fixed either by breaking it apart into two separate sentences or by adding a comma and/or a conjunction such as *and, or, but, so,* or *yet.* For example:

Incorrect: I wonder if I'll ever see a killer whale I doubt that I will.

Correct: I wonder if I'll ever see a killer whale, but I doubt that I will.

Correct: I wonder if I'll ever see a killer whale. I doubt that I will.

V. WRAP-UP

Take a moment at the end of the lesson for students to reflect using the **Readers' Checklist.** This checklist asks students to self-assess their **enjoyment** of "Killer Whales" and models for them the type of questions good readers ask of themselves after they've finished a selection.

Assessment

To test students' comprehension, use the **Assessment** blackline master on page 95.

Name _____

VOCABULARY
Words from the Selection

DIRECTIONS Answer these questions that use the words from the selection.

1. If you have <u>offspring</u>, do you have pets or children?
   _____

2. If you are <u>transient</u>, do you remain in one place or travel around?
   _____

3. When you <u>display</u> anger, do you show it or keep it hidden?
   _____

4. If you <u>assert</u> your opinion, do you firmly express it or mention it casually?
   _____

5. When you <u>irritate</u> others, do you make them laugh or annoy them?
   _____

Strategy Lesson: Word Analysis

DIRECTIONS Write the word from the list at the right that correctly answers each question.

6. Which word means both "a feather" and "a column of water"? _____

7. Which word has a prefix meaning "out"?
   _____

8. Which word means both "regions at the ends of the earth" and "long metal bars"?
   _____

9. Which word means both "a seed case" and "a group of whales"? _____

10. Which word contains a root meaning "master"?
    _____

poles

dominance

plume

pod

exhale

Name _____

COMPREHENSION
Graphic Organizer

DIRECTIONS Use this graphic organizer to help you find important details from Caroline Arnold's article, "Killer Whales."

1. Find and circle the most important sentence in each paragraph of the article. (There are 11 paragraphs.)

2. Write the sentences in the boxes below. Use quotation marks.

3. Use this organizer to help you write your summary.

Notable Quotes: "Killer Whales"

paragraph 1 "Killer whales are found in oceans all over the world, ranging from the icy waters near the poles to regions near the equator."	
paragraph 2	**paragraph 7**
paragraph 3	**paragraph 8**
paragraph 4	**paragraph 9**
paragraph 5	**paragraph 10**
paragraph 6	**paragraph 11**

Name _____

PREWRITING
Writing a Summary

To write a good summary, you must select the most important ideas and combine them into clear, easy-to-understand sentences.

DIRECTIONS Follow these steps to write a summary for "Killer Whales."

STEP 1. REREAD. Go over the article carefully. Highlight key words and phrases.

STEP 2. LIST. Make a list of the most important facts and opinions in the article.

Important facts and opinions:

• _____

• _____

• _____

• _____

STEP 3. CHOOSE. Select the most important fact or opinion from your list and make this the main idea of your summary. Write a topic sentence that states the main idea.

Caroline Arnold's main idea in "Killer Whales":

_____

_____

STEP 4. FIND DETAILS. Gather important details from the article. Physical characteristics, information about habits, and facts about killer whales' environment are all examples of important details.

Arnold's important details:

1. _____ 6. _____

2. _____ 7. _____

3. _____ 8. _____

4. _____ 9. _____

5. _____ 10. _____

STEP 5. WRITE. Now write your summary on pages 47 and 48 of your book.

⇒ Begin with the topic sentence.

⇒ Then summarize the details that support this topic sentence.

⇒ End with a concluding sentence that ties things together.

Name _____

ASSESSMENT

Multiple-Choice Test

DIRECTIONS On the blanks provided, write the letter of the best answer for each question.

_____ 1. Where are whales found?
- A. rivers
- B. lakes
- C. oceans
- D. streams

_____ 2. How do whales live?
- A. in groups
- B. alone
- C. in pairs
- D. all of the above

_____ 3. Who leads the other whales?
- A. a younger male
- B. a younger female
- C. an older male
- D. an older female

_____ 4. How many whales might be in a resident pod?
- A. 100 to 200
- B. 5 to 50
- C. 20 to 100
- D. 1 to 5

_____ 5. What do whales in resident pods eat?
- A. fish
- B. seals
- C. plants
- D. other whales

_____ 6. How do killer whales usually hunt?
- A. alone
- B. in pairs
- C. in groups
- D. They aren't hunters.

_____ 7. How might killer whales show their power?
- A. by leaping out of the water
- B. by shoving
- C. by splashing
- D. all of the above

_____ 8. Why do whales breach?
- A. to knock off parasites
- B. for fun
- C. to communicate
- D. all of the above

_____ 9. What do whales need in order to breathe?
- A. oxygen
- B. water
- C. a blowhole
- D. A. and C.

_____ 10. What is the longest time killer whales have stayed under water?
- A. 5 minutes
- B. 15 minutes
- C. 2 minutes
- D. 30 minutes

Short-Essay Test.

You have read two informational articles on whales. Which article did you prefer and why?

Walter Dean Myers

Unit Background   WALTER DEAN MYERS (pages 49–66)

This unit contains excerpts from two Walter Dean Myers books: "Joshua" from *The Journal of Joshua Loper* and "The Man" from *Somewhere in the Darkness*.

Walter Dean Myers was born in Martinsburg, West Virginia, was adopted at age three, and grew up in Harlem. He now lives with his family in Jersey City, New Jersey.

His first book, *Where Does the Day Go?*, was published after he entered and won a contest sponsored by The Council on Interracial Books for Children. He has won the Coretta Scott King Award five times, and three of his books, including *Somewhere in the Darkness*, have been chosen Newbery Honor Books. Among his most recent books are *Harlem: A Poem* (1997), *Amistad: A Long Road to Freedom* (1998), *At Her Majesty's Request: An African Princess in Victorian England* (1999), and *145th Street: Short Stories* (2000).

Teaching the Introduction

A Harlem neighborhood, a young boy, the cover of Walter Dean Myers's book, and a photo of African American cowboys are shown on page 49.

1. Ask someone to read the unit introduction aloud while the rest of the class follows along.

2. Ask how many students have read a Walter Dean Myers book. Then ask them to give their opinions about his books and stories.

3. Some students may have read about African-American cowboys. If so, ask them to tell what they know.

Opening Activity

Since the first excerpt is from a book titled *The Journal of Joshua Loper,* the point of view is first person. The first entry in the ***Sourcebook*** is dated 1871. Ask students to imagine that they are living in the western United States in 1871. Ask them to think about where they would be living, how they got there, and what they would be doing to earn a living or raise a family. Remind them that the Civil War is over. Ulysses S. Grant is president, California has entered the Union, but Colorado, Arizona, New Mexico, Montana, North Dakota, South Dakota, Oklahoma, and Utah are not yet states. Ask students to write a journal entry as if they were living in the West in 1871.

STUDENT PAGES 50-57

Skills and Strategies Overview

THEME	Walter Dean Myers
READING LEVEL	average
VOCABULARY	◆acre ◆keen ◆crew ◆herd ◆argument
PREREADING	think-pair-and-share
RESPONSE	question
COMPREHENSION	story frame
PREWRITING	web
WRITING	character sketch / commas
ASSESSMENT	depth

BACKGROUND

"Joshua," an excerpt from Walter Dean Myers's novel *The Journal of Joshua Loper,* tells the story of an African–American teenage boy who is desperate to join a cattle drive to Abilene, Kansas. Joshua sees the drive as a way to prove to himself that he is finally a man.

Myers's novel, which is set in 1871, is comprised of a series of journal entries that Joshua makes before and during the cattle drive. Although the journal entries are fictional, the obstacles that 16-year-old Joshua faces—including the bigotry of the cattle boss and the danger of driving cattle across a barren land—were a very real part of life in the West during the 1800s.

UNIT THEME Walter Dean Myers explores the themes of growing up and facing adversity in this work of historical fiction.

GRAPHIC ORGANIZER A sequence organizer can help readers keep track of the important events in a work of fiction or nonfiction. You might have students complete an organizer similar to this one.

Captain Hunter asks Joshua his name and age.

↓

Mama tells Joshua that Mr. Muhlen, the boss of the ranch, wants Joshua to ride on the next cattle drive.

↓

Joshua readily agrees.

↓

Captain Hunter argues with Mr. Muhlen about taking three African Americans on the drive.

↓

Muhlen insists that Joshua be allowed to go.

↓

Hunter defers to Muhlen's wishes and informs the crew that it's important the drive be successful.

BEFORE YOU READ

Read through the introduction to the lesson with students. Offer background information about Walter Dean Myers and his writing style as you see fit. Then have students begin the prereading activity, a **think-pair-and–share**. (Refer to the **Strategy Handbook** on page 40 for more help.)

Motivation Strategy

Borrow from the library a book that relates to the topic of *The Journal of Joshua Loper.* You might choose *Bill Pickett, Bulldogger: The Biography of a Black Cowboy* (C. Bailey); *Black Cowboy, Wild Horses: A True Story* (Julius Lester); or *Cowboys of the Wild West* (Russell Freedman). As a class, do a picture walk of the book you've chosen. This quick activity will make for an engaging warm-up to the story "Joshua."

ENGAGING STUDENTS Explain that "Joshua" is the story of a boy who is eager to prove that he can do the work of a man. Have students tell about a time they did an adult's job. How did the experience make them feel? Did others (family or friends) treat them differently as a result? Help students make a personal connection to the theme of the selection before they begin reading.

Vocabulary Building

Read aloud the key vocabulary words for this selection: *acre, keen, crew, herd,* and *argument.* (*Argument*, page 53, is not footnoted.) Have students circle these words in the text. These words are featured on the **Vocabulary** blackline master on page 102. Encourage students to familiarize themselves with the definition of each word. Later, they can practice using these words in sentences.

STRATEGY LESSON: IDIOMS As an additional vocabulary lesson, you might spend some time discussing idioms. An idiom is a phrase or expression that means something different from the ordinary meanings of the words. For example, to indicate a person is causing trouble, some people say he is "making waves." For some students, especially students who speak English as a second language, idiomatic expressions are perplexing. You might offer this advice: To understand an idiom, try picturing the action described. For example, if you visualize "making waves," you get a picture of rough water. More than likely this visualization of the idiom will provide valuable clues about what the idiom means. Ask students to visualize these idioms: "laying low" (page 51) and "short of hands" (page 52). See how close they can come to defining what the idiom means.

For additional practice on this strategy, see the **Vocabulary** blackline master on page 102.

Prereading Strategies

Students are asked to complete a **think-pair-and-share** before reading "Joshua." A think-pair-and-share can help readers become actively involved in a selection *before* they begin reading. In addition, this activity can refine students' ability to work cooperatively in a group. During the "pair" exercise, students should build upon other's ideas and help the group reach consensus on the ordering of the statements from the text. Each student should then make his or her own prediction about the story. Finish the activity by asking each group to share their ideas with the rest of the class.

Spanish-speaking Students

Joshua Loper es un joven negro que trabaja en un rancho en los años después de la Guerra Civil. Su jefe, Señor Muhlen, le respeta y quiere que le ayude en mover el ganado vacuno a Kansas. El Capitán que está encargado del manejo es racista, pero Joshua no deja que estropee la aventura.

II. READ

Response Strategy

Before students begin to read, walk through the process of responding to literature. Introduce the strategy of **questioning** and point out the example given on page 51. Explain that each time a question occurs to them, students should make a note of it in their **Response Notes**. If you like, read the first paragraph of "Joshua" as a group, and then ask volunteers to suggest questions they have about the text. It may surprise your students to hear that you are interested in even the most trivial questions.

Comprehension Strategies

Students are asked to fill out a series of **story frames** as they are reading "Joshua." Story frames can help readers get a handle on plot. Rather than simply asking students to "tell what happens," a story frame provides an actual framework for response. In addition, it can prod readers into thinking carefully about elements of setting, character, and even theme. Encourage students to reread their story frame notes once they have finished the selection. Their notes will come in handy when it comes time to plan their character sketch of Joshua.

DIRECTED READING As an alternate comprehension strategy, try doing a directed reading of the selection. In a directed reading, you or a group leader directs a silent reading of the text. Readers pause every once in a while to answer **stop and think** questions designed to elicit factual and inferential responses. A directed reading will help you see what (if anything) is causing problems for readers. Using students' comments as a guide, you might speed up or slow down the pace of future readings, or spend more time clarifying the facts and details of this selection. Many of the Discussion Questions below will work well for a directed reading of "Joshua."

For more help, see the **Comprehension** blackline master on page 103.

Discussion Questions

COMPREHENSION 1. Who writes the journal entries in "Joshua"? (*Joshua*)

2. Why do Mr. Muhlen and Captain Hunter argue? (*Hunter does not want to take three African Americans along on the drive.*)

CRITICAL THINKING 3. Why does Joshua want to go on the cattle drive? (*Answers will vary. Possible: He likes the excitement of a drive and hopes to prove that he is a man.*)

4. What inferences can you make about Joshua and Captain Hunter? (*Remind students to support what they say with evidence from the text. If students are struggling, teach a brief lesson on making inferences. See the Literary Skill section below.*)

Literary Skill

INFERENCES Students should know that no writer will spell out everything in a story. Readers are expected to make inferences (reasonable guesses) based on the evidence provided. If an inference can be supported with evidence from the selection, then it should be considered valid. For practice, ask students to make three or more inferences about these characters: Joshua, Mr. Muhlen, and Captain Hunter. Students might infer that Joshua is levelheaded, well behaved, and a hard worker. They might infer that Mr. Muhlen is loyal, frank, and fair. Captain Hunter, on the other hand, might be seen as prejudiced, hard-hearted, and arrogant. Each of these inferences is supportable with evidence from the reading.

III. GATHER YOUR THOUGHTS

Prewriting Strategies

Use the prewriting activities on page 55 to help students prepare to write a **character sketch** of Joshua. As a first activity, students will create a **web** about Joshua. Remind them that Myers has not told them everything they need to know about the character. They will have to make inferences about Joshua based on the information provided. If you like, ask students to finish their work on the character web by stating their opinion of Joshua. Do they admire him? Does he remind them of someone from their own lives? Does he seem realistic? Students should formulate an opinion before they write their topic sentences.

Next students will use two words from their web (or opinion) in a topic sentence about Joshua. Using a graphic organizer, they'll find two details from the selection that support each word. If you feel it would help, check each student's graphic organizer before having them begin. Be sure they have a clearly worded topic sentence and strong supporting details.

Have students use the **Prewriting** blackline master on page 104.

IV. WRITE

Students should understand what's involved in writing a **character sketch**. Explain that a character sketch is a short piece of writing that describes a real person or a fictional character. Each point students make in their character sketches about Joshua should be supported with evidence from the selection.

WRITING RUBRIC Use this writing rubric to help you evaluate the quality of students' writing.

Do students' character sketches

- open with a topic sentence that identifies two characteristics of Joshua?

- contain two or more supporting details for each characteristic?

- end with a closing sentence that ties things together?

Grammar, Usage, and Mechanics

When they are ready to proofread their work, refer students to the **Writers' Checklist.** At this point, you might want to introduce a brief lesson on comma usage. Remind the class that commas are used in a series of three or more, and that a comma is always placed before the *and*, *or*, and *nor*. In addition, commas are used to separate the month from the year or the day from the year in a date. A comma also separates city names from state names.

Incorrect: In May 1871 Joshua was ready willing and able to ride to Abilene Kansas.

Correct: In May, 1871, Joshua was ready, willing, and able to ride to Abilene, Kansas.

V. WRAP-UP

Take a moment at the end of the lesson for students to reflect on the **depth** of their understanding, using the **Readers' Checklist.** Explain how important it is for students to recognize whether or not they were able to apply what they learned to their own lives.

Assessment

To test students' comprehension, use the **Assessment** blackline master on page 105.

Name _____

VOCABULARY

Words from the Selection

DIRECTIONS To build vocabulary, answer these questions that use words from the selection.

1. If you buy an <u>acre</u>, are you buying land or food? _____

2. When someone is <u>keen</u> on an idea, are they enthusiastic or unenthusiastic?

    _____

3. If you are working on a <u>crew</u>, are you working alone or in a group?

    _____

4. If you are in charge of a <u>herd</u>, are you watching a group of cattle or children?

    _____

5. When you have an <u>argument</u> with a friend, do you agree or disagree?

    _____

Strategy Lesson: Idioms

An **idiom** is a phrase or expression that means something different from what the words actually say. For example, some people say "She was walking on air" to mean "She was excited and happy."

DIRECTIONS Draw a line between the underlined idioms in Column A and their meanings in Column B.

Column A

6. We decided to <u>lie low</u> until the boss left.

7. We <u>ran out of</u> flour and sugar.

8. He was <u>short of hands</u> at the carwash.

9. She <u>ran across</u> a friend she hadn't seen in years.

10. He never <u>spit out</u> a bad word about anyone.

11. We were asked to <u>lend a hand</u> at the bake sale.

Column B

A. had no more

B. help

C. met by chance

D. stay out of the way

E. in need of more help

F. said

12. Use one of the idioms in Column A in a sentence of your own:

_____

_____

_____

Name _____

COMPREHENSION
Making Inferences

DIRECTIONS Make some inferences (reasonable guesses) about Joshua.

1. Skim the story. Highlight things that Joshua says, thinks, and does.

2. Then record these details on the chart. Say what you think Joshua's words and actions show about him.

My inferences about Joshua

Things the character says, thinks, does	What his words and actions show
1. "I had been laying low since Captain Hunter came to the ranch."	He is cautious.
2.	
3.	
4.	
5.	

Word Web

DIRECTIONS Now look over the chart you just completed. Write 5–10 words that describe your character on the web below.

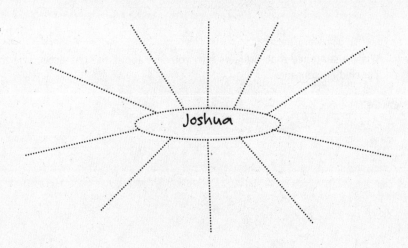

Joshua

Name _____

PREWRITING
Writing a Character Sketch

Open your character sketch with a topic sentence. The topic sentence lets readers know what to expect.

DIRECTIONS Follow these steps to write a character sketch.

STEP 1. WRITE A TOPIC SENTENCE. Use this sentence starter:

_____ is important to the story because .

(character name)

STEP 2. Write three details that show how your character is important. Record them here.

detail #1: _____

_____

_____

detail #2: _____

_____

_____

detail #3: _____

_____

_____

STEP 3. Write a sentence that explains how you feel about the character. Use this as your concluding sentence.

My concluding sentence: _____

_____

_____

Name _____

ASSESSMENT

Multiple-Choice Test

DIRECTIONS On the blanks provided, write the letter of the item that best answers each question or completes each statement.

_____ 1. What does Joshua think is strange when he returns home from church?
   A. The house is locked.   C. There is a party at his house.
   B. There is nothing special to eat. D. There is a strange man in his house.

_____ 2. Whom does Joshua try to stay away from?
   A. Mr. Muhlen   C. Charlie Taggert
   B. Captain Hunter D. Mama

_____ 3. Who bought Mama's freedom?
   A. Mr. Muhlen   C. Charlie Taggert
   B. Captain Hunter D. Nehemiah

_____ 4. Where does Mr. Muhlen want to send Joshua?
   A. to another farm C. north on the trail
   B. down south   D. into town

_____ 5. Why does Mr. Muhlen want to put Joshua on the crew?
   A. Joshua is eager to go.   C. Mr. Muhlen is short on help.
   B. Joshua is a troublemaker.   D. Captain Hunter wants to get rid of Joshua.

_____ 6. Joshua wants to show that he is . . .
   A. a man.   C. a talented worker.
   B. a slave. D. honest.

_____ 7. Why do the Captain and Mr. Muhlen argue?
   A. The Captain wants more men.   C. The Captain doesn't want to take three African–
                                            American men.
   B. The Captain wants to go a   D. The Captain doesn't want to go to Kansas.
      different way.

_____ 8. What does Mr. Muhlen say about Joshua?
   A. He is a good boy.   C. He is very smart.
   B. He makes trouble.   D. He knows how to drive.

_____ 9. What does Joshua's friend tell him he should practice?
   A. camping   C. running
   B. hunting   D. all of the above

_____ 10. When Mr. Muhlen calls the crew together, what does he say he wants?
   A. a quick drive   C. a safe drive
   B. a successful drive   D. a fun drive

Short-Essay Test

Why do you think Joshua is so excited about the journey?

STUDENT PAGES 58–66

Skills and Strategies Overview

THEME Walter Dean Myers

READING LEVEL average

VOCABULARY

◇glistening ◇banister ◇approvingly ◇down payment ◇battered

PREREADING story impression

RESPONSE mark or highlight

COMPREHENSION predict

PREWRITING quickwrite

WRITING letter / letter-writing form

ASSESSMENT style

BACKGROUND

"The Man" is an excerpt from Walter Dean Myers's realistic novel, *Somewhere in the Darkness*. In this story, Jimmy, who is 14 years old, has been raised by his dependable Mama Jean, a friend of the family. Jimmy's mother is dead, and his father (who is nicknamed "Crab") is in prison for killing a man during an armed robbery.

When Crab suddenly shows up at Jimmy's house, Jimmy doesn't recognize him. He also wonders how Crab was able to make parole so early. Slowly Jimmy begins to trust his father and agrees to join him on a trip to Chicago. Jimmy's world falls apart, however, when he learns that Crab, who is very ill with kidney disease, has actually escaped from prison.

Myers's novel is as thought-provoking as it is grim. Crab is a hardened criminal, yet the reader can't help but feel sympathy for him. Jimmy, who was on his way to becoming a "tough" before his father's unexpected arrival, ends up learning some valuable lessons.

UNIT THEME Myers explores themes of loyalty, trust, and growing up in this provocative work.

GRAPHIC ORGANIZER A character attribute map can help readers make a careful analysis of a fictional character.

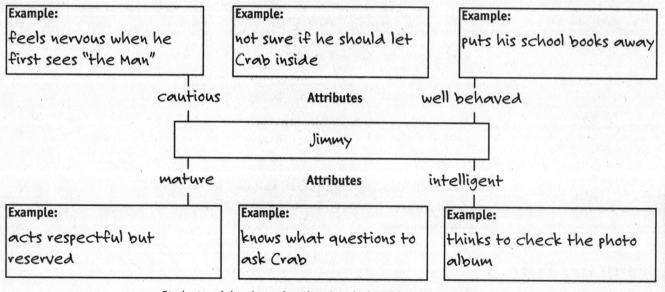

Example:
feels nervous when he first sees "the Man"

Example:
not sure if he should let Crab inside

Example:
puts his school books away

cautious   Attributes   well behaved

Jimmy

mature   Attributes   intelligent

Example:
acts respectful but reserved

Example:
knows what questions to ask Crab

Example:
thinks to check the photo album

BIBLIOGRAPHY Students might also enjoy these works by Walter Dean Myers: *At Her Majesty's Request: An African Princess in Victorian England* (historical fiction, 1999); *145th Street* (short stories, 2000); and *Monster* (novel, 2000).

BEFORE YOU READ

Before you begin the lesson, tell students that they are about to read a second selection by Walter Dean Myers. Be sure to explain that "The Man" is realistic fiction, in contrast to "Joshua," which is historical fiction. Then have students complete the prereading activity, a **story impression**. (Refer to the **Strategy Handbook** on page 40 for more help.)

Motivation Strategy

In "The Man," a boy named Jimmy meets up with someone he hasn't seen in years. Ask students to tell about a time they visited with a long, lost friend or relative. What made the encounter difficult? What made it enjoyable? Help students connect the events of the story to their own lives.

ENGAGING STUDENTS Explain that "The Man" is a story about a father and son. Ask students to complete this sentence: "I think parent-child relationships are often _____." Students' ideas may relate to Myers's theme.

Vocabulary Building

Help students use **context clues** as they read to figure out the meanings of difficult words, especially the key vocabulary words for this lesson: *glistening, banister, approvingly, down payment,* and *battered*. Have students circle these words in the text. Encourage students to get into the habit of defining in context before checking the footnoted or dictionary definition. Remind them that defining in context is easier and faster. For additional practice with these words, see page 110.

STRATEGY LESSON: HOMOGRAPHS A homograph is a word that has the same spelling as another word, but a different origin and meaning. For example, *kind* (meaning "type" or "considerate") is a homograph. Tell students that the meaning of such words is usually made clear by context. (Students who speak English as a second language may have a fair amount of trouble with homographs, however.) For practice with this strategy, see the **Vocabulary** blackline master on page 110.

Prereading Strategies

The purpose of a **story impression** is to help students begin thinking about the mood and topic of a selection before they begin reading. An author's word choices contribute to the mood. Funny words make for a humorous story. (Think of Lewis Carroll, for example.) Serious-sounding words make for a serious story. After students glance through the story, ask them to read the list of words on the left-hand side of page 58. Do they give the impression of mirth or grief or trouble, or something else entirely? Have students work together or alone to write sentences for each of the seven words. The words are simple enough that students probably won't need the help of a dictionary.

WORD WEB As an alternate prereading strategy, ask students to do a quick word web for the word *teenager*. What images and impressions come to mind? Students might be surprised to see that 14-year-old Jimmy in "The Man" doesn't fit all of their preconceived notions.

Spanish-speaking Students

En "El hombre," un joven conoce a su padre por la primera vez. Regresa a casa después de un día en la escuela y se encuentra con un hombre extraño esperando en el umbral. El joven le deja entrar, pero se preocupa un poco porque la madre no está en casa. Además, sabe que su padre había estado en la cárcel y no está seguro de por qué ha visitado. Los dos hablan hasta llegar la madre.

II. READ

Before students begin reading, have a volunteer read aloud the directions at the top of page 59. Be sure every student understands the response strategy of **mark or highlight**. Remind them to pay careful attention to clues about character. Each time they make an inference about Crab or Jimmy, they should make a note about it in the **Response Notes**.

Response Strategy

VISUALIZE   How do students picture Jimmy? How do they picture Crab? As an alternate response strategy, ask them sketch the characters and setting of "The Man." Students can use these sketches to help them keep track of the characters and action of the story.

Comprehension Strategies

At several different points in the novel excerpt, students will **stop and predict** what they think will happen next. Making predictions can help readers feel more directly involved in what they are reading. This is an especially effective strategy to use when a selection is suspenseful and the outcome is uncertain.

STORY FRAME   As an additional or alternate prewriting strategy, ask students to create a story frame that helps them keep track of the setting, characters, conflict, and resolution of the story. Although "The Man" is an excerpt from a longer work, students should be able to get a good sense of what the chief conflict will be. In addition, they may be able to predict how they think that conflict will be resolved. Have students keep their thoughts organized on a story frame.

For more help, see the **Comprehension** blackline master on page 111.

Discussion Questions

COMPREHENSION   1. Why is Jimmy initially frightened of the man? *(He is a stranger.)*

2. What is the relationship between Jimmy and this stranger? *(He is Jimmy's long-lost father.)*

CRITICAL THINKING   3. Why do you think Jimmy agrees to allow Crab to come up to the apartment? *(Answers will vary. Possible: He is curious to know whether this is his real father.)*

4. What convinces Jimmy that Crab is telling the truth about his identity? *(Possible: Crab tells the story about buying a new car. Jimmy hears this and believes that Crab may be telling the truth after all.)*

5. What kind of person is Jimmy? What kind of person is Crab? Support your answers. *(Answers will vary. Students might note that Jimmy seems friendly, although he's cautious and careful. Crab also seems friendly, but there's an air of mystery surrounding him.)*

Literary Skill

POINT OF VIEW   To introduce a literary skill with this lesson, explain to students that any story can be told from more than one vantage point, or point of view. "The Man" is told from the point of view of Jimmy. We see into his thoughts and understand his emotions. The character he encounters is more of a mystery. Ask students in what ways "The Man" would be different had it been told through Crab's eyes. Your more advanced students might rewrite a descriptive paragraph from the selection using Crab's point of view. What parts of the story change? What stays the same?

III. GATHER YOUR THOUGHTS

The purpose of the prewriting activities on page 65 is to prepare students to write a **letter** to a person they haven't seen for a long time. Before they write their letters, students will choose a recipient and then decide what they want to tell this person.

To brainstorm ideas, students will do a **one-minute quickwrite**. In a quickwrite, the writer lets his or her thoughts flow freely. Some of these thoughts or ideas can then be used in the more formal writing assignment.

Prewriting Strategies

NARROWING A TOPIC If you feel students will benefit, you might work with them to narrow the focus of their writing. Inexperienced writers tend to try to cover too much in their writing. Ask students to choose a narrowed topic to write about—school this week, family doings, and so on— rather than try to cover everything about their lives. Students can cover one narrowed topic in each of the two paragraphs of the letter.

For more help, see the **Comprehensive** blackline master or page 112

IV. WRITE

Ask the class to read the directions at the top of page 66, and then have a volunteer summarize the assignment requirements.

WRITING RUBRIC After students have completed a first draft, have them stop and think carefully about what they've written. You might have them answer the questions on this writing rubric before they begin revising.

Do students' letters

- begin with an opening appropriate for a long-lost friend or family member?
- contain two main ideas, each in its own paragraph?
- include interesting details as support for these main ideas?

Grammar, Usage, and Mechanics

When is time for students to proofread their work, refer them to the questions on the **Writers' Checklist** at the left of page 66. Remind the class to capitalize each word in the greeting but only the first word in the closing. Both the greeting and the closing are followed by a comma. In addition, students should remember that the date appears at the top right-hand corner, with a comma separating the day from the year. For practice, put a sample letter on the board and ask students to correct errors.

V. WRAP-UP

Take a moment at the end of the lesson for students to reflect on and discuss Walter Dean Myers's writing **style**. Have them use the **Readers' Checklist** as a starting point for their discussion. What do they think about Myers's style? Is it difficult? Why or why not?

Assessment

To test students' comprehension, use the **Assessment** blackline master on page 113.

Name _____

VOCABULARY
Words from the Selection

DIRECTIONS To build vocabulary, answer these questions about five words from the selection.

1. When an object is <u>glistening</u>, is it shining brightly or looking pretty dull?

   _____

2. If you slide down a <u>banister</u>, are you inside a building or on a playground?

   _____

3. If your father nods <u>approvingly</u>, is he giving you permission or telling you "no"?

   _____

4. When you put a <u>down payment</u> on a house, have you paid the full amount or only part?

   _____

5. Is a <u>battered</u> coffee pot dented or brand new? _____

Strategy Lesson: Homographs

A **homograph** is a word that has the same pronunciation and sometimes the same spelling as another word but a different origin and meaning. For example, *ring* can mean "jewelry you wear on your finger" or "the sound a telephone makes." The context surrounding the word can tell you which meaning is correct.

DIRECTIONS Use the clues in each sentence to tell you the correct meaning of the underlined word. Draw a line matching each word to its correct definition.

6. I had to <u>strain</u> to hear his quiet voice.   A. type

7. We saw his uniform and thought he might be   B. believe
   some <u>kind</u> of police officer.
                                                                C. a person who counts
8. I <u>figure</u> it's best to take the highway.
                                                                D. coated with egg for frying
9. We sat at the <u>counter</u> to eat dinner.
                                                                E. try very hard
10. My shoes were old and <u>battered</u>.
                                                                F. beat up

                                                                G. a kind of table

                                                                H. separate out unwanted material

                                                                I. nice

                                                                J. shape

Name _____

COMPREHENSION
Story Frame

DIRECTIONS Use this story frame to show what you know about "The Man."

Setting		
When does the story take place?	Where does it take place?	What do you know about this time and place?

Characters

Who are the main characters?

Plot

What are the three most important events of the story?

1.	2.	3.

Name _____

PREWRITING
Writing Sensory Details

When you write, try to make your details as meaningful and interesting as possible. If your details are boring, your writing will be boring. Sensory details can make your writing interesting. Sensory details are details that appeal to the five senses (smell, touch, taste, hearing, and sight).

EXAMPLE: *On our nature walk, I saw a deer with a brown-and-white tail and could smell the sharp odor of a frightened skunk.*

DIRECTIONS Think about one event or experience to tell about in your letter. Write words that describe what you saw, smelled, heard, tasted, and touched.

I saw _____

_____

_____

_____

I smelled _____

_____

_____

The event or experience _____

_____

I touched _____

_____

_____

I heard _____

_____

_____

I tasted _____

_____

_____

Name _____

ASSESSMENT
Multiple-Choice Test

DIRECTIONS On the blanks provided, write the letter of the best answer for each question.

_____ 1. Who is waiting for Jimmy at his house?
   A. Mama Jean
   B. his father
   C. his uncle
   D. his sister

_____ 2. What do people call "the man"?
   A. Crab
   B. Cephus
   C. Mama Jean
   D. James

_____ 3. Why does Jimmy doubt the man?
   A. The man looks like he is lying.
   B. The man doesn't know Jimmy's name.
   C. The man doesn't look like the father Jimmy remembers.
   D. Jimmy has never heard of him.

_____ 4. How does Jimmy feel as he leads the man upstairs?
   A. happy
   B. scared
   C. unsure
   D. B. and C.

_____ 5. Where has the man been?
   A. away on a job
   B. out of the country
   C. with another family
   D. in jail

_____ 6. What does Jimmy plan to do if the man tries something funny?
   A. run away
   B. jump out the window
   C. lock him in the bathroom
   D. call the police

_____ 7. Who is in the picture Jimmy finds?
   A. the man
   B. Jimmy's mother
   C. Mama Jean
   D. all of the above

_____ 8. What does the man say he and Jimmy's mother were planning to buy the day the picture was taken?
   A. a house
   B. a bedroom set
   C. a living room set
   D. a car

_____ 9. What does the man remember doing with Jimmy?
   A. putting him on top of the refrigerator
   B. reading to him
   C. playing catch
   D. teaching him to fish

_____ 10. How does Jimmy feel about the man?
   A. helpful
   B. fearful
   C. nervous
   D. pleasant

Short-Essay Test

How do you think Jimmy feels about the man coming back into his life? Use details from the story to support your answer.

113

Decisions

Unit Background   DECISIONS (pages 67–82)

A short story by Jim Heynen and a novel excerpt from *Family Secrets* by Susan Shreve appear in this unit.

Jim Heynen was born in 1940 in Sioux County, Iowa, and has taught English at Calvin College and the University of Oregon. He lives in Saint Paul, Minnesota, and teaches at St. Olaf College. His books for young people include *One-Room Schoolhouse* (1995), *Being Youngest* (1997), and *Cosmos Coyote and William the Nice* (2000).

Susan Shreve is a graduate of the University of Pennsylvania and a professor of English at George Mason University. She lives in Washington, D.C., with her husband and four children. She writes for adults and young people. Her young-adult books include *The Bad Dreams of a Good Girl* (1982), *Lucy Forever and Miss Rosetree* (1995), *The Goalie* (1996), and *Ghost Cats* (1999).

Teaching the Introduction

Illustrations on page 67 show a page from a mathematics book, a young man and a boy, and icicles hanging from a roof.

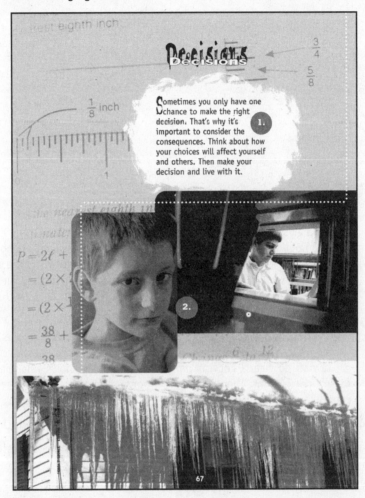

1. After reading the introduction to students, tell them that both selections in this unit involve making decisions but that one decision made was the wrong one.

2. Ask students to make two lists on the board. One list should contain decisions that others used to make for students, such as what they should wear and eat and where they should go to school. The other list should contain decisions that students can now make for themselves.

Opening Activity

Tell students that there are three possible ways to make a decision: flip a coin, carefully investigate the pros and cons of the possible outcomes of a decision, and ask for advice. Have students discuss which of the following decisions could be made by a flip of a coin, which ones should be thought about carefully, and which ones might require asking advice: what to order in a fast food restaurant, what movie to see, how much of one's allowance to save, whether to cheat on a test, whether to study for a test, whether to try to stop a fight at school, whether to skip school, whether to lie to a parent, whether to follow the crowd or act on one's own, and how to deal with a bully.

What Happened During the Ice Storm

Skills and Strategies Overview

THEME	Decisions
READING LEVEL	average
VOCABULARY	✦ livestock ✦ huddled ✦ pheasants ✦ glazed ✦ crouching
PREREADING	picture walk
RESPONSE	predict
COMPREHENSION	double-entry journal
PREWRITING	brainstorming
WRITING	journal entry / capitalization
ASSESSMENT	meaning

BACKGROUND

Jim Heynen's short story, "What Happened During the Ice Storm," was originally published in an anthology of short stories called *You Know What Is Right*—a book about making decisions. Heynen uses sensory language and embedded dialogue to tell the story of a group of boys who set out to hunt a group of freezing pheasants. When they find the pheasants, however, the boys are moved by their plight and give them their coats instead of clubbing them to death.

The decision the boys make is in many ways representative of the kinds of decisions young people make every day. This story presents the thematic question: Do I do what I know I *can do,* or do I do what I know is *right?* Heynen's story shows what happens when one chooses to do what is right. There are ramifications, of course (the boys are soaked), but they have clearly made the correct decision.

UNIT THEME   A group of boys make a surprising decision in the middle of an ice storm.

GRAPHIC ORGANIZER   An organizer like the one below can help students explore an abstract word or thematic idea.

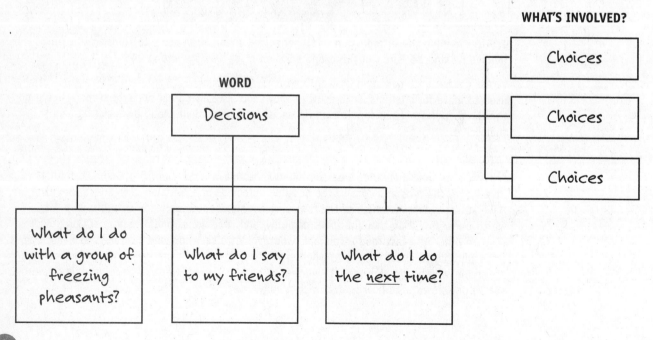

WHAT'S INVOLVED?

WORD

Decisions

Choices

Choices

Choices

What do I do with a group of freezing pheasants?

What do I say to my friends?

What do I do the <u>next</u> time?

BEFORE YOU READ

Read through the introduction to the lesson (page 68) with students. The purpose of this opening paragraph is to motivate and focus students, as well as to forge an initial connection between the reading and the student's own life. Then introduce the prereading activity, a **picture walk**. (Refer to the **Strategy Handbook** on page 40 for more help.)

Motivation Strategy

ENGAGING STUDENTS In "What Happened During the Ice Storm," a group of boys have to choose between doing what's right and doing what's "cool." Ask students to think of a time they had to make this kind of choice. What decision did they make, and why? A short discussion on this topic will help students connect the theme of the selection to their own lives.

Vocabulary Building

Discuss with students the key vocabulary words for this selection: *livestock, huddled pheasants, glazed,* and *crouching.* Have them circle these words in the text and then encourage them to define the words in context before checking the footnote definition. Students will benefit from the additional work with using **context clues**.

STRATEGY LESSON: PRONUNCIATION Knowing the pronunciation of a word is as important as knowing its correct meaning. Write the following words from the selection and their pronunciations on the board. Ask students to practice saying the words: *pounce* (POWNS), *glistened* (GLISS nd), and *pheasants* (FEZ nts).

For additional practice on this strategy, see the **Vocabulary** blackline master on page 120.

Prereading Strategies

As a prereading activity, students are asked to take a **picture walk** of the selection. Explain that during a picture walk, the reader looks only at the art, photographs, and captions. In many instances, these elements can give valuable clues about the plot, characters, and author's message. When they have finished their picture walks of "What Happened During the Ice Storm," students might work together to explain how the photographs made them feel. In addition, they should use the pictures to make predictions about the topic. After they have read the story, you might have students return to the pictures and explain the connections they see between the photographs and the mood of Heynen's writing. Do they think the art matches the mood? Why or why not? What pictures would students have chosen to accompany this story if they were the designers of the book?

QUICKWRITE As an alternate prereading strategy, ask students to think about a time they had to make an important decision. Ask them to write for one minute about the decision and how it made them feel. Remind the class that quickwriting means jotting down whatever words, phrases, and images come to mind about a topic. Sentence structure and grammar are not as important as getting some ideas down on paper. This quick activity will help students connect the theme of the selection and unit to their own lives. In addition, it may give them ideas for the writing activity they are asked to complete on page 73.

Spanish-speaking Students

En "Lo que sucedió durante la tormenta de hielo," dos chicos intentan salvar a unos faisanes que se están muriendo. Hace mucho frío y todo está cubierto de hielo. Los faisanes no pueden volar ni ver porque los ojos se han congelado. Los chicos, sin embargo, están determinados a calentar los pájaros y ayudarlos por el resto de la tormenta.

II. READ

Before students begin reading, remind them of how valuable **predictions** can be. Predictions can help strengthen the bond between readers and text, give the reader a purpose for reading, and motivate them to continue reading until the end of the selection to see whether their predictions come true.

Response Strategy

MARK OR HIGHLIGHT You may also want students to mark or highlight important passages as they read. Have them make a note each time they come to sensory language, and help students see that writers use sensory details to bring vibrancy to their writing.

Comprehension Strategies

Using a **double-entry journal** encourages active response to text. Students read quotations from the selection and then write their thoughts and feelings. They can respond by saying what the quote reminds them of, what they think it means, or how it makes them feel. (Remind them to go beyond "I like/don't like this sentence or idea." They can use an opinion like this as a starting point if they like, but they should elaborate a bit and then offer support.) Point out the sample entry on page 70, read it aloud to the class, and explain that this is one reader's reaction to the quote. Every reader's reaction will be slightly different, of course, so students should feel free to write whatever comes to mind. Later in the *Sourcebook,* students will be asked to find quotations from the text that they think are interesting or important and then react to them using the same format.

For more help, see the **Comprehension** blackline master on page 121.

Discussion Questions

COMPREHENSION 1. What is the town's initial reaction to the ice storm? (*"How beautiful!"*)

2. How does that reaction change as the storm continues? (*People begin to worry about the safety of their livestock. The storm becomes more troublesome than beautiful.*)

3. Why do the boys go out into the freezing rain? (*Heynen doesn't say what their actual intent is, but it is possible that they want to harvest the pheasants as their parents have done, or they may want to scare the pheasants in order to have some fun.*)

CRITICAL THINKING 4. Why do you think the boys decide to cover the pheasants with their coats? (*Answers will vary. Possible: They are moved by the helplessness of the pheasants.*)

5. What is the mood of Heynen's story? (*Answers will vary. Remind students that mood is the overall effect created by an author's words. Students might note that the mood is quiet or hushed. Heynen's description of the ice on the fields and birds contributes to this mood.*)

Literary Skill

SIMILE To introduce a literary skill with this story, you might teach a short lesson on simile. A *simile* is a comparison of two things that are basically different but that have some similarities. Similes usually contain the words *like* or *as*. Heynen's similes add a poetic flavor to his prose and make his descriptions easy to visualize. Ask students to look for similes in the story and discuss their effectiveness. Students might suggest these: "Tree branches . . . broke like glass." "The grass seeds looked like little yolks. . . . " "And the pheasants looked like unborn birds glazed in egg white."

III. GATHER YOUR THOUGHTS

The goal of the prewriting activities on page 72 is to encourage students to reflect on what they have read and then use those reflections to help them do some writing of their own. First, students will think carefully about the boys' kindness to the pheasants. What motivated these children to help the birds rather than hurt them?

Next, students will **brainstorm** topics for a journal entry about a time they performed an act of kindness. Have students work alone or in pairs during their brainstorming session. Ask them to make a list of several acts of kindness in the margin of their books. They can then choose one from the list that they'd like to tell about in some detail. The **graphic organizer** on page 72 will help them consider their topic.

Prewriting Strategies

WORD BANK   Ask students to build a word bank of sensory words that they can use in a journal entry about their act of kindness. Have them look at their during-reading notes and then model their sensory language on the author's. They might make a bank of words that describe time, place, or even the people involved in the act of kindness. Some writers may also want to try writing some similes that they can use in their journal entries.

Have students use the **Prewriting** blackline master on page 122.

IV. WRITE

Students will write a **journal entry** about their act of kindness. Remind them to consult their notes on page 72 as needed. Also remind your writers to be as specific as possible.

WRITING RUBRIC   You might use this rubric to evaluate students' writing.

Do students' journal entries

- open with a statement about the act of kindness?
- offer details about the who, what, where, when, and why of the kindness?
- include a discussion of how things ended and how the writer felt once it was over?

Grammar, Usage, and Mechanics

After students have written a rough draft, encourage them to consult the **Writers' Checklist** for help with capitalization. Remind them that proper nouns (names of specific persons, places, and things) are always capitalized, as are names of the days of the week and months of the year. (In contrast, names of the seasons of the year are not capitalized unless they appear at the beginning of a sentence.) For practice, ask students to decide which of these words should be capitalized.

the farm   shady brook farm   rio Grande   san diego   winter

V. WRAP-UP

Take a moment at the end of the lesson and ask students to respond to the selection. Have them consider what the story **meant** to them personally. They might answer the questions on the **Readers' Checklist** aloud so that you have a sense of whether or not they were able to make a personal connection to the reading.

Assessment

To test students' comprehension, use the **Assessment** blackline master on page 123.

Name _____

VOCABULARY

Words from the Selection

DIRECTIONS Using context clues, fill in each blank with the most appropriate word from the box.

> ✦livestock   ✦huddled   ✦pheasants   ✦glazed   ✦crouching

1. The animals _____ together to keep warm during the ice storm.

2. We herded all the _____ into the barn to get them out of the rain.

3. Because their eyes were frozen shut, the _____ couldn't see us.

4. We were _____ behind the bush to surprise the birds.

5. The branches of the trees were _____ with a thin coat of ice.

Strategy Lesson: Pronunciation

DIRECTIONS Each sentence below contains the pronunciation of a word in parentheses. From the list on the right, choose the word that is pronounced. Write that word on the blank.

6. The farmers had to (POWNS) _____ on the pheasant so he didn't get away.

7. I used (JEL uh tin) _____ to make my dessert.

8. The ice on the trees (GLISS nd) _____ in the sunlight.

9. Summer is the season in which we (HAR vest) _____ the corn.

10. The boys saw five (FEZ nts) _____ sitting on a fence.

> glistened
>
> pheasants
>
> harvest
>
> pounce
>
> gelatin

Name _____

COMPREHENSION
Graphic Organizer _____

Directions Use this story pyramid to show what you know about Heynen's story.

1. _____
Name of story

2. _____ _____
Two words about the character

3. _____ _____ _____
Three words about the setting

4. _____ _____ _____ _____
Four words about the problem

5. _____ _____ _____ _____ _____
Five words about the solution

Word Bank _____

DIRECTIONS Now think of words that you might use to describe your act of kindness. Try to think of words that appeal to the five senses.

WORD BANK

Name _____

PREWRITING
Gathering Details

DIRECTIONS Think of a time you helped someone who was in trouble.

1. Use this organizer to show what happened and how you felt.

2. Then write about the event in your journal entry.

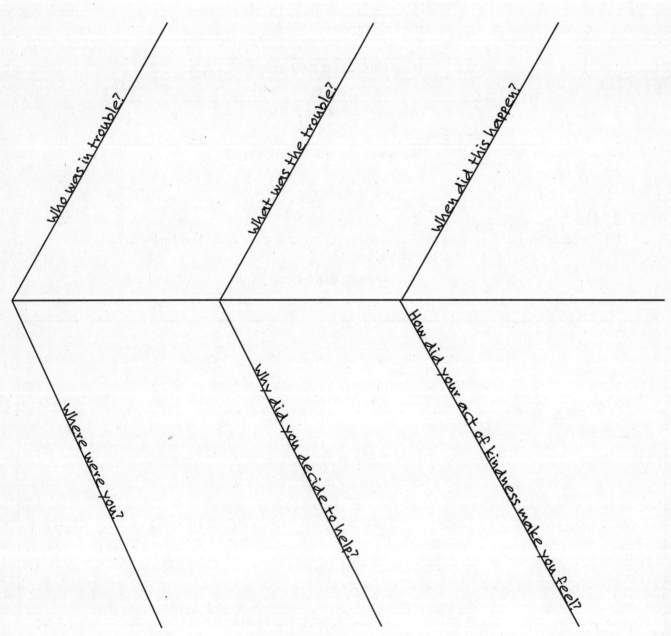

Name _____

ASSESSMENT

Multiple-Choice Test

DIRECTIONS On the blanks provided, write the letter of the best answer for each question.

_____ 1. When the freezing rain first begins to fall, what do people think?
    A. It is beautiful.   C. They are going to lose their power.
    B. It is dangerous.   D. Time to get inside.

_____ 2. What do the farmers do with their livestock?
    A. put them in a pen   C. put them in the barns
    B. tie them up   D. bring them in the house

_____ 3. Which creatures are not safe from the storm?
    A. cows   C. pheasants
    B. chickens   D. horses

_____ 4. What happens to the pheasants?
    A. Their wings freeze together.   C. Their feet freeze to the ground.
    B. Their eyes freeze shut.   D. They fly south.

_____ 5. What do the farmers take with them to kill the pheasants?
    A. clubs   C. ropes
    B. sacks   D. all of the above

_____ 6. Where do the boys find the pheasants?
    A. along the road   C. along a fence
    B. in the barn   D. on a tree branch

_____ 7. How many pheasants do the boys see?
    A. two   C. four or five
    B. three or four   D. five or six

_____ 8. What happens when trees or grass blades become too heavy with ice?
    A. They break like glass.   C. They begin to melt.
    B. They begin to bend.   D. all of the above

_____ 9. What do the pheasants do with their heads?
    A. stretch them up   C. turn them around
    B. keep them still   D. bury them between their wings

_____ 10. What happens to the boys as they run back to the house?
    A. They lose their coats.   C. They fall on the ice.
    B. Ice begins to freeze on them. D. They drop the pheasants.

Short-Essay Test

Why do you think the boys decide to throw their coats over the pheasants? Support your answer.

STUDENT PAGES 75–82

Skills and Strategies Overview

THEME Decisions

READING LEVEL easy

VOCABULARY ◇ core ◇ decent ◇ clinch ◇ hedge ◇ absolutely

PREREADING anticipation guide

RESPONSE react and connect

COMPREHENSION story frame

PREWRITING sequencing

WRITING story ending / dialogue

ASSESSMENT enjoyment

BACKGROUND

Susan Shreve is a novelist who is fascinated by plots. She attributes this fascination to her early years. As a child, Shreve lay in bed for months recovering from polio. The only entertainment she had was to listen to soap operas on the radio. The soap operas stories showed Shreve how important a good plot could be. She has kept this knowledge and writes with the attitude that if the plot is dull, no one will bother reading the story.

Shreve's story "Cheating" was first published in a book called *Family Secrets*. The stories in this anthology are all based on real events from her children's lives or Shreve's own life. The story described in "Cheating" happened to Shreve as a child. She remembers cheating on a math test and how frightened she felt afterward. The main character of this story (Sammy) experiences the same fears and worries that Shreve herself felt as a child.

UNIT THEME A young boy cheats on a math test and then must decide if he can live with himself.

GRAPHIC ORGANIZER A word web can help students explore the connotative and denotative meaning of a word. Before they begin reading, you might ask students to complete a web for the word *cheating*.

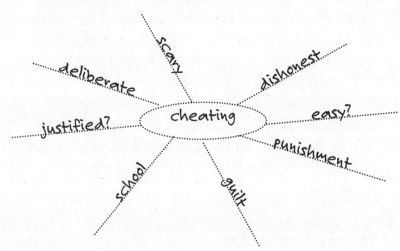

BIBLIOGRAPHY Students might also enjoy these works by Susan Shreve: *Family Secrets* (average, 1979); *The Gift of the Girl Who Couldn't Hear* (average, 1993); *The Flunking of Joshua T. Bates* (easy, 1995); *Goodbye, Amanda the Good* (easy, 2000).

BEFORE YOU READ

Read through the introduction to the lesson with students to motivate and focus students. Then introduce the prereading activity, an **Anticipation Guide**. (Refer to the **Strategy Handbook** on page 40 for more help.)

Motivation Strategy

Borrow a copy of *Family Secrets* from your library and read aloud another story about Sammy. Use the read-aloud to introduce students to his character and some of his problems.

ENGAGING STUDENTS Ask students to silently think about a time they were tempted to cheat on a test at school. Have them consider the situation and what happened. Why did they make the decision they did? Students should keep this memory in mind as they read about Sammy and the outcome of his cheating episode.

Vocabulary Building

Good writers have at their fingertips a large vocabulary that they can call on if they get stuck for a word. (They also know that using the same word over and over again makes for writing that is dull and uninspired.) Learning **synonyms** can help a new writer build vocabulary. Have students get into the habit of automatically thinking of a synonym or two for words that they use in their own writing. You might have them practice by writing synonyms for these key vocabulary words: *core, decent, clinch, hedge, and absolutely. Core* ("the central part") on page 76 is not footnoted. Have students circle these words in the text.

STRATEGY LESSON: ANTONYMS Explain that sometimes learning the antonym for a word can be a shortcut to memorizing the word's full dictionary definition. Give students a list of words that relate to the selection, such as *criminal, worried,* and *reveal.* Have volunteers suggest antonyms for each word. Students can use these antonyms to help them better understand the selection.

word	antonym
criminal	law-abiding
worried	confident
reveal	hide

For additional practice on this strategy, see the **Vocabulary** blackline master on page 128.

Prereading Strategies

Anticipation guides are easy to create and interesting for students to do. They work especially well with thought-provoking selections such as "Cheating" because they give students a head start on the topic and theme of the work. The six statements in the box on page 75 will help students think about cheating and how they feel about it. Because every student will have a slightly different attitude toward the topic, have readers work individually on this anticipation guide. Remind students that you are interested in hearing how they really feel about the topic—not how they think they are *supposed* to feel. When they have finished Shreve's story, students will return to the guide and react to the statements once again. Have they changed any of their answers? If so, why did they? Help students see that readers really can be affected by what they read.

Spanish-speaking Students

"Engañar" muestra el tumulto personal que resula de ser deshonesto. Un joven se siente culpable y horrible durante todo el día después de hacer trampa en un examen en la escuela. No puede comer ni hablar con sus padres. Se siente como si fuera el peor ser humano del mundo. Por fin, confiesa a sus padres y al maestro que haya sido engañoso y se siente muchísimo mejor.

II. READ

Response Strategy

Ask a volunteer to read aloud the directions at the top of page 76. Have another student explain what it means to **react and connect** to a piece of literature. (If you feel students will benefit, have them review the react and connect work they did while reading "Mother" on page 22–30 of their *Sourcebook*.)

Comprehension Strategies

As they read "Cheating," students will keep track of the elements of the story on four **story frames** that are scattered throughout the text. These story frames will reinforce students' knowledge of the essential elements of a story: setting, character, conflict, and resolution. Remind the class that understanding these elements is an important first step in analyzing a work of fiction.

DIRECTED READING As an alternate comprehension strategy, you might do a directed reading of "Cheating." A directed reading can help low-level readers better understand what they are reading. If you anticipate problems with the selection, then oversee the reading process of the whole class or a small group. Interrupt students' reading occasionally in order to ask questions that assess students' comprehension. Even simple questions, such as "What's happening here?" can help students get a handle on the action of the story.

For more help, see the **Comprehension** blackline master on page 129.

Discussion Questions

COMPREHENSION 1. What do you know about the narrator of this story? (*He's a "pretty decent" kid who is kind and respectful. He is introspective and intelligent and very worried about this cheating episode.*)

2. What happens at school that makes the narrator feel he's turned into a criminal? (*He cheated on a math test.*)

CRITICAL THINKING 3. Did the narrator cheat deliberately, or was it a mistake? (*The cheating was deliberate. He tells Mr. Burke that he planned it the night before.*)

4. Why do you think the narrator decides to tell his dad about the cheating? (*Answers will vary. Possible: He couldn't keep it in any longer and felt he had to talk about it.*)

5. What would you have done if you had been in this boy's shoes? Explain why. (*Answers will vary. Ask students to say what they would have done and why that action might be preferable to what the narrator does in "Cheating.")*

Literary Skill

PLOT For extra work on sequence and plot, have students record the events of "Cheating" on a plot line similar to the one below.

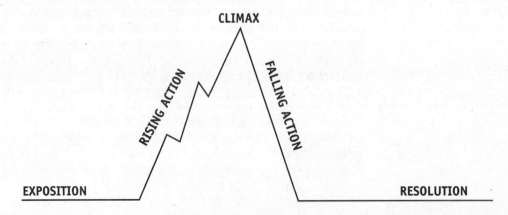

III. GATHER YOUR THOUGHTS

Students should work alone or in pairs to create a new **story ending** for "Cheating." As a prewriting activity, they will plan what will happen on a **storyboard** that shows the **sequence of events** in the story. Since a storyboard combines both writing and drawing, it is particularly useful for students who have trouble getting started on a writing project.

Prewriting Strategies

BRAINSTORMING If you feel students need an additional prewriting activity, have the class work as a group to think up possible ideas for a new ending of Shreve's story. To help, ask the class to think about answers to these questions: What will the narrator say first to Mr. Burke? Who else might be in the room on Saturday during the test make-up? How will the narrator act? How will Mr. Burke act?

Have students use the **Prewriting** blackline master on page 130.

IV. WRITE

Be sure students understand that their assignment is to write a new **story ending** for "Cheating." Read aloud the directions at the top of page 81. Remind the class that their story should sound like Shreve's story. Students should remember to use the first-person throughout.

WRITING RUBRIC Use this writing rubric to help students focus on the assignment requirements and for assistance with a quick assessment of their writing.

Do students' story endings

- read as if they are natural continuations of "Cheating"?
- demonstrate a knowledge of the rules of dialogue?
- show that students fully understood the plot of the original story?

Grammar, Usage, and Mechanics

After students have written a first draft, have them stop and think carefully about what they've written. Is there anything they should add? Is there any part that they should take out?

When they are ready to proofread their work, refer students to the **Writers' Checklist.** At this point, you might want to introduce a brief lesson on writing dialogue. For practice, ask students to correct this dialogue from Shreve's story:

My stomach is feeling sort of upset I hedge.

Okay he says and he pats my leg and gets up.

V. WRAP-UP

Take a moment at the end of the lesson for students to reflect using the **Readers' Checklist.** This checklist asks students to self-assess their **enjoyment** of "Cheating" and models for them the type of questions good readers ask of themselves after they've finished a story.

Assessment

To test students' comprehension, use the **Assessment** blackline master on page 131.

Name _____

VOCABULARY
Words from the Selection

DIRECTIONS Substitute a synonym from the word box for the underlined word or words in the sentences below, and write it on the line.

> ✦core ✦decent ✦clinch ✦hedge ✦absolutely

1. I think most people thought I was a fairly <u>good</u> person.

   _____

2. At the <u>central part</u> of me, I really wasn't so great, however.

   _____

3. It took the math test to <u>prove</u> it. _____

4. I was afraid I was a <u>completely</u> bad person. _____

5. I'm not going to <u>say it unconvincingly.</u> I was worried.

   _____

Strategy Lesson: Antonyms

An *antonym* is a word that means the opposite of another word. For example, *stop* is an antonym for go.

DIRECTIONS Find the word or words in Column B that mean the opposite of the word underlined in Column A. Then draw a matching line between the two. If there is a word you don't know, skip it and come back to it when you've finished the whole column.

Column A

6. I felt like a <u>criminal</u>.

7. I was <u>worried</u> about my math grade.

8. I had to <u>reveal</u> my dishonesty.

9. I was <u>reluctant</u> to do this.

10. Cheating is a <u>bad</u> thing to do.

Column B

confident

good

law-abiding person

hide

eager

Name _____

COMPREHENSION
Graphic Organizer

DIRECTIONS Use this character map to show what you know about the narrator and Mr. Burke.

1. Feel free to check details in your book if you need to.

2. Your knowledge of these characters will help you write a new story ending for "Cheating."

his personality	how he acts toward others

narrator

how I feel about him	how others feel about him

his personality	how he acts toward others

Mr. Burke

how I feel about him	how the narrator feels about him

Name _____

PREWRITING
Writing Dialogue

DIRECTIONS Write some dialogue for your new story ending. When writing dialogue, you need to consider these three questions:

1. Who is there?

2. What are they saying? (What topic are they discussing?)

3. How are they saying it? (Are they angry? tired? excited?)

STEP 1: Which characters will be in your story ending?

_____

_____

STEP 2: What are the characters talking about?

_____

_____

STEP 3: What do they actually say? (Remember that the directions on page 81 ask you to begin with Mr. Burke's first words.)

Character #1 says:

_____

Character #2 responds:

_____

Character #1 says:

_____

Character #2 responds:

_____

STEP 4: How do they say it? (Are they muttering, laughing, murmuring, questioning, shouting, whispering, replying, giggling, or crying?)

Character #1 talks in a _____ voice.

Character #2 talks in a _____ voice.

Name _____

ASSESSMENT

Multiple-Choice Test

DIRECTIONS On the blanks provided, write the letter of the item that best answers each question or complete each statement.

_____ 1. What question or questions does the narrator ask himself?
A. Could I steal?   C. Am I bad to the core?
B. Could I hurt someone on purpose?   D. all of the above

_____ 2. Why does the narrator think he is not a wonderful kid?
A. He has a bad temper.   C. He likes to lie to his parents.
B. He gets in a lot of fights.   D. He talks back to his teachers.

_____ 3. What does the narrator say are some of his good characteristics?
A. He works hard.   C. He tells the truth.
B. He sticks up for little kids.   D. all of the above

_____ 4. What does the narrator wish he was better at?
A. basketball   C. making friends
B. math   D. drawing

_____ 5. Why does the narrator feel he is a criminal?
A. He stole candy from a store.   C. He cheated on a math test.
B. He lied to his parents.   D. He beat up a little kid.

_____ 6. The narrator is afraid he will never again . . .
A. have a friend.   C. feel good about himself.
B. tell the truth.   D. all of the above

_____ 7. The narrator says his mom drives him crazy because she always . . .
A. wants to help.   C. asks too many questions.
B. knows when something is wrong.   D. yells a lot.

_____ 8. What does the narrator tell his dad he is going to have to do?
A. run away   C. fight another student
B. tell the truth   D. drop out of school

_____ 9. After the narrator confesses to his father, what does he have to do?
A. come to dinner   C. tell his mom
B. go to bed   D. call his teacher

_____ 10. Who is Mr. Burke?
A. the school principal   C. a neighbor
B. a teacher   D. a coach

Short-Essay Test

What lessons does the narrator learn from the cheating episode? Explain them here.

Civilizations

Unit Background   CIVILIZATIONS (pages 83–100)

Two selections about mummies appear in this unit, one by Charlotte Wilcox from *Mummies and Their Mysteries,* and one by Patricia Lauber from *Tales Mummies Tell.*

Charlotte Wilcox has written about many topics, including a series of books about various breeds of dogs, books about horses, and another book about mummies: *Mummies, Bones, and Body Parts* (2000). She was born in Harris, Minnesota, in 1948 and has worked as a freelance writer and graphic designer.

Patricia Lauber, also a prolific writer, has written more than 60 books for young readers. Her books include *Volcano: The Eruption and Healing of Mount St. Helens* (1986), *Great Whales: The Gentle Giants* (1995), and *The Tiger Has a Toothache: Helping Animals at the Zoo* (1999). She has been editor of *Junior Scholastic,* editor-in-chief of *Science World,* and chief editor of science and mathematics for *The New Book of Knowledge.* She was born in 1924 in New York, is a graduate of Wellesley College, and lives in Connecticut.

Teaching the Introduction

Illustrations on this page show pyramids in Egypt, a case containing an Egyptian mummy, and a map showing the location of Egypt.

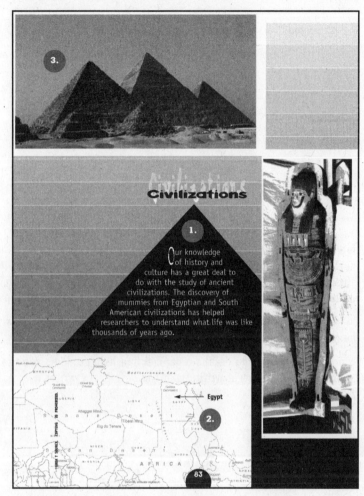

1. Many students will be immediately interested in the topic of this unit. Ask someone to read the unit introduction, and then ask for ideas about what we might learn from the study of 1000-year-old mummies, whether from South America or Egypt.

2. Depending on recent experiences, such as the death of a friend or of a relative, some students may be uncomfortable at first about viewing or discussing mummies. If so, focus initial discussion on Egyptian civilization in general and topics such as Egyptian writing or art. Ask, for example, what students know about papyrus and about what Egyptian writing looks like and what it is called. What do they know about how artists depicted people?

3. Ask someone to explain the connection between Egyptian pyramids and Egyptian mummies.

Opening Activity

Some students may be interested in talking about or investigating what researchers have learned from mummies: what the person ate, the person's age, sex, and physical condition, what objects or implements the person used, and what the person died from. They can find information in the books from which the excerpts were taken or from other more recent sources. Others might like to research and explain carbon-14 dating or report on how scientists can sometimes use DNA to find out more about mummified bodies.

LESSON 9

Egyptian Mummies

STUDENT PAGES 84–91

Skills and Strategies Overview

THEME Civilizations

READING LEVEL challenging

VOCABULARY ✧legends ✧preserve ✧embalmed ✧decay ✧lavish

PREREADING preview

RESPONSE clarify

COMPREHENSION directed reading

PREWRITING web

WRITING descriptive paragraph / verb pairs

ASSESSMENT understanding

BACKGROUND

The informational article "Egyptian Mummies" is an excerpt from Charlotte Wilcox's popular book, *Mummies and Their Mysteries* (1993). In addition to describing the process of mummification (both real and accidental), Wilcox offers specific information about burial rituals in ancient Egyptian, Chinese, and Indian cultures. She explains how mummies that are hundreds or thousands of years old can provide valuable clues to past ways of life.

UNIT THEME Charlotte Wilcox offers information about the who, what, where, when, why, and how of mummies.

GRAPHIC ORGANIZER A main idea/supporting details organizer can help students see the relationship between the central idea of a piece of writing and the details the writer uses as "proof" that this idea is true.

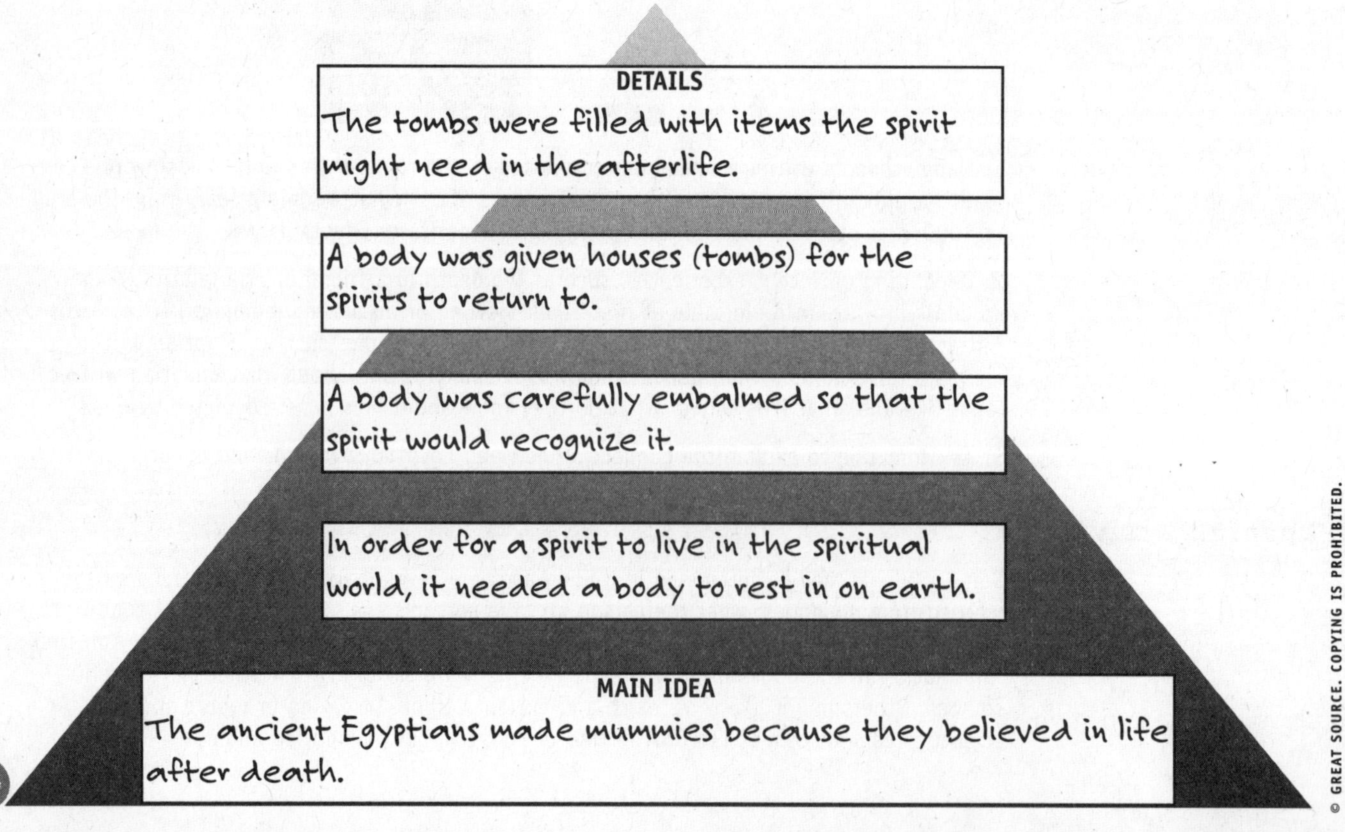
DETAILS
The tombs were filled with items the spirit might need in the afterlife.
A body was given houses (tombs) for the spirits to return to.
A body was carefully embalmed so that the spirit would recognize it.
In order for a spirit to live in the spiritual world, it needed a body to rest in on earth.
MAIN IDEA
The ancient Egyptians made mummies because they believed in life after death.

1. BEFORE YOU READ

Ask a volunteer to read aloud the introduction to the lesson. Have students talk about what they know about mummies. Make a "fact" and "fiction" chart on the board and sort what they know into the two categories (or allow students to do their own sorting). Then have them complete the prewriting activity, a **preview**. (Refer to the **Strategy Handbook** on page 40 for more help.)

Motivation Strategy

Ask students to tell about scary (or funny) mummy movies they've seen on TV or at the movie theater. Why do they suppose mummies are such a popular topic for filmmakers? If students were to make a movie about mummies, what would their plot be? Which Hollywood actors would star in the film? Give students the chance to explore the fictional aspect of mummies before reading about Egyptian mummies.

Vocabulary Building

Help students use **context clues** as they read to figure out the meanings of difficult words, especially the key vocabulary for this lesson: *legends, preserve, embalmed, decay,* and *lavish.* Have students circle these words in the text. If you feel students will benefit, model using context clues. For example, you might say: "I don't know the meaning of the word *lavish*. I see, however, that it is used as an adjective to describe the preparations a pharaoh made for life after death. I also see that these lavish preparations included gathering clothing, gold, jewels, furniture and 'other things he enjoyed in life.' Could *lavish* mean 'fancy'? I can check the footnote definition to see if my guess is correct." For additional practice with these words, see page 138.

STRATEGY LESSON: IRREGULAR VERBS Most verbs are "regular"; that is, the past tense is formed by adding *-ed.* But the past tense of some verbs is formed in other ways. The forms of these verbs sometimes can cause trouble for speakers and writers. For example, the word *saw,* the past tense of *see,* appears on page 85. Other troublesome verbs include *run-ran, flee-fled, give-gave, leave-left,* and *teach-taught.* The best way for non-native speakers to learn these troublesome verbs is to memorize them.

For additional practice with irregular verbs, see the **Vocabulary** blackline master on page 138.

Prereading Strategies

Before they read, students will do a **preview** of "Egyptian Mummies." A preview is a helpful prereading strategy because it gives readers a glimpse of what's to come. Thumbing through the pages they are about to read can help students learn about the subject and anticipate any comprehension problems they might have. (This is a particularly helpful strategy to use with students who are intimidated by nonfiction.) To that end, you might have students note any underlined words that are unfamiliar.

PICTURE WALK As an alternate strategy, ask students to do a **picture walk** of the selection. (For help with this strategy, see the **Strategy Handbook**, page 40.) A picture walk is similar to a preview in that it asks students to take a quick look through the selection they're about to read. A picture walk can also reveal valuable clues about the topic of the article and, in some cases, the author's main idea. These clues can help readers later, when they'll need to think carefully about how the details of the piece work together to support one central idea.

Spanish-speaking Students

Charlotte Wilcox escribe de la civilización egipcia en esta selección. Explica que hace más de dos miles de años, los egipcios creían en la importancia de perservar a los muertos. Los cuerpos fueron embalsamados o secados naturalmente. El proceso de momificarse ha sido estudiado por los siglos y es una prueba de la inteligencia de los egipcios y de su cultura avansada.

READ

Before students begin their close readings, explain again the purpose of making notes that **clarify** the point the author makes. Ask them to note in particular their thoughts about how mummies are formed and why the Egyptians wanted to create them. Students should write their comments of clarification in the **Response Notes**, along with any questions that come up during the reading.

Response Strategy

VISUALIZE As an alternate response strategy, students might visualize and then sketch the contents of the elaborate tombs Wilcox describes. Making sketches may help maintain students' interest in Wilcox's article.

Comprehension Strategies

You may find that the best comprehension strategy to use with nonfiction is a **directed reading**. The reason for this is simple. Some students are afraid of nonfiction and avoid reading it. They worry that it will be too hard or that they will miss important details. A directed reading allows you to closely monitor students' reading progress. In addition, it helps you gauge students' understanding of a text. If you feel students will benefit, have them work as a group to answer the three **stop and think** questions. Review their work as a class after they have finished.

For more help, see the **Comprehension** blackline master on page 139.

Discussion Questions

COMPREHENSION 1. How were mummies formed before 2500 B.C.? *(Most formed naturally in the desert. The wind and sun dried the bodies before they could decay.)*

2. Who were the pharaohs? *(Egyptian kings)*

3. Why did the ancient Egyptians build tombs? *(to house the corpses of important people such as pharaohs)*

CRITICAL THINKING 4. Explain why the ancient Egyptians created mummies. *(The ancient Egyptians believed a person lived on in spirit after death and that that person needed a physical body and home on earth as a place of rest—thus the Egyptian mummies and tombs.)*

5. What information did you find most interesting or surprising in this article? *(Answers will vary. Encourage students to explain their individual responses to the text.)*

Literary Skill

NONFICTION If your students have a hard time reading nonfiction, use this opportunity to explain that nonfiction (both narrative and expository) doesn't have to be difficult. A graphic organizer or fact chart can make the reading process easier. Show students a few graphic organizers that will work well with "Egyptian Mummies." For example, you might suggest they fill out a who, what, where, when, why, and how organizer or a word web with the word *mummy* in the center. Students can then use their organizer notes to help them uncover the main idea (and supporting details) of the writing.

III. GATHER YOUR THOUGHTS

Prewriting Strategies

Use the prewriting activities as a warm-up for the writing activity, a **descriptive paragraph**, which is assigned on page 90. Have them use the web at the top of page 89 to analyze the information in Wilcox's article. Ask the class: "What is Wilcox's most important idea? What message does she have for readers?"

After students finish their webs, have them create a **word bank** of descriptive words that they can use in a paragraph about mummies. Word banks are extremely helpful to writers who tend to get stuck for a word or for writers who don't use a variety of words in their writing. If you like, have students use a thesaurus to help them complete their word banks.

Have students use the **Prewriting** blackline master on page 140.

IV. WRITE

Read aloud the directions on page 90 to be sure students understand the assignment. Remind them that their **descriptive paragraphs** should begin with a topic sentence that tells the topic of the paragraph and their thoughts and feelings about it. In the body of the paragraph, they'll offer details that help readers "see" what they are describing.

After students have written a first draft, have them stop and think carefully about what they've written. They should ask themselves: Have I used adequate details? Have I given my readers a sense of what mummies look like and how they are formed? Have I made my writing as interesting as I can?

WRITING RUBRIC You can use this rubric to help students focus on the assignment requirements and for assistance with a quick assessment of their writing.

Do students' descriptive paragraphs

- begin with a topic sentence?

- include specific details from Wilcox's article?

- stay focused on the topic throughout?

Grammar, Usage, and Mechanics

When they are ready to proofread their work, refer students to the **Writers' Checklist.** At this point, you might want to introduce a brief lesson on confusing verb pairs. Review *bring/take* and *leave/let*. Then ask students to correct verb problems in this sentence:

He will have you take that video to me, but you can't bring it home.

V. WRAP-UP

Take a moment at the end of the lesson for students to reflect using the **Readers' Checklist.** Its intent is to help students ask the questions good readers ask of themselves to determine their **understanding** of a piece of writing.

Assessment

To test students' comprehension, use the **Assessment** blackline master on page 141.

Name _____

VOCABULARY
Words from the Selection

DIRECTIONS Use context clues and your knowledge of the article to find the meaning of the underlined words. Circle the correct definition of each word.

1. "Egyptian mummies have been the subject of <u>legends</u> for thousands of years."

(a) tests   (b) stories   (c) classes   (d) books

2. "It was once believed that ancient Egyptians used secret spells to <u>preserve</u> bodies."

(a) dress up   (b) bury   (c) destroy   (d) protect

3. The mummies were <u>embalmed</u> to prevent rotting.

(a) filled with a substance   (b) thrown away   (c) dumped in the ocean (d) dried out

4. "Warm desert winds and hot sun heating the sand caused bodies to dry out very quickly, so they did not <u>decay</u>."

(a) rot   (b) walk   (c) speak   (d) sleep

5. "During his life, a pharaoh made <u>lavish</u> preparations for the life he expected to live after death."

(a) dull   (b) few   (c) fancy   (d) reasonable

Strategy Lesson: Irregular Verbs

The past tense of most verbs is formed by adding –ed: *walk/walked; talk/talked*. But the past tense of some verbs is formed in other ways.

DIRECTIONS The verbs in Column A are in the present tense. The past tense of these verbs are in Column B. Draw a line between the present tense verb in Column A and its past tense in Column B.

Column A (present tense)	Column B (past tense)
6. have	wrote
7. is	became
8. write	had
9. find	grew
10. become	thought
11. do	drank
12. grow	found
13. think	did
14. build	built
15. drink	was

Name _____

COMPREHENSION
Group Discussion

DIRECTIONS Get together with a partner or a small group. Discuss what you know about mummies.

1. Make a list of mummy "facts" and mummy "fictions."

2. Try to come up with at least ten items for each column.

3. Then use details from the "facts" column for your paragraph.

MUMMIES

Facts	Fictions
1. Mummies can be thousands of years old.	Mummies can get up and walk around.
2.	
3.	
4.	
5.	
6.	
7.	
8.	
9.	
10.	

Name _____

PREWRITING
Word Web

DIRECTIONS Imagine you are an archeologist. You have just opened an ancient Egyptian tomb and have discovered a mummy. What do you see, hear, smell, and touch. How do you feel?

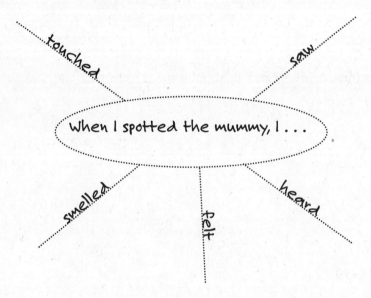

When I spotted the mummy, I . . .

touched
saw
smelled
felt
heard

Why I felt this way: _____

_____

_____

_____

_____

_____

_____

Name _____

ASSESSMENT

Multiple-Choice Test

DIRECTIONS On the blanks provided, write the letter of the item that best answers each question or completes each statement.

_____ 1. The ancient Egyptians believed that_____could preserve dead bodies.
   A. the gods   C. doctors
   B. secret spells   D. the sun

_____ 2. The oldest mummies were formed by . . .
   A. the hot sun.   C. chemicals.
   B. desert winds.   D. A. and B.

_____ 3. The ancient Egyptians believed . . .
   A. the dead were not important.   C. mummies came back to this life.
   B. in life after death.   D. in one god.

_____ 4. What did the ancient Egyptians put in the graves?
   A. gold   C. jewelry
   B. food   D. all of the above

_____ 5. A pharaoh was a . . .
   A. king.   C. priest.
   B. woman.   D. mummy.

_____ 6. The ancient Egyptians also believed that the pharaohs were . . .
   A. evil.   C. gods.
   B. fools.   D. none of the above

_____ 7. What was needed for a spirit to live in the spirit world?
   A. permission   C. a body on earth to rest in
   B. a family on earth   D. none of the above

_____ 8. The pyramids were . . .
   A. the largest of all tomb houses.   C. built by the pharaohs.
   B. constructed with stone.   D. all of the above

_____ 9. What is Charlotte Wilcox's main idea in "Egyptian Mummies"?
   A. Burial practices in ancient   C. The Great Pyramid is the largest one.
      Egypt are very interesting.
   B. Mummies can be found   D. Osiris was the god-king of the dead.
      only in Egypt.

_____ 10. "Egyptian Mummies" is an example of . . .
   A. fiction.   C. biography.
   B. nonfiction.   D. historical fiction.

Short-Essay Test

Explain the ancient Egyptian attitude toward death.

STUDENT PAGES 92–100

Skills and Strategies Overview

THEME	Civilizations
READING LEVEL	challenging
VOCABULARY	✦rapid ✦multiply ✦prying ✦trade ✦providing
PREREADING	K-W-L
RESPONSE	question
COMPREHENSION	graphic organizer
PREWRITING	using graphic organizers
WRITING	compare and contrast paragraph / subject-verb agreement
ASSESSMENT	ease

BACKGROUND

In *Tales Mummies Tell,* the award-winning children's author Patricia Lauber explains how opening a mummy's tomb can be like opening the pages of an ancient diary. "Mummies" is an excerpt from the first part of this popular book.

Lauber offers much information about mummies in this selection, including a description of how mummies are formed, where they are most often found, and what ancient people buried along with the bodies of their loved ones. She also gives specifics about some famous mummies, such as Copper Man, Little Alice, and the 8,000 men, women, and children found buried in the Capuchin Catacombs.

UNIT THEME Patricia Lauber reveals some fascinating insights about mummies.

GRAPHIC ORGANIZER A chart like the one below can help students keep track of important facts as they read.

Mummy	Found where?	Found when?	Died when?	Manner of death?	Other facts
Copper Man	Atacama Desert of northern Chile	1899	c. A.D. 800	died when the tunnel he was mining collapsed	Found with his arms in a working position, hair was neatly braided and he was wearing a loincloth.
8,000 men women, and children	Capuchin Catacombs in Palermo, Sicily	?	1800s	unknown	All dressed in their best clothes, their bodies preserved by dry air
Little Alice/ Little Al	Salts Cave in Kentucky	1875	2,000 years ago	unknown	Child who died at the age of 9 or 10
the Basket Makers	the American Southwest	1900s	c. A.D. 100–700	unknown	Sandals, beads, baskets, weapons, and pipes were buried alongside these men, women, and children.

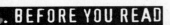

BEFORE YOU READ

Remind students of the theme of this unit (civilizations), and ask a volunteer to summarize the information contained in Charlotte Wilcox's "Egyptian Mummies." Then have the class complete the prereading activity, a **K-W-L.** (For help with this strategy, see the **Strategy Handbook**, page 40.)

Motivation Strategy

In "Mummies," Patricia Lauber describes ancient burial practices. Ask students to discuss burial practices of today. What rituals have they heard about? How long would they say these rituals have been around? A brief discussion on this topic will help students make a connection between the topic of the article and contemporary society.

ENGAGING STUDENTS Ask students to think about famous graveyard scenes in movies, TV shows, and books. (For example, they might mention the graveyard scene from the book or movie version of *Tom Sawyer* or *A Christmas Carol.*) What is the prevailing mood in these scenes? What are modern attitudes about death? A brief discussion of this topic may pique students' interest in Lauber's article.

Vocabulary Building

Read aloud to students the key vocabulary words for this lesson: *rapid, multiply, prying, trade,* and *providing.* Ask students to circle these words in the text. These words are featured on the **Vocabulary** blackline master on page 146. Encourage students to familiarize themselves with the definition of each word. Later, they can practice using these words in sentences.

STRATEGY LESSON: ROOT WORDS As you know, a root is a base upon which a word is built.

root	meaning	word
–cycl–	circle, ring, wheel	tricycle, cyclone, recycle
–sim–	like	similar, simile, simulate

Show students these words and their roots: *recycled, cycle, similar, cyclone,* and *cyclical.*

For additional practice on this strategy, see the **Vocabulary** blackline master on page 146.

Prereading Strategies

The purpose of a **K-W-L** is to activate prior knowledge and allow students to take responsibility for their own learning gaps. In the K column, students will make notes about mummies. (If you like, allow students to review notes they made while reading "Egyptian Mummies" pages 84–88 of the *Sourcebook*). Later, they'll chart what they learned about the topic in the L column. A K-W-L can show students that ultimately they are responsible for their own learning.

SKIM As an alternate prereading strategy, ask students to do a prereading skim of "Mummies." You might tell them to skim for an answer to these questions: "Where can mummies be found?" "Which mummies does Lauber describe?" Have students make notes about words, phrases, or ideas that pop out at them. Also have them look carefully at the footnoted material and the interrupter questions. A quick skim beforehand will make the article seem like familiar territory during their close readings.

Spanish-speaking Students

Los egipcios no eran los únicos que creaban momias. Patricia Lauber explica que hay momias por todo el mundo, especialmente donde hay desiertos. Los cuerpos muertos secan fácilmente en lugares donde hay mucho sol y poco agua. El carecer de bacteria y humedad impide putrefacción.

II. READ

Before students begin reading "Mummies," read aloud the directions at the top of page 93. Be sure students understand the response strategy of **questioning**. Remind them to note any question that occurs to them, even if they think it will be answered later in the reading. This strategy can help keep students focused on the reading and can also slow down those who tend to skim haphazardly rather than read closely.

Response Strategy

MARK OR HIGHTLIGHT As an alternate or additional response strategy, ask students to mark or highlight important facts or details that can help them answer questions they have written on the **K-W-L** chart. In particular, students should make notes about how mummies are made, where many of them have been found, and names and characteristics of specific mummies.

If students need to do a second reading of the article, have them use a different colored pen to write their additional set of notes. This will help them see that doing another reading can strengthen their understanding of the author's topic.

Comprehension Strategies

Graphic organizers keep students organized and on task as they read. For this selection, students will complete three different informational webs that will help them track information about the mummies Lauber describes. Students should write as many important facts and details as they can think of on each web, adding spokes as necessary. Students will want to refer to these organizers when working on the **Venn diagram** in Part III.

For more help, see the **Comprehension** blackline master on page 147.

Discussion Questions

COMPREHENSION 1. How are most mummies formed? *(by rapid drying)*

2. What does it mean when a mummy forms "naturally"? *(It means they have formed without the help of humans. Many mummies formed naturally in the desert, thanks to the hot, dry sands and wind.)*

3. Who is Copper Man? *(He's a South American mummy who formed naturally with the help of dry air and salts. See page 94 of the **Sourcebook** for specifics.)*

4. What mistake did researchers make when they named Little Alice? *(They thought Alice was a female mummy, when in fact it is the mummy of a male child.)*

CRITICAL THINKING 5. What do mummies from all over the world seem to have in common? *(Ask students to think about common characteristics, including the fact that mummies have dried naturally in many parts of the world; that many mummies have been found buried with items to be used in the afterlife; that most cultures mummified not only important men, but women and children as well, and so on.)*

Literary Skill

ANECDOTE To introduce a literary skill with this lesson, you might teach a brief lesson on anecdote. Explain that an anecdote is a very short story that an author tells in order to make a point, clarify an idea, or pique a reader's interest. Lauber uses several different anecdotes in "Mummies," all of which serve to illustrate her point that mummies have been found in many places in the world. For practice, ask students to find two anecdotes in Lauber's article. (They might mention the stories of Copper Man, Little Alice, or the Basket Makers.) How do these anecdotes help support Lauber's main idea?

III. GATHER YOUR THOUGHTS

Prewriting Strategies

The prewriting activities on page 98 will help students gather what they've learned about mummies and prepare them to write a **compare and contrast paragraph** in which they discuss different types of mummies.

To begin, students will complete a **Venn diagram** using details from Lauber's article. (You'll probably also want to have them include information from Wilcox's piece.) Encourage students to be as detailed as possible in making their notes. They may even want to use a few direct quotations from the text.

Next, students will write a topic sentence that names the comparison to be made. If students need help, suggest a few sentence starters such as:

Egyptian mummies and mummies from other parts of the world are . . .

Have students use the **Prewriting** blackline master on page 148.

IV. WRITE

Remind students that the purpose of a **compare and contrast paragraph** is to show readers the ways in which two things are similar or different. Explain that their paragraphs should begin with a topic sentence that sets up the comparison. In the sentences that follow, they'll provide support from their Venn diagrams.

WRITING RUBRIC Use this rubric to help students focus on the assignment requirements and for assistance with a quick assessment of their writing.

Do students' compare and contrast paragraphs

- thoroughly explore the similarities and/or differences between Egyptian mummies and mummies from other parts of the world?

- include adequate supporting details?

- stay focused on the comparison named in the topic sentence?

Grammar, Usage, and Mechanics

When they are ready to proofread their work, refer students to the **Writers' Checklist.** At this point, you might want to introduce a brief lesson on subject-verb agreement. Remind the class that a singular subject needs a singular verb. A plural subject needs a plural verb.

Incorrect: Lauber's article describe mummies.

Correct: Lauber's article describes mummies.

V. WRAP-UP

At the end of the lesson, point out the **Readers' Checklist** and ask students to answer both questions. Have the class explain what they found **easy** or challenging about the reading.

Assessment

To test students' comprehension, use the **Assessment** blackline master on page 149.

Name _____

VOCABULARY
Words from the Selection

DIRECTIONS Write a vocabulary word from the word box for the underlined word or words.

> ◇rapid ◇multiply ◇prying ◇trade ◇providing

1. "These may mean that the Basket Makers believed in a life after death and were <u>giving</u> the dead what they might need." _____

2. Bacteria need water in order to <u>increase in number</u> and grow.

   _____

3. Mummies are formed from a process of <u>fast</u> drying. _____

4. One miner died while <u>digging</u> out copper ore. _____

5. My <u>job</u> was to locate and study mummies from around the world.

   _____

Strategy Lesson: Root Words

DIRECTIONS Read this list of common roots and their definitions. Then use what you've learned to fill in the blanks.

Roots
-cycl- = circle, ring
-sim- = like

6. Dad bought an old <u>motorcycle.</u> A motorcycle has two _____ and a motor.

7. We <u>recycled</u> our paper and bottles. This meant they could be used

   _____.

8. A <u>cyclone</u> is a storm that moves around in a _____.

9. Mummies across the globe have formed in <u>similar</u> ways or ways that are

   _____.

10. A computer <u>simulation</u> of a car crash looks _____ the real thing.

Name _____

COMPREHENSION
Word Bank
....

DIRECTIONS With a partner, make a word bank of transition words and phrases that you can use when writing your compare and contrast paragraph. (Transitions help readers move along from one sentence to the next in a piece of writing.) Try to think of at least ten. (Three transition words are shown.)

Word Bank
therefore
although
in contrast

Reflect
....

DIRECTIONS Complete these statements about "Mummies."

This is what I've learned about Egyptian mummies: _____

_____

_____

This is what I've learned about mummies from other cultures: _____

_____

_____

I'd still like to know: _____

_____

_____

Places I could go to find out more: _____

_____

Name _____

PREWRITING
Comparing and Contrasting

DIRECTIONS Follow theese steps to write a paragraph that compares and contrasts different types of mummies.

STEP 1. WRITE A TOPIC SENTENCE. Write a topic sentence that prepares the reader for the comparison you want to make. Use this sentence starter:

Egyptian mummies and mummies from other parts of the world are

_____

STEP 2. LIST SIMILARITIES. List three important similarities between the mummies.

similarity #1: _____

similarity #2: _____

similarity #3: _____

STEP 3. LIST DIFFERENCES. List three important differences between the mummies.

difference #1: _____

difference #2: _____

difference #3: _____

STEP 4. WRITE A CLOSING SENTENCE. Write a closing sentence that sums up the comparison and leaves your readers with something to think about.

My closing sentence: _____

_____

WRITING TIP

If you want to emphasize the **similarities** between different mummies, discuss them last. If you want to emphasize the **differences** between them, then you should discuss *them* last.

Name _____

ASSESSMENT

Multiple-Choice Test

DIRECTIONS On the blanks provided, write the letter of the best answer for each question.

_____ 1. Which mummies are the most famous?

    A. Native-American mummies   C. Egyptian mummies

    B. Sicilian mummies   D. South American mummies

_____ 2. How are most mummies formed?

    A. by rapid drying   C. with leather

    B. with bandages   D. with chemicals

_____ 3. What do bacteria need in order to begin the decaying process?

    A. water   C. wind

    B. sun   D. minerals

_____ 4. Besides mummies, what else do we use the drying process for?

    A. preserving books   C. preserving meat

    B. preserving fish   D. B. and C.

_____ 5. Where have mummies formed naturally?

    A. in deserts   C. in the rain forest

    B. under water   D. all of the above

_____ 6. Where was Copper Man found?

    A. Egypt   C. Arizona

    B. Chile   D. China

_____ 7. When Copper Man was found, how did he look?

    A. His arms were in working position.   C. He was wearing a loincloth.

    B. His hair was braided.   D. all of the above

_____ 8. Why was he named Copper Man?

    A. His body was stained green.   C. He was a policeman.

    B. He was holding copper ore.   D. all of the above

_____ 9. What are the walls of the Capuchin Catacombs lined with?

    A. skulls   C. mummies

    B. skeletons   D. all of the above

_____ 10. What helped scientists to know the age of Little Alice?

    A. information in history books   C. drawings on the wall of a cave

    B. carbon-14 dating   D. all of the above

Short-Essay Test

What do all mummies have in common?

Jan Hudson

Unit Background   JAN HUDSON (pages 101–120)

Two selections from Jan Hudson's book *Sweetgrass* appear in this unit.

Jan Hudson (1954–1990) was born in Calgary, Alberta, Canada. She received a B.A. degree from the University of Calgary in 1978 and an LL.B. in 1983 from the University of Alberta. She worked as a legal editor and writer and was an administrative assistant and editor for the attorney general of British Columbia. *Sweetgrass*, the fictional name of a Blackfoot Indian girl, was named the Best Children's Book of the Year by the Canadian Association of Children's Librarians in 1984 and was chosen a Notable Book and Best Book for Young Adults by the American Library Association when the book was published in the United States in 1989. Her only other book, *Dawn Rider* (1990), is also about the Blackfoot and set in the early 1700s. Hudson was married to a Native American and adopted his daughter, to whom *Sweetgrass* is dedicated.

In the book, Sweetgrass is 15 years old in 1837. In 1837, a smallpox pandemic spread among Blackfoot camps and almost one-third of the people died, a fact not mentioned in these excerpts.

Teaching the Introduction

The cover of *Sweetgrass*, Native-American girls picking berries, and Plains Indians in front of tepees are shown on page 101. Although for many people, tepees (or tipis) are thought of as the only type of Indian dwelling, in fact Native Americans had many types of houses. The conical tents pictured on page 101 were most common on the Great Plains and the type of housing erected by the Blackfoot.

1. Much information on the Blackfoot Indians is included with the first lesson plan for this unit; however, you may want to give students a little information on the Sun Dance, mentioned in the second excerpt. The Sun Dance is a religious ceremony, often sponsored by an individual who takes a vow with the hope of being cured of worry or illness or of being blessed. It is usually performed in late spring or early summer. Dancers do not eat or drink during the three or four days of the dance.

2. After reading the introduction, you might tell students that, though the label *Indian* was inaccurate when Columbus named the people he found (he called them *Indios*), Indians themselves are divided on the use of the term *Native American*, and many use both terms.

Opening Activity

Ask students what they know about the Indians who inhabited or inhabit the area in which they now live. If you have Native Americans in your class, encourage them to talk about their people.

Summer Berries

Skills and Strategies Overview

THEME Jan Hudson

READING LEVEL average

VOCABULARY ◇shame ◇sacrificed ◇daintily ◇plucking ◇sorrow

PREREADING word web

RESPONSE visualize

COMPREHENSION graphic organizer

PREWRITING organize a paragraph

WRITING personal experience paragraph / possessives

ASSESSMENT style

BACKGROUND

Jan Hudson's 1989 novel *Sweetgrass* is the story of a 15-year-old Blackfoot girl (named Sweetgrass) who longs to be married to a brave warrior. Sweetgrass's protective father feels she is too young to marry, so Sweetgrass sets out to prove to her father and other elders that she is mature enough to make her own decisions.

Students may benefit from some background information on the Blackfoot Nation. Explain that the Blackfoot were originally a nomadic Algonquin Indian people who lived mostly in the northern Plains. The name *Blackfoot* (an English term) probably comes from this group's tradition of using ashes to stain their moccasins.

Although the history of the Blackfoot is a long one, the tribe reached the height of its power in the mid-1800s. During this period, most Blackfoot Indians lived in Montana, where they had gone in search of buffalo. Today, many Blackfoot live on a reservation in Montana, adjacent to Glacier National Park.

Hudson's *Sweetgrass* is set near Montana, on the western Canadian prairie. The story takes place some time in the mid- to late nineteenth century.

UNIT THEME Jan Hudson explores themes of growing up and self-confidence in this coming-of-age story.

GRAPHIC ORGANIZER A story organizer like the one below can help prepare lower-level readers for the reading. Share this organizer with the class or have students create their own after they finish reading.

Characters	Setting	Plot
Sweetgrass: the narrator Pretty-Girl: Sweetgrass's friend Shy-Bear: a warrior Pretty-Girl wants to marry him Eagle-Sun: a warrior Sweetgrass wants to marry him	place: a prairie in western Canada time: mid- to late-1800s	Pretty-Girl and Sweetgrass worry they won't be able to marry the men they want. The two girls discuss their fears and begin thinking about how they might convince their elders that Shy-Bear and Eagle-Sun would make good husbands for them.

BEFORE YOU READ

Read through the introduction to the lesson with students. Offer background information on Jan Hudson and the novel *Sweetgrass* as you see fit. You may want to explain the concept of a bride price. The man Pretty Girl marries must be able to give her father some valuable asset in exchange for his daughter. Then have students complete the prereading activity, a **word web**. (Refer to the **Strategy Handbook** on page 40 for more help.)

Motivation Strategy

Tell students that "Summer Berries" is the story of a girl who must prove to her parents that she is mature enough and intelligent enough to make her own decisions. Have students tell about a time they wanted to prove they were all grown up. What was the situation and what happened? How did the event change the student's feelings about himself or herself? A brief discussion on this topic will help students make a personal connection to the theme of "Summer Berries" before they begin their reading.

Vocabulary Building

Discuss with students the key vocabulary words for this selection: *shame, sacrificed, daintily, plucking,* and *sorrow.* (Note that *shame* is used as a verb in "Summer Berries.") Have them circle the words in the text, and then encourage them to define the words in context before checking the footnote definition. Students will benefit from additional work with using **context clues.**

STRATEGY LESSON: SUFFIXES If you feel students need some additional vocabulary work, you might write these suffixes on the board: *–ful* ("full of"), *–ness* ("quality or condition of being"), and *–ous* ("like, having, possessing"). Write the following words on the board, and ask students to underline the suffixes and tell what the words mean: *meaningful, gentleness, perilous.*

For additional practice on this strategy, see the **Vocabulary** blackline master on page 156.

Prereading Strategies

Word webs give students the chance to explore abstract words or concepts that are important to a selection. Creating a web can help make the abstraction or concept much more concrete. In a word web, the writer lists phrases, situations, experiences, and emotions that he or she associates with the word or words to be defined. (On page 102, students are asked to make a web for the words "Growing Up.") The items or details students write on their webs can come from what they have read or seen or from their own ideas and experiences. When finished, students will have created their own definitions for the word or concept.

Spanish-speaking Students

Pretty-Girl y Sweetgrass son jóvenes indias norte americanas que se preocupan por el futuro. Como su nombre sugiere, Pretty-Girl es muy bonita y el tribu le admira mucho. Está angustiada que no se pueda casar con el hombre a que ama, Shy-Bear. Sweetgrass está angustiada porque piensa que nunca se va a casar.

II. READ

Response Strategy

As students begin to read, walk through the process of responding to literature. Introduce the strategy of **visualizing** and point out the example given on page 103. Students' sketches might be as simple as the one in the *Sourcebook,* or they can be very detailed. Their purpose here is to try to picture the people, places, and events the author describes. Good readers do this automatically (and often unconsciously) as they are reading. Help your students to develop this habit.

Comprehension Strategies

The **graphic organizers** on pages 104, 105, 106, and 108 will help students keep track of what they have learned about the two main characters in the story, Pretty-Girl and Sweetgrass. Students will see that some of their ideas will change or take on a sharper focus the further they read in the story. This is an excellent way to show students that even good readers must build their way toward comprehension of a story or article. Understanding doesn't come all at once.

PREDICT   As an alternate or additional comprehension strategy, ask students to make predictions about characters and events as they read. Have them stop at the bottom of every page and make a quick prediction about Sweetgrass, Pretty-Girl, or an upcoming event. Making predictions can help readers feel more directly involved in what they're reading. Predictions can also help readers make inferential responses to a text.

For more help, see the **Comprehension** blackline master on page 157.

Discussion Questions

COMPREHENSION   1. What is the relationship between Sweetgrass and Pretty-Girl? *(They are girlfriends in the same Native-American tribe.)*

2. What problem does Pretty-Girl face? What problem does Sweetgrass face? *(Pretty-Girl is afraid her father won't let her marry Shy-Bear. Sweetgrass is afraid her father will never treat her like an adult.)*

CRITICAL THINKING   3. Pretty-Girl says Sweetgrass is "spoiled." What do you think she means by this? *(Her father has been accused of giving her too much attention and bending to her will on most matters.)*

4. Which girl—Sweetgrass or Pretty-Girl—would you say is the wiser of the two? *(Answers will vary according to students' inferences about the two characters. Encourage the class to support their opinions with evidence from the text.)*

5. Do you predict that Sweetgrass will be able to convince her father to allow her to marry? Explain your prediction. *(Answers will vary. Possible: She probably will be able to change her father's mind, since it seems that she can usually get him to do what she likes. This battle may be a bit more difficult, however.)*

Literary Skill

CHARACTERIZATION   The method an author uses to develop characters is called *characterization*. An author may describe how characters look or reveal them through their actions, thoughts, and dialogue. Discuss with students how this author distinguishes one girl from the other in this excerpt, especially in their attitudes toward Pretty-Girl's marriage.

III. GATHER YOUR THOUGHTS

Prewriting Strategies

The prewriting activities on page 109 will help prepare students to write a **personal experience paragraph** about a time they disagreed with the plans their families had for them. To begin, students will reflect on Sweetgrass's and Pretty-Girl's disagreements with their families. Then students will think about a time they disagreed with a family decision. The three questions at the top of the page can show students how easy it is to make a link between literature and self. Encourage them to take their time answering each question.

Next, students will **organize** the paragraph they are assigned to write in Part IV. They'll begin by stating the disagreement they had with their family. This statement can and should be used as the topic sentence. Then they will list two reasons for the disagreement. This will be their support. Remind students to explain how the conflict was resolved and how they felt about this resolution.

Have students use the **Prewriting** blackline master on page 158.

IV. WRITE

Read aloud the directions on page 110 to be sure that students understand that their assignment is to write a **personal experience paragraph** about a time they disagreed with plans their family had for them. Have students follow the paragraph plan they created on page 109.

WRITING RUBRIC Consider using this rubric to help students focus on the assignment requirements and for assistance with a quick assessment of their writing.

Do students' personal experience paragraphs

- tell about an event from their own life?
- show a clear progression—a beginning, a middle, and an end?
- include adequate details about the event?
- also include a discussion of the effect the event had on the writer?

Grammar, Usage, and Mechanics

When students are ready to proofread for grammatical and mechanical errors, refer them to the **Writers' Checklist** and consider teaching a quick lesson on possessives. Review the rules for creating possessives and then have students edit the following sentence for errors:

My fathers irritation about Beths decision was plain to see.

V. WRAP-UP

Before they leave this first excerpt from *Sweetgrass,* have students discuss Hudson's writing **style.** Students might enjoy having the chance to comment on a published writer's word choices and grammatical structures.

Assessment

To test students' comprehension, use the **Assessment** blackline master on page 159.

Name _____

VOCABULARY

Words from the Selection

DIRECTIONS Using context clues, fill in each blank with the most appropriate word from the list.

◇shame ◇sacrificed ◇daintily ◇plucking ◇sorrow

1. She picked the flowers _____ and put them in her basket.

2. All of the people in her camp will _____ her if she is not happy about her husband-to-be.

3. Her _____ over her marriage made me want to cheer her up.

4. I would have _____ everything I had to marry Eagle-Sun.

5. We sat in the field talking and _____ flowers.

Strategy Lesson: Suffixes

DIRECTIONS Study the suffixes and their meanings in the box. Circle the suffix in each word, and then write the meaning of the word on the line.

> –ness = quality or condition of being _____
>
> –ous = like; having; possessing
>
> –ful = full of; showing

6. I sighed with <u>happiness</u> as we picked the berries. _____

7. We had to be <u>careful</u> not to step in the poison ivy. _____

8. There was a <u>thunderous</u> noise in the distance. _____

9. We admired the shiny, red <u>roundness</u> of the fruit. _____

10. The flowers looked <u>beautiful</u> in her hair. _____

Name _____

COMPREHENSION
Retell

DIRECTIONS Retell "Summer Berries" on this organizer. Be sure to include all important details.

BEGINNING

MIDDLE

END

Name _____

PREWRITING
Writing a Personal Experience Paragraph

DIRECTIONS On this story frame, tell about a time you disagreed with your family's plans for you. Then use the completed story frame to help you write your personal experience paragraph.

The disagreement took place _____

(where)   (when)

_____ **was there when it happened.** _____ **was also there.**

(who)   (who)

Here's what I was doing or saying during the disagreement:

_____

The main problem was _____

Another problem was _____

The problems were solved when _____

The whole thing ended when _____

Name _____

ASSESSMENT

Multiple-Choice Test

DIRECTIONS On the blanks provided, write the letter of the item that best answers each question or completes each statement.

_____ 1. Who is upset about her parents' choice for a husband?
A. Pretty-Girl   C. Shy-Bear
B. Sweetgrass   D. Eagle-Sun

_____ 2. Who is excited at the thought of a marriage?
A. Pretty-Girl   C. Shy-Bear
B. Sweetgrass   D. Eagle-Sun

_____ 3. Sweetgrass compares the two girls' lives to . . .
A. a song.   C. an old tale.
B. a beaded design.   D. B. and C.

_____ 4. What is Pretty-Girl supposed to start making?
A. a dress   C. a tipi
B. moccasins   D. a basket

_____ 5. Pretty-Girl's eyes look like that of a . . .
A. buffalo.   C. deer.
B. baby.   D. bird.

_____ 6. Why will Pretty-Girl's parents not give her to Shy-Bear?
A. Shy-Bear already has many   C. He does not have enough horses.
   wives.
B. Shy-Bear lives far away.   D. Her parents don't like Shy-Bear.

_____ 7. What is Pretty-Girl afraid will happen?
A. She will become a slavewife. C. She will never have children.
B. She will never see her family. D. She will be laughed at.

_____ 8. Where is Shy-Bear as the girls are speaking?
A. He is in a great battle.   C. He is at the camp.
B. He is sitting with the girls. D. He is returning from a horse raid.

_____ 9. How does Sweetgrass feel as she watches her friend cry?
A. strange   C. unmoved
B. excited   D. fearful

_____ 10. According to Sweetgrass, good Blackfoot girls are . . .
A. obedient.   C. hardworking.
B. quiet.   D. all of the above

Short-Essay Test

Compare Sweetgrass and Pretty Girl. How are they similar? How are they different?

Summer Berries, continued

Skills and Strategies Overview

THEME	Jan Hudson
READING LEVEL	average
VOCABULARY	◇ wove ◇ dizzying ◇ eerie ◇ jagged ◇ sprawling
PREREADING	anticipation guide
RESPONSE	prediction
COMPREHENSION	directed reading
PREWRITING	forming an opinion
WRITING	review / commas
ASSESSMENT	depth

BACKGROUND

Tell students that they are about to read a second excerpt from Jan Hudson's *Sweetgrass*. Before they begin, you might want to offer some additional information about the Blackfoot Indians. The Blackfoot men were expert horseback riders, fierce buffalo hunters, and courageous, gifted warriors. They were feared by other Native-American groups and warred frequently with the Cree, Crow, Sioux, and other tribes. (Notice that Shy-Bear and the others are returning from a horse raid against the Crow.)

Except for growing tobacco, the Blackfoot did no farming. Instead, their men made weapons (sometimes used for trading) and hunted for buffalo and elk, while the women managed the household and gathered wild plants for food. As you might infer from the reading, the Blackfoot practiced polygamy. An important warrior or powerful chief might have had several wives. Arranged marriages were the norm; much of the time, a marriage was arranged or agreed upon with an eye to the wealth of the suitor and prospective bride.

UNIT THEME Jan Hudson explores themes of growing up and self-confidence in this coming-of-age story.

GRAPHIC ORGANIZER A theme and supporting details organizer like the one below can help students see the relationship between a central theme in "Summer Berries" and Hudson's supporting details. Encourage students to look for a theme (or main idea) each time they read. Help them reach the point where they do this automatically.

THEME STATEMENT:

Growing up can be difficult and wonderful at the same time.

DETAIL #1:

Pretty-Girl looks forward to marrying but is worried about who will be her husband.

DETAIL #2:

Sweetgrass is overjoyed to be maturing but is afraid her father will always think of her as immature.

DETAIL #3:

Both girls want to test their independence but are afraid of alienating their loved ones.

BEFORE YOU READ

Open the lesson by asking a volunteer (or group of students) to refresh the class's memory of the first excerpt from *Sweetgrass*. Be sure your volunteers discuss both characters and plot (plus conflict). Then ask the class to turn to the prereading activity, an **anticipation guide**. (Refer to the **Strategy Handbook** on page 40 for more help.)

Motivation Strategy

If you think your students will be comfortable doing so, ask for volunteers to read aloud the personal experience paragraphs they wrote at the end of Lesson 11. Have the reader then comment on how their disagreements were similar to or different from the conflict that Sweetgrass and Pretty-Girl have with their families.

ENGAGING STUDENTS One of the best motivation strategies you can use for a continuation of a work of fiction or nonfiction is to have students make a series of predictions about outcomes. Set up a chart similar to the one below on the board. Invite students to fill in the blank. When the class has finished reading, return to the chart to see which predictions actually came true.

I PREDICT . . .	WHAT REALLY HAPPENS . . .
Pretty-Girl will decide this about Shy-Bear . . .	
Sweetgrass will make this decision about her father . . .	
The horse raid against the Crow Indians will turn out to be . . .	
The story will end on a happy / sad note.	

Vocabulary Building

Help students use **context clues** as they read to figure out the meanings of difficult or unknown words, especially the key vocabulary for this lesson: *wove, dizzying, eerie, jagged,* and *sprawling*. Ask students to circle these words in the text. Although the footnotes define these words for students, you'll want to encourage them to try defining on their own before checking the footnoted definition. For additional pratice with these words see page 164.

STRATEGY LESSOON: COMPOUND WORDS AND WORD ANALYSIS Tell students that it is often possible to figure out the meaning and pronounciation of a compound word (a word made up of two or more words) by analyzing the parts. For example, a *campsite* is a "site (place) for camping." Have students practice analyzing the parts of the following compound words: *carefree, killjoy, letterhead, blue–green, outburst, globetrotter, doubleheader,* and *ringmaster*.

By now, students have learned a number of strategies for defining new words, analyzing word parts, and understanding roots. To help students review some of these strategies, assign the **Vocabulary** blackline master on page 164.

Prereading Strategies

The purpose of an **anticipation guide** is to explore students' ideas about a theme or topic before they read. The statements on the guide have been chosen to pique students' interest and help them begin thinking about the theme of "Summer Berries." Once they've finished reading the story, students should return to their guides and look at their ratings again. Show students that the predictions they make about a reading beforehand can help them become more careful readers.

Spanish-speaking Students

En la continuación de "Fruta de verano" Pretty-Girl y Sweetgrass esperan ansiosamente el regreso de los guerreros que fueron a hacer una incursión para conseguir caballos. Las dos están preocupadas que la incursión haya sido un fracaso y que unos hombres se hayan muerto. Pretty-Girl está desilusionada descubrir que tenga que casarse con un hombre a que no ama, solo porque consiguió los más caballos. Teniendo esta tragedia en cuenta, Sweetgrass le promete a sí misma que siempre va a controlar su propia vida.

II. READ

Read aloud the directions on page 112 to students. Tell them to share the reading (and responding) process with their partners. Explain how important it will be for readers to make **predictions** about characters and events as they are reading. Each time the reader makes a new prediction, he or she should make a note of it in the **Response Notes**. When everyone has finished, discuss the predictions as a group. Which came true? Which were far off the mark? Show the class that making predictions can make reading more enjoyment.

Response Strategy

QUESTION Tell students to write the questions they want to ask the author, another reader, and you in the **Response Notes**. When they've finished reading, have volunteers read their questions aloud. Work as a class to find answers.

Comprehension Strategies

A **directed reading** can help reluctant or low-level readers better comprehend what they are reading. In a directed reading, you guide the reading by posing open-ended questions. You will notice that several different comprehension and inferential questions interrupt the text of "Summer Berries." Use these questions, plus a few of your own, such as: "What is Sweetgrass's biggest problem?" and "What are Sweetgrass's greatest strengths? What are her greatest weaknesses?"

For more help, see the **Comprehension** blackline master on page 165.

Discussion Questions

COMPREHENSION 1. Why does Sweetgrass think summer is the best time of the year? *(She likes the heat, the flowers, the fragrant air, the summer Sun Dance, and so on.)*

2. Who or what, according to Blackfoot tradition, gave power to the people? *(The Blackfoot believed that the sun was the giver of power. The Sun Dance was a way of honoring the sun for its gifts.)*

3. What "omen" does Pretty-Girl see in her mind? *(She sees Five-Killer's nephew tying horses to his uncle's tipi. Pretty-Girl takes this as a sign that her marriage to Five-Killer is inevitable.)*

CRITICAL THINKING 4. What does Sweetgrass mean when she says she will "control her own days"? *(Answers will vary. Possible: She alone will decide what her future will be.)*

5. Which girl—Sweetgrass or Pretty-Girl—would you say is stronger? *(Answers will vary. Students will probably suggest Sweetgrass, since it is she who decides to "control her own days.")*

Literary Analysis

SETTING *Setting* is the time and place in which the events of a story or novel occur. Setting can contribute to the mood or feeling of a work and reveal character. Ask students to describe the setting of "Summer Berries," tell how the season contributes to our understanding of Sweetgrass, and describe what mood the setting conveys.

III. GATHER YOUR THOUGHTS

Prewriting Strategies

The purpose of the prewriting activities on page 118 is to prepare students to write a **review** of both parts of "Summer Berries." Remind the class that a reviewer usually comments on one or more of these elements in a story: plot, character, setting, and theme. In the first activity, students will rate three of these elements on a scale of one to five. Students will then write an **opinion statement** that says how they feel about one aspect of "Summer Berries." Have them begin by choosing the element they'd like to focus on: plot, character, or theme. Them ask them to write their opinion statement. For example:

opinion statement: The characters in "Summer Berries" are very realistic.

Students will finish the prewriting process by thinking of three or more details that support their opinion.

Have students use the **Prewriting** blackline master on page 166.

IV. WRITE

Read aloud the directions on page 119 to be sure students understand what is expected of them. After students have written a first draft, have them exchange papers with an editing partner. Student editors should read the review with these two questions in mind: Is the opinion clear? Is the support adequate?

WRITING RUBRIC Use this rubric when assessing the quality of students' writing.

Do students' reviews

• begin with a clear opinion statement?

• include two or more details that support the opinion?

Grammar, Usage, and Mechanics

Next, have students proofread their work. Refer them to the **Writers' Checklist** and ask that they check carefully for problems with comma usage. You might want to teach a brief lesson on this topic, since commas usually cause problems for inexperienced writers. (They often use too many or two few.) You might offer this as a practice sentence:

Incorrect: Pretty-Girl I told you to stop worrying and say hello to your love Shy-Bear.

Correct: Pretty-Girl, I told you to stop worrying and say hello to your love, Shy-Bear.

V. WRAP-UP

Invite students to reflect on the **depth** of their understanding. As a starting point, have them answer the questions on the **Readers' Checklist**. Its intent is to help students think about the bridge they've created between the literature and their own lives.

Assessment

To test students' comprehension, use the **Assessment** blackline master on page 167.

Name _____

VOCABULARY
Words from the Selection

DIRECTIONS To build vocabulary, answer these questions about five words from the selection.

1. If you <u>wove</u> something together, did you tie it or staple it?

   _____

2. If you have a <u>dizzying</u> experience, are you thinking clearly or is your mind spinning?

   _____

3. When you have an <u>eerie</u> feeling, do you feel happy or scared?

   _____

4. If a piece of glass has a <u>jagged</u> edge, is it rough or smooth?

   _____

5. When a person is <u>sprawling</u> on the ground, is she curled up or spread out?

   _____

Strategy Lesson: Word Analysis

DIRECTIONS Write the word from the list at the right that correctly answers each question.

6. Which word means both "a season" and "to jump"? _____

7. Which word has a suffix meaning "full of" or "showing"? _____

8. Which word contains a root that means "conquer"? _____

9. Which word is a compound word?

   _____

10. Which word contains a prefix meaning "again"? _____

sweetheart

reassurances

graceful

victory

spring

Name _____

COMPREHENSION
Graphic Organizer

DIRECTIONS Decide what you liked and didn't like about "Summer Berries."

1. Use this chart to keep track of your ideas.

2. Explain your reasons.

3. Then answer a question about the story.

"Summer Berries"

	characters	setting	plot	theme
What I liked about the . . .				
What I didn't like about the . . .				
My reasons				

If you had written the story, what would you have done differently? _____

_____

_____

Name _____

PREWRITING
Writing a Review

In a review, you give your opinion, offer support for your opinion, and then say whether or not you could recommend the piece.

DIRECTIONS Follow these steps to write a review.

STEP 1. WRITE AN OPINION STATEMENT. In your opinion statement, say whether you liked the story.

My opinion statement: _____

STEP 2. GATHER SUPPORT FOR YOUR OPINION. Now support your opinion. Your support should come directly from the story.

fact or detail #1: _____

fact or detail #2: _____

fact or detail #3: _____

STEP 3. PLAN YOUR INTRODUCTION. In the first few sentences of your review, you should tell a little about the story. Write some facts about "Summer Berries" on the fact card.

FACT CARD
Story name:
Author's name:
What the story is about:

STEP 4. PLAN YOUR CLOSING. In your closing sentence, say whether or not you want to recommend the story.

My closing sentence: _____

_____

Name _____

ASSESSMENT
Multiple-Choice Test

DIRECTIONS On the blanks provided, write the letter of the item that best answers each question or completes each statement.

_____ 1. The sweetgrass plant is described as . . .
   A. sprawling.
   B. beautiful.
   C. fragrant.
   D. colorful.

_____ 2. When does Sweetgrass hope her marriage will be arranged?
   A. next winter
   B. at the Sun Dance
   C. on her birthday
   D. in a few years

_____ 3. What does Sweetgrass feel is the best time of year?
   A. spring
   B. summer
   C. fall
   D. winter

_____ 4. What do Sweetgrass and Pretty-Girl see on the ground of the Red Deer River badlands?
   A. cactus
   B. flowers
   C. rocks
   D. a skull

_____ 5. According to Sweetgrass and her people, what gives power and victory?
   A. the wind
   B. the flowers
   C. the sun
   D. the rain

_____ 6. What do the girls see on the horizon?
   A. the returning warriors
   B. a herd of buffalo
   C. an enemy tribe
   D. just the sun

_____ 7. What do the warriors capture on the horse raid?
   A. stallions
   B. men
   C. mares
   D. A. and C.

_____ 8. The horse raid was important to Otter because . . .
   A. he needed to gain power.
   B. he wanted to take a wife.
   C. it was his first.
   D. all of the above

_____ 9. Pretty-Girl is afraid her father will marry her to . . .
   A. Otter.
   B. Five-Killer.
   C. Eagle-Sun.
   D. Shy-Bear.

_____ 10. This piece of writing is an example of . . .
   A. autobiography.
   B. mystery.
   C. nonfiction.
   D. historical fiction.

Short-Essay Test

How do you think Sweetgrass will manage to "control her own days"?

Becoming Champions

Unit Background **BECOMING CHAMPIONS** (pages 121–140)

Excerpts from books about two sports figures make up this unit. The first is from *Sammy Sosa, A Biography* by Bill Gutman; the second is from *Stealing Home: The Story of Jackie Robinson* by Barry Denenberg.

Bill Gutman was born in New York City and grew up in Stamford, Connecticut. He is a graduate of Washington College and has been a reporter and feature writer for *Greenwich Time* and has written more than 100 books about sports, including works about Greg Landry, Chris Evert, and Nadia Comeneci, as well as Sammy Sosa. A recent book is *Tiger Woods: Golf's Shining Young Star* (1998).

Jackie Robinson, the first African American to play baseball in the major leagues, joined the Brooklyn Dodgers at the age of 28 and helped lead the team to six World Series appearances. He was playing in the Negro National League with the Kansas City Monarchs when Dodgers general manager Branch Rickey assigned him to the Dodgers' farm team. The first year Robinson played for the Dodgers (1947), they won their first pennant since 1941 and Robinson was named Rookie of the Year. In 1949 he was the National League batting champion and named Most Valuable Player. He was elected to the Baseball Hall of Fame in 1962.

Teaching the Introduction

A picture of a neighborhood, possibly like the one in which Sammy Sosa grew up, and photos of Jackie Robinson and Sammy Sosa are shown on this page.

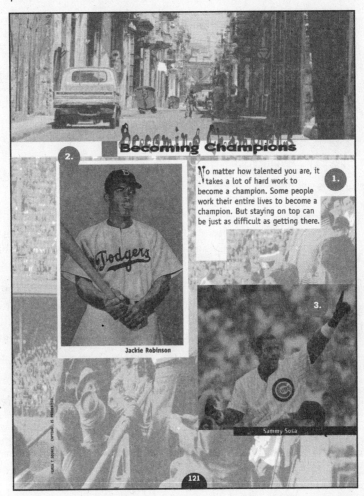

1. Read the unit title and introduction with students, and ask them to tell what they know about the two sports champions pictured.

2. Ask someone to list on the board what it takes to be a champion as other students call out suggestions.

3. Ask students to offer current information on Sammy Sosa.

Opening Activity

Have students name current sports champions, both male and female, and ask what they know about the background of these people. Then ask students to debate the statement:

"There is too much emphasis on professional sports champions in the United States."

Skills and Strategies Overview

THEME	Becoming Champions
READING LEVEL	average
VOCABULARY	◇survive ◇equivalent ◇instill ◇adversities ◇manicured
PREREADING	skim
RESPONSE	highlight or mark
COMPREHENSION	directed reading
PREWRITING	graphic organizer
WRITING	speech / capitalization
ASSESSMENT	understanding

BACKGROUND

Students might be surprised to learn that Sammy Sosa, the successful baseball player whom they enjoy watching on TV and reading about in the newspaper, had an extraordinarily difficult childhood.

In *Sammy Sosa, A Biography*, Bill Gutman describes Sosa's humble beginnings in the Dominican Republic, his tough childhood, his decision to play baseball, and his meteoric rise to superstardom as one of the sport's greatest hitters of all time. Gutman's book finishes with a detailed description of Sosa's record-breaking year (1998) in the major leagues.

"A Better Life" is an excerpt from Gutman's book. This excerpt, which is taken from the first part of the biography, describes Sammy Sosa's early years.

UNIT THEME Young Sammy Sosa must overcome a great deal of adversity before he can fulfill his dream of playing professional baseball.

GRAPHIC ORGANIZER On page 128 of their books, students will make notes similar to the ones below. Cards like these help readers keep track of important facts and details.

> topic: Sammy Sosa   #1
> **I. EARLY YEARS**
> **born when and where:** Nov. 12, 1968, in the Dominican town of San Pedro de Macoris
> **information about family:** Sammy is ~~fifth~~ of seven children. Father and mother hardworking, devoted.

> topic: Sammy Sosa   #2
> **II. SCHOOL YEARS**
> **important events:** Father dies when Sammy is seven
> **accomplishments:** Helps support family. Excels at sports.
> **challenges:** Poverty; worries about family; struggles to survive.

> topic: Sammy Sosa   #3
> **III. ADULT YEARS**
> **important events:** Begins playing baseball in earnest at age 14
> **accomplishments:** Breaks home run record at age 30. Named MVP and receives many awards.
> **challenges:** constantly competing with himself

BIBLIOGRAPHY Students might also enjoy these sports biographies: *Standing Fast: Battles of a Champion* by Michelle Akers (1997); *Alex Rodriguez: Slugging Shortstop* by Stew Thornley (1998); *Picabo Street: Downhill Dynamo* by Joel Dippold (1998); *Home Run Heroes: Mark McGwire and Sammy Sosa* by Joseph Layden (1998); *Women's Soccer: The Game and the World Cup* by Jim Trecker (1999); and *Parcells; A Biography* by Bill Gutman (2000).

BEFORE YOU READ

Have students read the introduction to the lesson on page 122. Ask students to offer what they know about Sammy Sosa. (Consider creating a "Sosa Stats" chart on the board that students can add to at their leisure.) Then assign the prereading activity, a **skim**. (Refer to the **Strategy Handbook** on page 40 for more help.)

Motivation Strategy

Several biographies of Sammy Sosa are available, many of which may be shelved in the juvenile section of your library. Check out a few and bring them in for the class to thumb through. Students can do quick picture walks of each or choose one to borrow for some outside reading. Use the pictures in these books to pique students' interest in Sosa's life.

ENGAGING STUDENTS Borrow a Cubs highlights or Sammy Sosa video from your library. (Or ask students if they have one at home.) Show the video to the class and give students a chance to see Sosa in action. Ask: "What qualities does he have that make him a champion?"

Vocabulary Building

As students read, point out key vocabulary words such as *survive, equivalent, instill, adversities,* and *manicured.* Have students circle these words in the text, and ask for volunteers to pronounce and offer definitions for them. Then ask for sample sentences for each. Help students become accustomed to hearing the words in many different contexts.

STRATEGY LESSON: IDIOMS As an additional vocabulary lesson, you might spend some time discussing idioms. Remind students that an idiom is a phrase or expression that means something different from the ordinary meanings of the words. For example, in the first paragraph of "A Better Life," Gutman says that sports and education could "pave the way to a better life." Write this idiom on the board and ask students to picture what it says. (Some may suggest they picture a road being paved. This may help them see that the idiom can be translated as "moving toward.") Write some idioms on the board and ask for translations of each.

all of the children *chipped in*

iron out a problem

he was *all thumbs*

she was *all ears*

For additional practice on this strategy, see the **Vocabulary** blackline master on page 174.

Prereading Strategies

Skimming can be used to introduce readers to the selection topic and at the same time alert them to any problems they might have (such as challenging vocabulary) during their close readings. When they skim, students should look quickly at the first sentence of every paragraph. They should pay particular attention to key words and phrases and watch for repeated or unfamiliar words. Have students use the chart on page 122 for their skimming notes.

Spanish-speaking Students

"Un mejor vida" retrata parte de la vida de Sammy Sosa, uno de los mejores jugadores de beísbol. El nació en la República Dominicana, donde luchaba para sobrevivir. Tenía que trabajar duramente por toda su vida, vendiendo naranjas y lavando coches cada día. No jugó al beísbol hasta que tenía catorce anos, cuando era obvio que era talentoso. Sosa ha dicho que el estres de jugar profesionalmente no compara con el estres de ganar la vida en la República Dominicana.

II. READ

Before students begin reading, have a volunteer read aloud the directions at the top of page 123. Be sure every student understands the response strategy of **mark** or **highlight**. Remind them to pay careful attention to Sosa's "championship" qualities. Each time they see a clue to these qualities, they should make a note of it in the **Response Notes**.

Response Strategy

VISUALIZE How do students picture Sosa's childhood home? How do they picture him as a boy? As an alternate response strategy, ask them to make quick sketches of everything they "see" in the **Response Notes**. Students may want to use these sketches to help them with the speech they will write in Part IV.

Comprehension Strategies

Since some students may find it challenging, **directed reading** is a perfect comprehension strategy to use with this selection. Ask students to read silently, perhaps one page at a time. At each **stop and think** or **stop and retell** question, have the class pause and write answers. Then briefly discuss the question as a group. If there is time, ask students to work together on a round-robin reading of the article. This may help those who missed important facts or details on their first readings.

For more help, see the **Comprehension** blackline master on page 175.

Discussion Questions

COMPREHENSION 1. Where and when was Sammy Sosa born? *(in the Dominican town of San Pedro de Macoris on November 12, 1968)*

2. What were some of the challenges Sosa faced as a child? *(His father died when he was seven. The family struggled to earn enough money for food. Sosa and his siblings went to work to support the family.)*

3. What were some of Sammy's jobs? *(shining shoes, selling oranges, and washing cars)*

4. What is Sosa's attitude toward pressure on the baseball field? *(He says it does not compare to the pressure of working to earn enough to pay for food for the next meal.)*

CRITICAL THINKING 5. What adjectives would you use to describe Sammy Sosa? *(Answers will vary. Possible: hard working, humble, driven, loyal. Remind students to support what they say with evidence from the selection.)*

Literary Skill

CHRONOLOGICAL ORDER Gutman uses chronological order to tell Sammy Sosa's life story. You might take this opportunity to teach a lesson on time order and the use of transitions in a narrative. Remind students that when writers use chronological order, they usually use transitional words and phrases to help their narrative read smoothly. Words and phrases such as *first, last, later, when, after that, the next day*, and *a week later* cue readers as to where they are in the story. You might want to keep a list of transitional words and phrases posted on the board. Students can refer to the list as they write their speeches.

III. GATHER YOUR THOUGHTS

The purpose of the prewriting activities on page 128 is to prepare students to write a **speech** about a person they admire. Begin by asking them to work together to brainstorm a short list. Remind them to think of people from their own lives in addition to famous people.

After they have chosen a topic for their speech, ask students to complete the **graphic organizer** cards. Point out that they will divide the large topic (someone's life) into three subtopics: early years, school years, and adult years. Students should take these cards with them to the library, computer, or interview and use them to keep track of their notes.

Prewriting Strategies

MAIN IDEA After students have researched their topics, you may want to help them write a main-idea statement for their speeches. Remind them that the main idea is the central, or most important, idea in a piece of writing. It is what the author wants his or her readers to remember most. Have students work together to write their main-idea statements. Check students' work before they begin drafting their speeches.

Have students use the **Prewriting** blackline master on page 176.

IV. WRITE

Be sure students understand that the purpose of their **speeches**, is to tell about a person they admire. Also review with them the balloon tips on pages 129 and 130. Students should know the function of each of the three paragraphs of the speech. When students have finished writing, allow time for them to give their speeches to the class.

WRITING RUBRIC Use this rubric to help students focus on the assignment requirements and for assistance with a quick assessment of their writing.

Do the students' speeches

- open with a topic sentence that names the person to be described and explains what makes him or her admirable?

- include descriptive details about this person, including a discussion of his or her early years, school years, and adult years?

Grammar, Usage, and Mechanics

When students are ready to proofread their work, refer them to the **Writers' Checklist.** At this point, you might want to introduce a mini-lesson on capitalization. Remind the class that abbreviations and titles before a name are always capitalized. For example:

Incorrect: mr. Sammy Sosa   Martin Luther King, jr.

Correct: Mr. Sammy Sosa   Martin Luther King, Jr.

V. WRAP-UP

Take a moment at the end of the lesson for students to reflect on their **understanding** of "A Better Life." Ask them to use the **Readers' Checklist** to help them decide what they thought about the reading and which (if any) parts caused difficulty..

Assessment

To test students' comprehension, use the **Assessment** blackline master on page 177.

173

Name _____

VOCABULARY
Words from the Selection

DIRECTIONS To build vocabulary, read these sentences and then answer the questions. Use context clues and your knowledge of the selection to help you understand the meaning of each underlined word.

1. Sammy and his family struggled to <u>survive</u> without Mr. Sosa. Does this mean they were doing everything they could or giving up? _____

2. The family lived in the <u>equivalent</u> of a one-bedroom apartment. How big was their home? _____

3. Sosa's mother tried to <u>instill</u> in her children a sense of pride. Did she take away or build up their sense of pride? _____

4. Sammy Sosa's family had to overcome <u>adversities</u>. Did they have many troubles or an easy life? _____

5. As a child, Sammy did not play on <u>manicured</u> fields. Were the fields trimmed or messy? _____

Strategy Lesson: Idioms

An **idiom** is a phrase or expression that means something different from what the words actually say. For example, "Do you get the picture? " means "Do you understand?"

DIRECTIONS Draw a line between the idioms in Column A to their meanings in Column B.

Column A	Column B
6. Sammy did not <u>lose his temper</u>.	A. He was very surprised.
7. His eyes <u>popped out of his head</u>.	B. eager to listen
8. It's a secret, so <u>keep it under your hat</u>.	C. contributed
9. Marge was <u>all ears.</u>	D. Don't tell anyone.
10. We each <u>coughed</u> up a dollar.	E. get mad

Name _____

COMPREHENSION
Graphic Organizer

DIRECTIONS Use this character map to show four of Sammy Sosa's most important qualities.

1. Refer to your book as needed.

2. Then answer a question about Sosa.

quality: _____

example: _____

_____

_____

_____

_____

quality: _____

example: _____

_____

_____

_____

_____

Sammy Sosa

quality: _____

example: _____

_____

_____

_____

_____

quality: _____

example: _____

_____

_____

_____

_____

What do you admire most about Sammy Sosa? _____

_____

Why? _____

_____

Name _____

PREWRITING
Outlining

DIRECTIONS Use this outline to plan your speech.

1. Make notes about what you want to say on the writing lines.

2. Refer to your speech cards on page 128.

Introduction

_____

_____

_____

I. Early years

_____

A.

_____

B.

_____

II. School Years

_____

A.

_____

B.

_____

III. Adult Years

_____

A.

_____

B.

_____

Conclusion

_____

_____

Name _____

ASSESSMENT

Multiple-Choice Test

DIRECTIONS On the blanks provided, write the letter of the item that best answers each question or completes each statement.

_____ 1. Where was Sammy Sosa born and raised?
A. Puerto Rico
B. The Dominican Republic
C. The United States of America
D. Mexico

_____ 2. How many children were in Juan Montero and Mireya Sosa's family?
A. one
B. five
C. seven
D. eleven

_____ 3. As a young child, Sammy . . .
A. read about baseball heroes.
B. ran barefoot through the streets.
C. played baseball all day long.
D. all of the above

_____ 4. What event changed Sammy's carefree life?
A. His mother died.
B. His father died.
C. He was picked on in school.
D. He broke his arm.

_____ 5. How did the Sosa family feel when life became difficult?
A. angry
B. sad
C. hopeless
D. determined

_____ 6. What job did Sammy do in order to bring home money for his family?
A. He shined shoes.
B. He washed cars.
C. He sold oranges.
D. all of the above

_____ 7. Why does Sammy spend so little time during his childhood playing baseball?
A. He had to work.
B. His mother wouldn't let him play.
C. He never heard of the game.
D. He didn't like sports.

_____ 8. What sport originally attracted Sammy?
A. football
B. soccer
C. boxing
D. track and field

_____ 9. For his first baseball glove, Sammy used . . .
A. his dad's old glove.
B. an old milk carton.
C. his own pillow.
D. his bare hands.

_____ 10. How does Sammy feel about the "pressure" of playing in the major leagues?
A. It isn't as bad as his childhood.
B. It is much harder than he thought.
C. He doesn't notice.
D. He has trouble handling it.

Short-Essay Test

What qualities does Sammy Sosa have that make him a champion?

Jackie Robinson's First Game

STUDENT PAGES 131–140

Skills and Strategies Overview

THEME Becoming Champions

READING LEVEL average

VOCABULARY ◇accommodations ◇concentrate ◇debut ◇erratic ◇reputation

PREREADING walk-through

RESPONSE react and connect

COMPREHENSION graphic organizer

PREWRITING character map

WRITING biographical paragraph / capitalization

ASSESSMENT meaning

BACKGROUND

"Jackie Robinson's First Game" is an excerpt from Barry Denenberg's biography, *Stealing Home*. In this selection, Denenburg describes many of the difficulties Robinson faced as the first African–American baseball player on a national league team.

Students may benefit from some background information on Jackie Robinson (1919–1972). Robinson was born in Cairo, Georgia. His parents were sharecroppers who struggled constantly to put food on the table. Robinson attended the University of California at Los Angeles (UCLA), where he demonstrated remarkable athletic ability. He was the first UCLA student ever to win varsity letters in four sports: football, basketball, baseball, and track. In 1941, Robinson left college to join the army. Bothered by the discrimination he saw all around him, Robinson protested the Army's discriminatory practices. He received an honorable discharge in 1944 and began his professional baseball career with the Kansas City Monarchs, one of the leading teams of the Negro League. In 1946, Robinson was recruited by Branch Rickey, general manager of the Brooklyn Dodgers (now the Los Angeles Dodgers), and assigned to the Montreal Royals, a farm team.

UNIT THEME Jackie Robinson overcomes tremendous obstacles to become the first African American to play in a professional baseball league.

GRAPHIC ORGANIZER A sequence organizer like the one below can help students keep track of important facts and details in a piece of writing.

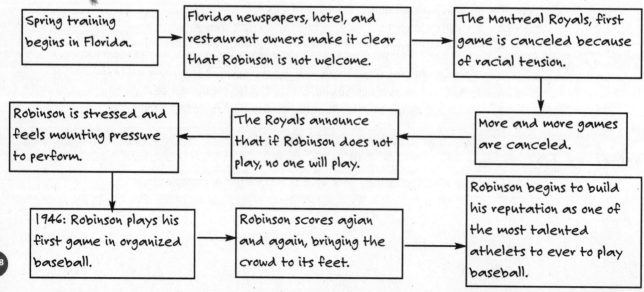

© GREAT SOURCE. COPYING IS PROHIBITED.

1. BEFORE YOU READ

Open the lesson by reminding students of the theme of the unit (Becoming Champions). As they read the article, students should watch to see if Jackie Robinson exhibited championship qualities. Then assign the prereading strategy, a **walk-through**. (Refer to the **Strategy Handbook** on page 40 for help with the prereading strategy.)

Motivation Strategy

Ask students to brainstorm a short list of today's sports champions, both men and women. What qualities do these sports stars all have in common?

ENGAGING STUDENTS Have students discuss their own personal sports experiences. What are some of their triumphs? What are some of their defeats? How would students feel if someone tried to stop them from playing because of the color of their skin, their gender, or their religion? A brief discussion on this topic will be an excellent warm-up to the theme of "Jackie Robinson's First Game."

Vocabulary Building

Help students use **context clues** as they read to figure out the meanings of difficult or unfamiliar words, especially the key vocabulary for this lesson: *accommodations, concentrate, debut, erratic,* and *reputation.* Have students circle these words in the text. If you think students will benefit, model using context clues and then checking your guess against the footnote. For additional practice with these words, see page 182.

STRATEGY LESSON: LATIN ROOTS As an alternate or additional vocabulary strategy, you might teach a short lesson on Latin roots. Since so many words in English contain these roots, students can't help but benefit from memorizing the definitions of a few of them. Put these words on the board: *tension, tendon, tendency, tense,* and *intend.* Explain that each contains the Latin root *–ten–,* which means "stretch" or "extend."

For additional practice on this strategy, see the **Vocabulary** blackline master on page 182.

Prereading Strategies

When readers do a **walk-through** of a text, they look at art, headings, footnotes, and any other elements on the page that attract their attention. This strategy allows readers to familiarize themselves with the topic and perhaps the main idea of the selection. Encourage students to take their time with their walk-through. The more they notice and think about now, the easier the reading process will be.

WORD WEB As an alternate prereading strategy, ask students to create a word web for the word *champion.* Have them think of words that appeal to the five senses. This short activity will encourage students to think carefully about the theme of this unit.

Spanish-speaking Students

Jackie Robinson es famoso por ser el primer negro a jugar al beísbol profesional. Los equipos eran segregados en los años cuarenta y había poco apoyo por Robinson. De hecho, no fue permitido que jugara en Florida, donde había mucho racismo. Pero él mostró su talento en el primer partido y rápidamente ganó la reputación de ser temerario.

READ

At this point, students should be very familiar with the process of responding as they read. Remind them that their job as reader will be to make note of their **reactions** to the article and any **connections** they find themselves making to the people and/or events described. In particular, students should feel free to jot down comments about their own team experiences or their own successes on the sports field.

Response Strategy

QUESTION Any time a question comes up, the reader should make a note of it, so that he or she doesn't lose track of the point of concern. As an alternate or additional response strategy, have students make note of the questions they want to ask the author, another reader, and you in the margins of their book. When they've finished reading, have volunteers read their questions aloud. Work as a class to find answers.

Comprehension Strategies

The **graphic organizers** that interrupt "Jackie Robinson's First Game" will help readers track the sequence of events that Denenberg describes. Explain to students that a sequence organizer like this one can be used along with any reading. Help students get into the habit of making quick sequence organizers every time they read a text that seems challenging or complex.

RECIPROCAL READING In a reciprocal reading, readers share the process of reading and responding to a text. This can make the activity easier and more enjoyable for students, as well as help refine their cooperative group skills. As an alternate or additional comprehension strategy, ask students to do a round-robin reading of "Jackie Robinson's First Game." Have them switch readers every page or so. Before they begin, invite students to review a list of questions that require them to make predictions, clarify action, and summarize events. Also ask them to be thinking of a question they'd like to ask you or the author about the selection. Some of the discussion questions below will work well for a reciprocal reading of the selection.

For more help, see the **Comprehension** blackline master on page 183.

Discussion Questions

COMPREHENSION 1. Explain what Denenberg means when he says that Florida was "segregated" in the 1940s. (*Blacks and whites were separated into two groups. They used different facilities and there was little if any mixing between the two groups. They could not compete against each other.*)

2. What were Daytona officials worried about? (*They were afraid the Dodgers might go elsewhere for spring training.*)

3. How did Robinson react to the tension swirling around him? (*He tried to concentrate on baseball.*)

CRITICAL THINKING 4. How do you think Jackie Robinson must have felt at the beginning of his baseball career? (*Student replies will vary.*)

Literary Skill

INFERENCES Remind students that making inferences is an important skill to use with nonfiction, as well as with fiction. The reasonable guesses that readers make can help deepen their understanding of the facts of the article or essay. After they read "Jackie Robinson's First Game," ask students to make inferences about Robinson and segregation. Remind them to support each inference with evidence from the selection.

III. GATHER YOUR THOUGHTS

The **character map** on page 138 gives students the opportunity to report on what they've learned about Jackie Robinson. They will choose four of Robinson's important qualities and write them on the map. For example, they might choose to write these qualities: courageous, determined, hardworking, and dedicated. Each of these four traits is supportable with evidence from the selection.

After they finish their character maps, students will formulate a topic sentence that they can use as an opening for a **biographical paragraph** about Robinson. Point out the sentence starter at the bottom of page 138.

Prewriting Strategies

DETAILS As an additional prewriting strategy, ask students to plan the details they want to use to support their topic sentences. Have students choose one piece of support for each of the two qualities they have attributed to Robinson.

Have students use the **Prewriting** blackline master on page 184.

IV. WRITE

The directions on page 139 ask students to write a **biographical paragraph** about Jackie Robinson. Remind students that a biographical paragraph should answer these essential questions: who, what, where, when, why, and how.

After students have written a first draft, have them stop and think carefully about what they have written. They should ask themselves: Have I used adequate details to describe Jackie Robinson? Do readers have an understanding of his championship qualities?

WRITING RUBRIC Use this rubric to help students focus on the assignment requirements and for assistance with a quick assessment of their writing.

Do students' biographical paragraphs

- open with a topic sentence that names Robinson's two finest qualities?

- provide adequate and convincing support for that topic sentence?

- prove that the writer has truly understood Denenberg's article?

Grammar, Usage, and Mechanics

When students are ready to proofread their work, refer them to the **Writers' Checklist.** Remind the class to capitalize names of buildings, monuments, institutions, ethnic groups, and languages.

> At the <u>u</u>nited <u>n</u>ations, you can hear almost any language of the world. On my tour, I listened to <u>f</u>rench, <u>g</u>erman, <u>r</u>ussian, and <u>s</u>wahili.

V. WRAP-UP

Spend a few minutes at the end of the lesson discussing what Denenberg's article **meant** to students. Refer them to the **Readers' Checklist** and have them answer each question as honestly as they can.

Assessment

To test students' comprehension, use the **Assessment** blackline master on page 185.

Name _____

VOCABULARY

Words from the Selection

DIRECTIONS To build vocabulary, answer these questions about five words from the selection.

1. When the team was looking for <u>accommodations</u>, were they in search of clothes or a place to stay? _____

2. If Robinson needed to <u>concentrate</u>, should he have daydreamed or focused?
   _____

3. If a player is making a <u>debut</u>, is this her first or her final appearance?
   _____

4. When Robinson's hitting became <u>erratic</u>, was it always the same or different every time?
   _____

5. If you have a good <u>reputation,</u> are others likely to trust you or to keep away from you?_____

Strategy Lesson: Latin Roots

DIRECTIONS The Latin root *-ten-* means "stretch." Study the words and their definitions in the box. Then write the word that correctly fits in each blank.

> *tension* = stress
>
> *tendon* = strong band of tissue that joins a muscle to a bone,
>
> *tendency* = a natural inclination to do something
>
> *tense* = having or causing strain
>
> *intend* = plan

6. It was a _____ moment when Jackie Robinson stepped out onto the field.

7. There was a lot of _____ in the South when Jackie Robinson came to play.

8. People have a _____ to judge others by their looks instead of their actions.

9. Jackie played first base because he was worried about tearing a _____ in his shoulder while playing shortstop and second base.

10. We _____ to camp out all night so we can get tickets to the game.

Name _____

COMPREHENSION
Graphic Organizer _____

DIRECTIONS Use this herringbone diagram to show what you learned from reading "Jackie Robinson's First Game." Check your book for details if you need to.

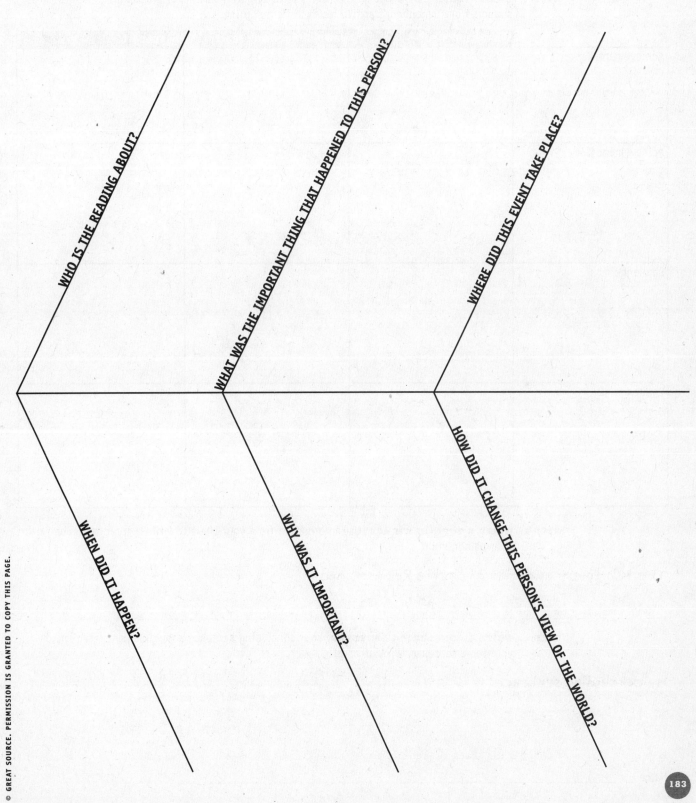

Name _____

PREWRITING
Writing a Biographical Paragraph

DIRECTIONS Follow these steps to write a biographical paragraph about Jackie Robinson.

STEP 1. BRAINSTORM. Make a list of Robinson's most important achievements and challenges. Give support from Denenberg's article for each item you list.

	What happened?	How did Robinson react?	My support
Achievement #1			
Achievement #2			
Challenge #1			
Challenge #2			

STEP 2. WRITE A TOPIC SENTENCE. Use information from your chart to write a topic sentence for your paragraph.

The two finest qualities of Jackie Robinson are _____

and _____ .

STEP 3. WRITE A CONCLUDING SENTENCE. Your concluding sentence should be a restatement of your topic sentence. Write it here.

My concluding sentence:

_____

_____

ASSESSMENT
Multiple-Choice Test

DIRECTIONS On the blanks provided, write the letter of the item that best answers each question or completes each statement.

_____ 1. Where does the action of this selection take place?
A. California   C. New York
B. Florida   D. Georgia

_____ 2. What time period does Denenberg describe in "Jackie Robinson's First Game"?
A. 1920s   C. 1940s
B. 1930s   D. 1950s

_____ 3. During this time period, African Americans might not be allowed in . . .
A. hotels.   C. waiting rooms.
B. restaurants.   D. all of the above

_____ 4. During the 1940s in the South, competition between whites and African Americans on the playing field was strictly . . .
A. forbidden.   C. encouraged.
B. ignored.   D. none of the above

_____ 5. How did Robinson feel about the problems that occurred as a result of his playing with the Royals?
A. He spoke out against the problems. C. He decided to quit baseball.
B. He didn't want to get involved.   D. He got in lots of fights.

_____ 6. What threat did the president of the Montreal Royals make?
A. He would cancel all games if   C. He would quit if Robinson didn't resign.
   Robinson couldn't play.
B. He would move spring training to   D. all of the above
   Pittsburgh if things didn't calm down.

_____ 7. Why did Daytona want the Dodgers to stay for spring training?
A. The city wanted the fame.   C. The city needed the money.
B. The people loved baseball.   D. all of the above

_____ 8. Robinson compared the first day of spring training to . . .
A. the day he got married.   C. the day his father died.
B. the day he was born.   D. his first day of school.

_____ 9. Why did Robinson switch positions when he tried out for the team?
A. He wanted to show how   C. He had hurt his leg.
   good he was.
B. He was nervous.   D. He had hurt his arm.

_____ 10. At his first official game, Robinson proved he was . . .
A. a daring base runner.   C. an accurate pitcher.
B. a wonderful coach.   D. a great catcher.

Short-Essay Test

Why do you think Branch Rickey went out of his way to make things easier for Jackie Robinson in the South?

Ancient Mexico

Unit Background   ANCIENT MEXICO (pages 141–160)

Two selections about the Aztec leader Moctezuma and Cortés's conquest of Mexico are included in this unit. The first selection is from *The Lost Temple of the Aztecs* by Shelley Tanaka and the second from *The Aztecs* by Donna Walsh Shepherd.

Donna Walsh Shepherd teaches at the University of Alaska in Anchorage and received a Best Children's Book award from the National Press Women in 1993 for *The Aztecs*. Her other works include *Uranus* (1994), *Auroras: Light Shows in the Night Sky* (1995), and *Tundra* (1996). She was born in Centralia, Washington, in 1948 and received an M.F.A. degree from the University of Alaska.

According to Aztec myth and legend, the Aztecs originated in Aztlan, somewhere in northern Mexico. Originally a nomadic people, they settled in central Mexico, and, after a series of military alliances, became a powerful group and built their capital in the marshes of Lake Texcoco in the Valley of Mexico in the fourteenth century. (The location became Mexico City.) Eventually the Aztecs extended their control over much of Mexico. They were superior architects and engineers, and their art, mathematics, and astronomy were highly developed. Their religion was polytheistic, but the deity of war, Huitzilopochtli, was the principal god, and his followers practiced human sacrifice.

Teaching the Introduction

The top illustration shows the ancient city of Teotihuacán located in the northeast corner of the Valley of Mexico. The city is a popular tourist site not far from Mexico City. Other images show the Aztec emperor Moctezuma and the Spanish conqueror Hernán Cortés superimposed on a map of Mexico. If you or your students are interested in ancient Mexico, the book *Archaeological Mexico: A Traveler's Guide to Ancient Cities and Sacred Sites* by Andrew Coe can provide information (Moon Travel Handbooks, Moon Publications, Inc., 1998).

1. To help establish the time period of these excerpts, ask students when Columbus arrived in what became the Americas. Then have someone read the unit introduction aloud.

2. Emphasize that the Aztecs, and other peoples in Mexico, probably had no idea about the vastness of the world and would have viewed with wonder the arrival of "foreign" men in ships. Similarly, the Spanish explorers would have been uncertain about what they would find. Ask students to give some reasons why the Spanish wanted to explore the Americas.

Opening Activity

Ask students to think about how the people of the Aztec empire in Mexico and the Spanish explorers from Europe would, in reality, have communicated. Even before they have read the excerpts, students might pantomime the first meeting of the two cultures when the Spanish ships arrive. Alternatively, some students might research the lives of Cortés or Moctezuma.

The Strangers Arrive

Skills and Strategies Overview

THEME Ancient Mexico

READING LEVEL challenging

VOCABULARY

◇ serpents ◇ momentous ◇ terror ◇ shimmering ◇ combat

PREREADING picture walk

RESPONSE clarify

COMPREHENSION reciprocal reading

PREWRITING research

WRITING expository paragraph /confusing words

ASSESSMENT ease

BACKGROUND

"The Strangers Arrive" is an excerpt from Shelley Tanaka's nonfiction book, *The Lost Temple of the Aztecs*. In this selection, Tanaka describes the events leading up to, and immediately following, Hernán Cortés's arrival in Tenochtitlán. Students will benefit from some background information about Moctezuma, Quetzalcoatl, and Cortés. Offer these facts:

Moctezuma—Moctezuma or Montezuma II (1480?–1520), was the ruler of the Aztec Empire of Mexico. When Spanish adventurer Hernán Cortés arrived in Mexico in 1519, Moctezuma was unsure of how to respond to the European force. Eventually, however, he decided to welcome Cortés. Some say that Moctezuma believed Cortés was actually the god Quetzalcoatl in disguise. Cortés quickly took control of Tenochtitlán, the Aztec capital. Later, Moctezuma was stoned to death by his angry subjects, who had come to understand that Cortés planned to take complete control of their empire.

Quetzalcoatl—According to Aztec legend, Quetzalcoatl (ket SAL ko AT ul) was a divine priest who, with his brother, Xoltol, created humans by grinding up the bones of the ancient dead and sprinkling them with his own blood. According to Aztec legend, Quetzalcoatl, in the guise of a light-skinned and bearded man, would return some day and resume his position as leader of the Aztec people.

Cortés—Hernán Cortés (1485–1547) was a Spanish explorer who conquered the Aztec Empire. On February 19, 1519, Cortés, with a force of some 600 men, 20 horses, and 10 wagons, set sail from Cuba, bound for the mysterious land of Mexico. In March, 1519, he landed in Mexico. Over the next several months, Cortés cut a swath of destruction from the Mexican coast inward. Eventually he arrived at the gates of Tenochtitlán and began "negotiations" with Moctezuma.

UNIT THEME The Aztecs hope against hope that the stranger who has recently arrived at the gates of their city might be their much-revered Quetzalcoatl.

Graphic Organizer A web like the one below can help students organize information about Moctezuma.

peaceful   Aztec leader

intelligent   Moctezuma   optimistic

afraid   cautious

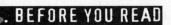

BEFORE YOU READ

Ask a volunteer to read aloud the introduction to the lesson on page 142. Offer additional background on Moctezuma, Cortés, and Quetzalcoatl as you deem necessary. Then assign the prereading activity, a **picture walk**. (Refer to the **Strategy Handbook** on page 40 for more help.)

Motivation Strategy

Prove to students that they really do know quite a bit about ancient Mexico even before they begin reading the two selections in the *Sourcebook*. Draw a quick **K-W-L** chart on the board. Work with the class to fill in the K column with names, dates, places, stories, people, and so on. Then help them make a list of questions that they'd like to find answers to.

ENGAGING STUDENTS Ask each student to bring in one Mexican "artifact" that they make or find sitting on the shelves of their home. Students might have a souvenir from a trip to Mexico, a postcard, a picture from a magazine, a travel guide, a piece of pottery, or something they brought with them when they arrived from Mexico. Give each student time to tell the class about his or her treasure.

Vocabulary Building

Remind students that learning the **synonym** for a word can be a shortcut to remembering a word's full definition. This information will be a boon to students who have trouble memorizing and/or adding new words to their vocabularies. Show students the key vocabulary words for this lesson: *serpents, momentous, terror, shimmering,* and *combat*. Have students circle these words in the text, and ask the class to come up with at least one synonym for each. Then assign the **Vocabulary** blackline master on page 192.

STRATEGY LESSON: WORD ANALYSIS By now, students should have at their fingertips several different strategies for defining new words, analyzing word parts, and understanding word origins. To help students review some of these strategies, ask them to complete the **Vocabulary** blackline master on page 192.

Prereading Strategies

A **picture walk** is an excellent prereading warm-up because it helps familiarize readers with the topic and possibly the main idea of a selection. Often a picture can give readers as much information as the text itself. Ask students to look carefully at each picture in this lesson. (You might also have them walk through the art for Lesson 16, "The Great Moctezuma.") Then have them choose the four pictures that they think are most interesting. They should write a question about each of the four and then record their questions on the chart on page 142.

PREVIEW As an alternate prereading strategy, ask students to do a preview of the selection. Ask them to read the first and last paragraphs of the selection and then skim the rest. What words, ideas, and phrases pop out at them? Like a picture walk, a preview can help introduce the topic of the piece. In addition, it can alert readers to any problem areas (such as difficult vocabulary) that they might encounter on their close readings.

Spanish-speaking Students

Shelley Tanaka describe uno de los sucesos más trágicos de nuestra historia en "Los extraños llegan." Los aztecas habían vivido por muchos años en lo que hoy día es Mexico, cuando los españoles llegaron en el siglo dieciseis. Guiado por Cortés, los conquistadores españoles querían destruir la civilización azteca. El líder de los indios, Moctezuma, pensaba que los conquistadores eran dioses, por eso, estuvo sorprendido que ellos quisieran luchar.

II. READ

As students begin to read, walk through the process of responding to literature. Remind students of the need to make notes that **clarify** the people and action the author describes. Have them pay particular attention to information that relates to questions they wrote on their picture walk chart on page 142.

Response Strategy

VISUALIZE Tanaka uses a great deal of descriptive detail in her article. As an alternate response strategy, ask students to visualize the people, places, and things she describes. What do they think the great Moctezuma looked like? What about the city of Tenochtitlán or the jewels and gifts that Moctezuma's men brought to Cortés? Have students make sketches of what they "see" in their **Response Notes**. These sketches may help them keep track of the main details of Tanaka's article.

Comprehension Strategies

In their **reciprocal readings** of "The Strangers Arrive," pairs of students will alternate reading aloud to each other. Occasionally the reader should interrupt in order to ask questions that will elicit either factual or inferential responses. Four types of questions are used in a reciprocal reading: 1. questions that ask readers to clarify the problem, characters, and setting; 2. questions that ask readers to predict outcomes; 3. questions that ask readers to summarize the events; and 4. questions about the literature, author's message, and main idea.

For more help, see the **Comprehension** blackline master on page 193.

Discussion Questions

COMPREHENSION 1. Who was Moctezuma? *(He was the ruler of the Aztec Empire.)*

2. What clues did Moctezuma have that "things were not well with the gods"? *(He saw a great tongue of fire streak across the sky, which terrified people. Also, temples burst into flames and the lake surrounding Tenochtitlán bubbled up.)*

CRITICAL THINKING 3. What would you say was Moctezuma's greatest mistake? *(Answers will vary. Possible: He assumed Cortés was the god Quetzalcoatl. who had promised to return to the Aztec people. As such, Moctezuma treated him as a friend rather than an enemy.)*

4. What do you think Cortés wanted from the Aztecs? *(Answers will vary. Students might suggest land, power, slaves, riches, and so on, all of which are true.)*

5. Does Tanaka present Cortés as a hero or a villain? *(Answers will vary. Most students will say that she presents him as a villain. Have students support what they say with evidence from the selection.)*

Literary Skill

SIMILE "The Strangers Arrive" presents an excellent opportunity to review simile. Remind the class that a *simile* is a comparison between two unlike things, in which the comparison words *like* or *as* are used. In "The Strangers Arrive," Tanaka says that "a great tongue of fire had streaked across the night sky, like a spear plunged in the very heart of the heavens." Tanaka's figurative language gives readers a strong sense of the world inhabited by the Aztecs. For practice, ask the class to look for other similes in the writing and then explain their effect. Students might point out these:

"They just appeared on the horizon one day, <u>as if</u> they had dropped from the sky." (p. 143)

". . . They floated toward the shore <u>like</u> small mountains." (p. 143)

"The great lake . . . swirled and bubbled up <u>as if</u> it were boiling with rage." (p. 145)

III. GATHER YOUR THOUGHTS

The goal of the prewriting activities on page 149 is to prepare students to write an **expository paragraph** about either Moctezuma or Cortés. To begin, students will choose their topic and then decide where to go to find information about their topic.

Once they have made their choices, students will locate at least two sources that contain information about their topic and then fill in a **research** organizer that asks them to respond to some basic questions. Students should feel free to use an additional piece of paper if they find information that doesn't fit in the organizer.

Prewriting Strategies

GRAPHIC ORGANIZER If you feel students need an additional prewriting activity, have them create a main idea/supporting details organizer similar to the one on page 46 of the *Sourcebook*. Remind them that their main idea statement will state the topic of the paragraph and then express some thought, feeling, or idea. Assign the **Prewriting** blackline master on page 194.

IV. WRITE

Be sure students understand they are to write an **expository paragraph**. Remind the class that an expository paragraph is one that presents facts, gives directions, defines terms, and so on. Also remind the class that their expository paragraphs should open with a topic sentence, include support for the topic sentence in the body of the paragraph, and then end with a concluding sentence that ties up any loose ends and acts as a restatement of the topic sentence. For support, students should offer details from Tanaka's article in addition to details from outside reading or research.

WRITING RUBRIC Use this writing rubric to help students focus on the assignment requirements and to assist with a quick assessment of their writing.

Do the students' expository paragraphs

- begin with a topic sentence and contain three or more details as support?

- present information and not opinions?

- stay focused on the topic of Cortés or Moctezuma?

Grammar, Usage, and Mechanics

When they are ready to proofread their work, refer students to the **Writers' Checklist.** You might want to introduce a mini-lesson on problems with *it's/its* and *there/their/they're*. Remind the class of the correct way to use each of these words, which tend to cause problems for inexperienced writers or students who speak English as a second language. For practice, ask students to choose the words that correctly complete this sentence:

(It's / Its) the birds over (they're / their / there) that made the children laugh and flap (they're / their / there) hands.

V. WRAP-UP

Take a moment at the end of the lesson for students to look at the **Readers' Checklist** and reflect on whether they read the selection with **ease**. If Tanaka's article was difficult, plan strategies for the nonfiction selection they will be reading next.

Assessment

To test students' comprehension, use the **Assessment** blackline master on page 195.

Name _____

VOCABULARY
Words from the Selection

DIRECTIONS Substitute a synonym (a word that means the same thing) from the word box for the underlined word or words.

> ✦serpents ✦momentous ✦terror ✦shimmering ✦combat

1. The jewels were <u>shining</u> in the sunlight. _____

2. The strangers wanted to see the messengers engaged in <u>fighting</u>.

   _____

3. Every night the people watched the dark skies with <u>fear</u>.

   _____

4. When the strangers arrived on the coast, it was a <u>very important</u>

   occasion._____

5. The ancient myth describes a god leaving on a raft of <u>snakes</u>.

   _____

Strategy Lesson: Word Analysis

DIRECTIONS Write the word from the list at the right that correctly answers each question.

6. Which word is a compound word? _____

7. Which word is a synonym for "thrown into"? _____

8. Which word has a prefix meaning "not"? _____

9. Which word is pronounced TER koyz? _____

10. Which word has a prefix meaning "back" and a root meaning "take"? _____

> reclaim
>
> plunged
>
> turquoise
>
> headdress
>
> unnatural

Name _____

COMPREHENSION
Main Idea

DIRECTIONS Answer these questions. They will help you think about the main idea of "The Strangers Arrive."

Why are Moctezuma and his people so anxious for the return of Quetzalcoatl?

_____

_____

_____

Why does Moctezuma send gifts to Cortés?

_____

_____

_____

What do you think Cortés wants from the Aztec people?

_____

_____

_____

Was Moctezuma a foolish or wise leader? Support your opinion.

_____

_____

_____

_____

Name _____

PREWRITING

Writing an Expository Paragraph

DIRECTIONS Use this organizer to plan your expository paragraph about Cortés or Moctezuma.

1. First write a main idea sentence that names the topic and tells something important about it.

2. Then look through your research notes for three pieces of support.

3. Finish by writing a closing sentence that says the main idea sentence in a slightly different way.

MAIN IDEA

DETAIL   **DETAIL**   **DETAIL**   **DETAIL**

MAIN IDEA

Name _____

ASSESSMENT

Multiple-Choice Test

DIRECTIONS On the blanks provided, write the letter of the item that best answers each question or completes each statement.

_____ 1. The visitors look strange to the Aztecs because they have . . .
A. short hair.   C. beards.
B. fair skin.   D. all of the above

_____ 2. Moctezuma thinks the strangers . . .
A. are from a neighboring tribe.   C. are European sailors.
B. represent an Aztec god.   D. none of the above

_____ 3. What helps Moctezuma know that big changes are about to occur?
A. Odd things in nature have been occurring.   C. A ghost told him so.
B. He had a dream about them.   D. all of the above

_____ 4. What natural event does Moctezuma describe as a "great tongue of fire"?
A. a hurricane   C. lightning
B. a tornado   D. a meteor

_____ 5. How does Moctezuma feel about the "unnatural happenings"?
A. They bore him.   C. They scare him.
B. They delight him.   D. They anger him.

_____ 6. Moctezuma sends his messengers to . . .
A. frighten the strangers.   C. question the strangers.
B. greet the strangers.   D. warn the strangers.

_____ 7. What do the messengers think when they first see Cortés?
A. They think he is a god.   C. They think he is deformed.
B. They think he is evil.   D. They think he is an animal.

_____ 8. What does Cortés think of the gifts?
A. He is grateful.   C. He is not impressed.
B. He is puzzled.   D. He is amused.

_____ 9. What has Cortés heard about the Aztec people?
A. They are kind and generous.   C. They are very tall.
B. They are great warriors.   D. They are very clever.

_____ 10. How do the messengers react to Cortés's demands?
A. They are surprised and confused.   C. They are excited.
B. They are happy.   D. all of the above

Short-Essay Test

The meeting between the strangers and the Aztec messengers did not go as planned. What do you think went wrong?

The Great Moctezuma

STUDENT PAGES 152–160

Skills and Strategies Overview

THEME	Ancient Mexico
READING LEVEL	challenging
VOCABULARY	◇legend ◇temples ◇monuments ◇massacred ◇mourned
PREREADING	think-pair-and–share
RESPONSE	question
COMPREHENSION	directed reading
PREWRITING	sequence of events
WRITING	summary / commas
ASSESSMENT	depth

BACKGROUND

In "The Great Moctezuma," an excerpt from a nonfiction book called *The Aztecs*, Donna Walsh Shepherd offers some fascinating details about the simmering tensions between Moctezuma, leader of the Aztecs, and Hernán Cortés, the Spanish adventurer.

How could this one leader, who had only 600 followers, have conquered a city with a population that numbered in the hundreds of thousands? This is a question students should ask themselves as they are reading Shepherd's article.

UNIT THEME Donna Walsh Shepherd explores the conflict between Moctezuma and Hernán Cortés.

GRAPHIC ORGANIZER The information on this sequence organizer may help students understand the events leading up to the fall of Tenochtitlán.

1. February 19, 1519: Cortés and some 600 men set sail for Mexico from Cuba.

2. March, 1519: Cortés lands in Mexico and conquers the coastal town of Tabasco. The people of Tabasco tell Cortés about the Aztec Empire and its ruler Moctezuma.

3. Late spring, 1519: Cortés orders that his own fleet be destroyed. He is concerned that some of his 600 men may desert him and return to Cuba. Cortés does not want Cuba to know of his successes in Mexico.

6. Winter of 1519–1520: Cortés and his men roam through Tenochtitlán and uncover treasures galore. Because he is afraid that the Aztecs might eventually oust him, Cortés kidnaps Moctezuma.

5. November 8, 1519: Cortés and his small force enter the city of Tenochtitlán. Some stories say the Aztecs may have believed Cortés was Quetzalcoatl, a god who was expected to return from the east.

4. Summer, 1519: Cortés begins his famous march inland through Mexico. Along the way, he conquers the native Tlaxcalans, who become his allies against the Aztecs, their enemies.

7. 1520: The Aztecs revolt against the Spaniards. At Cortés's request, Moctezuma addresses the Aztecs in an attempt to quell the revolt. Moctezuma is stoned and dies three days later.

8. June 30, 1520: On a dark, rainy night, the Spaniards are driven from Tenochtitlán by a group of Aztecs led by Moctezuma's nephew, Cuauhtémoc.

9. July, 1520: Cortés reorganizes his army and begins fighting his way back to the capital city. After three months of bloody battles, Tenochtitlán falls under complete control of the Spaniards. Not long after, Cortés begins rebuilding the ruined city, which eventually becomes Mexico City.

BEFORE YOU READ

Read aloud the introduction to the lesson on page 152. Ask students to explain how reading can "open up whole new worlds." Then have the class turn to the prereading activity, a **think-pair-and-share**. (For help teaching this strategy, see the **Strategy Handbook**, page 40.)

Motivation Strategy

Borrow Tanaka's *The Lost Temple of the Aztecs* and/or Shepherd's *The Aztecs* from the juvenile section of your library. As a class, do a careful picture walk through the book(s). Ask students to discuss the art and what the pictures reveal about ancient Mexico. This activity will help set the mood for students' reading of "The Great Moctezuma."

ENGAGING STUDENTS Show a film or video that relates to the topic of ancient Mexico. Some of your students—especially those who are visual learners—may find it helpful to be allowed to first "see" information about this theme. When it comes time to read Shepherd's selection, students will be more comfortable with the topic and feel less intimidated by the vocabulary and level of detail.

Vocabulary Building

The most efficient way to uncover the meaning of an unfamiliar word is to examine it in **context**. It's quicker and easier than turning to a dictionary. Good readers know that writers will often supply clues about a word somewhere in the word's environment. Sometimes these clues appear in the same sentence; other times they can be found in the preceding or following sentences. Ask students to practice defining these key vocabulary words in context: *legend, temples, monuments, massacred,* and *mourned*. Ask students to circle these words in the text. Although each of these words is footnoted, students should check the footnote only as a last resort. First they should try to define on their own. For more help with vocabulary work, see page 200.

STRATEGY LESSON: **PRONUNCIATION** Knowing the pronunciation of a word is as important as knowing the word's definition. Write the following words and pronunciations on the board, and ask students to practice saying them aloud: *omens* (O munz), *indecision* (IN di SIZ shun), and *chaos* (KAY os).

For additional practice on this strategy, see the **Vocabulary** blackline master on page 200.

Prereading Strategies

A **think-pair-and-share** can arouse interest in a reading and at the same time help students begin thinking about the author's message. The quotations on page 152 have been chosen to give readers clues about the topic and tone of the article. Ask students to work together to number the five sentences. Correct ordering of the sentences is not nearly as important as the ideas and feelings that they provoke in the reader. As such, there are no right or wrong answers. Think of the activity as a warm-up to Shepherd's message in "The Great Moctezuma."

READ-ALOUD As an alternate prereading strategy, have a volunteer read aloud the first few paragraphs of "The Great Moctezuma." After the read-aloud, ask students to help you make a list of "Moctezuma Facts" on the board. Students can consult this list as they are reading the rest of the selection and then use the facts from the list to help them write their summaries for Part IV.

Spanish-speaking Students

Esta selección describe la conquista de la civilización azteca. Los aztecas eran muy avansadas y les impresionaban mucho a los españoles. Pero los conquistadores querían convertir a los aztecas a la religión cristiana y anhelaban todos los tesoros. El líder español, Cortés, no tardó mucho tiempo en encargase de los aztecas. Eventualmente él y los otros conquistadores destruyeron la civilización que les habían impresionado tanto.

II. READ

Remind students to keep a running list of **questions** as they read. Some of their questions will be answered later on in the reading, of course. If this is the case, readers can jot down answers in the **Response Notes**. Questions that are not answered can be used as discussion starters at the end of the reading.

Response Strategy

MARK As always, students should be encouraged to mark or highlight anything that interests them, puzzles them, or surprises them. In particular, students should watch carefully for information about Moctezuma. What kind of leader was he? How did the Aztecs feel about him? How did the Spaniards feel about him? Students' notes will come in handy when they write their summaries of the selection.

Comprehension Strategies

Directed reading is a good comprehension strategy to use with this selection since some of your students may find it challenging. Your job as group leader will be to oversee the reading of the text and facilitate discussion as needed. Ask students to read silently, perhaps one page at a time. At each **stop and think** question, have students pause and write an answer. Then briefly discuss the question as a group. If there's time, ask students to read the selection a second time, at their own pace. If necessary, pull aside into one corner of the classroom a small group of students who seem to be struggling. You might do an oral reading with this group.

For more help, see the **Comprehension** blackline master on page 201.

Discussion Questions

COMPREHENSION 1. How many Aztecs lived in the city of Tenochtitlán at the time of the invasion? *(more than one million)*

2. What was the Spaniards' initial reaction to this city? *(They were awed by its beauty and size.)*

3. What does Moctezuma do when he realizes Cortés is not Quetzalcoatl? *(He bribes him with presents in the hope that he'll go away.)*

4. What was the Spaniards' "mission"? *(to save Indian souls)*

CRITICAL THINKING 5. Why do you think the Spaniards treated the Aztecs and their belongings so badly? *(Answers will vary.)*

6. Why do you think the Spaniards mourned Moctezuma's death? *(Answers will vary. Students may suggest that they had come to see him as a great leader of his people or respected him because of the magnificent city he built.)*

Literary Skill

MOOD To introduce a literary skill with this lesson, you might discuss mood with students. Remind the class that *mood* is the feeling a piece of literature arouses in the reader: happiness, sadness, anxiety, or peacefulness, for example. Writers create mood through their word choices. Have students say what they think the mood of "The Great Moctezuma" is. Point out that words such as *ruined*, *massacred*, and *stoned* build an atmosphere, or mood, of chaos that matches exactly the chaos the Aztec empire was thrown into upon Cortés's arrival. This mood also helps to evoke feelings of sadness, sympathy, and even anger in the reader. Shepherd wants to be sure her readers understand how horrifying the situation in Tenochtitlán actually was.

III. GATHER YOUR THOUGHTS

Use the prewriting activities as a warm-up for the writing activity (a **summary**), which is assigned on page 159 of the *Sourcebook*. Have students record the **sequence of events** on the organizer on page 158.

Prewriting Strategies

MAIN IDEA AND SUPPORTING DETAILS
If you feel students need an additional prewriting strategy, work with them to find the main idea of "The Great Moctezuma." Ask the class: "What is Shepherd's most important idea? What message does she have for readers?"

After students find the main idea, they should decide which facts and details directly support it. Have them create a main idea/supporting details organizer as a way of keeping track of their notes.

Have students use the **Prewriting** blackline master on page 202.

IV. WRITE

Be sure students understand that their assignment is to write a **summary** of events Shepherd writes about. Remind them that in a summary, the writer uses his or her own words and not the words of the author. Also be sure they know to include only the most important information in their writing, including names, dates, times and places.

Once students have written a first draft, ask them to watch carefully for problems with organization and level of detail. Remind the class that if their details are weak, the overall effect of the writing will be weak. Once they have finished, you might use this rubric to assess the quality of their writing.

WRITING RUBRIC
Do students' summaries

- clearly state the author's main idea?

- explain the events Shepherd describes in her article?

- include a discussion of the two key players in the drama—Moctezuma and Cortés?

Grammar, Usage, and Mechanics

Refer students to the **Writers' Checklist** and ask that they proofread carefully for problems with comma usage. Explain that commas are always used to set off explanatory and introductory phrases. In addition, they are used to separate interruptions from the rest of the sentence. For example:

Incorrect: Your lord I believe the Great Plumed Serpent also known as Quetzalcoatl is here.

Correct: Your lord, I believe the Great Plumed Serpent, also known as Quetzalcoatl, is here.

V. WRAP-UP

Invite students to reflect on the **depth** of their understanding using the **Readers' Checklist**. Its intent is to help students think about the "bridge" they were able to create between the literature and their own lives.

Assessment

To test students' comprehension, use the **Assessment** blackline master on page 203.

Name _____

VOCABULARY
Words from the Selection

DIRECTIONS To help you learn new words from the selection, answer each question. Write your answers on the lines.

1. Is a <u>legend</u> fact or fiction? _____

2. Do people go to <u>temples</u> to shop or pray? _____

3. Are <u>monuments</u> usually made of paper or stone? _____

4. When Shepherd says the Spanish <u>massacred</u> the Aztecs, does she mean they killed them or helped them? _____

5. When people <u>mourned</u> Moctezuma's death, how did they feel?

   _____

Strategy Lesson: Pronunciation

DIRECTIONS Each sentence below contains the pronunciation of a word in parentheses. From the list on the right, choose the word that is pronounced. Then write that word on the blank. You will not use one word.

6. Moctezuma worried that his (IN di SIZ shun)

   _____ would cost many lives.

7. The Spaniards said their (MISH un)

   _____ was to save the

   Aztecs' souls.

8. Many (O munz) _____

   pointed to the arrival of a stranger.

9. The Spanish were (BRYBD)

   _____ with gold.

10. (KAY os) _____

   occurred during the attack.

omens
indecision
embroidery
bribed
mission
chaos

Name _____

COMPREHENSION
Graphic Organizer

DIRECTIONS Use these webs to show what you know about Moctezuma and Hernán Cortés. Check your book for details.

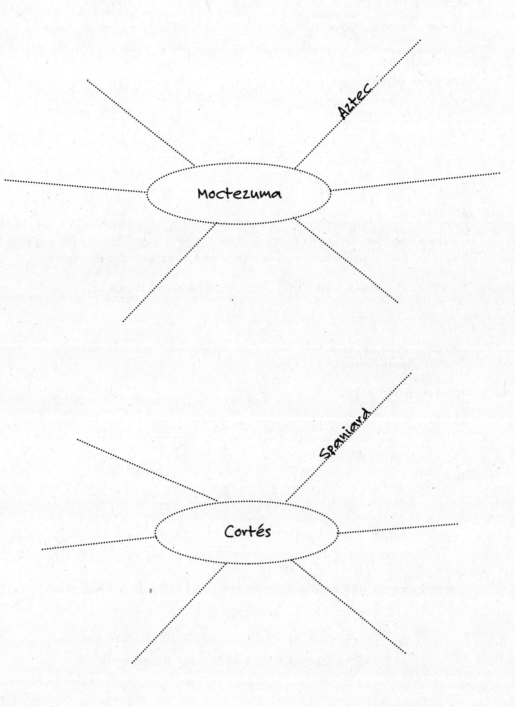

Name _____

PREWRITING
Writing a Summary

To write a good summary, select the most important ideas and combine them into clear, easy-to-understand sentences.

DIRECTIONS Follow these steps to write a summary for "The Great Moctezuma."

STEP 1. REREAD. Go over the article carefully. Highlight key words and phrases.

STEP 2. LIST. Make a list of the most important facts and opinions in the article.

Important facts and opinions: _____

- _____
- _____
- _____
- _____

STEP 3. CHOOSE. Select the most important fact or opinion from your list and make this the main idea of your summary. Write a topic sentence that states the main idea.

Donna Walsh Shepherd's main idea in "The Great Moctezuma" is:

_____

_____

STEP 4. FIND DETAILS. Gather important details from the article. Names, dates, times, and places are all examples of important details.

Shepherd's important details: _____

1. _____   6. _____

2. _____   7. _____

3. _____   8. _____

4. _____   9. _____

5. _____   10. _____

STEP 5. WRITE. Now write your summary on pages 159 and 160 of your book.

⇒ Begin with the topic sentence.

⇒ Then summarize the details that support this topic sentence.

⇒ End with a concluding sentence that ties things together.

Name _____

ASSESSMENT
Multiple-Choice Test

DIRECTIONS On the blanks provided, write the letter of the item that best answers each question or completes each statement.

_____ 1. What does Aztec legend say about Quetzalcoatl?
   A. He will die at a full moon.   C. He will return to rule.
   B. He will be born to a slave.   D. He will bring war.

_____ 2. Cortés and his men knocked down temples and replaced them with . . .
   A. forts.   C. pyramids.
   B. crosses.   D. flags.

_____ 3. What surprised the Spaniards about Tenochtitlán?
   A. It was huge.   C. It was orderly.
   B. It was beautiful.   D. all of the above

_____ 4. Why did Moctezuma greet Cortés and his men as friends?
   A. He didn't know what else to do.   C. He thought they were gods.
   B. He wanted to learn about their boats.   D. none of the above

_____ 5. What did Moctezuma do to welcome the Spaniards?
   A. He planned a celebration.   C. He took them to temples.
   B. He gave them beautiful gifts.   D. all of the above

_____ 6. What gift did the Spaniards seem to like the most?
   A. precious stones   C. gold
   B. featherworks   D. guns

_____ 7. What did Cortés do after he took charge of Tenochtitlán?
   A. He sent the city's gold to Spain.   C. He took the Aztec children away.
   B. He made the Aztecs learn Spanish.   D. all of the above

_____ 8. What made the Spanish soldiers think the Aztecs were ready to attack?
   A. They were gathering weapons.   C. They were dancing.
   B. They were painting their faces.   D. They were hiding.

_____ 9. It is said that Moctezuma died from being . . .
   A. stoned by his own people.   C. both A. and B.
   B. murdered by the Spaniards.   D. neither A. nor B.

_____ 10. How did the Aztecs and the Spaniards feel about Moctezuma's death?
   A. They were glad.   C. They were scared.
   B. They were sad.   D. all of the above

Short-Essay Test

Why do you think the Spaniards wanted to take over Moctezuma and his city?

Joseph Krumgold

Unit Background   JOSEPH KRUMGOLD (pages 161–180)

Two excerpts from . . . *and now Miguel* by Joseph Krumgold make up this unit.

Born in Jersey City, New Jersey, Joseph Krumgold (1908–1980) majored in English and history at New York University, received a degree in 1928, and went to Hollywood the next year. His father owned and operated movie theaters, and his older brother accompanied silent films on the organ; thus, Joseph seemed destined for some aspect of the movie business.

He became a publicity writer for MGM and a screenwriter and producer for various film companies. He was also a writer, director, and producer for CBS, NBC, and NET. During World War II, he worked for the Office of War Information and made documentary films. In 1947 he married Helen Litwin and they moved to Israel until 1951. While in Israel, he made 15 films, one of which, *The House in the Desert,* won a prize at the Venice Film Festival.

In 1952 he started his own production company and a year later made a film for the U.S. State Department about the life of sheep farmers in the Southwest. A publisher asked him to adapt the film into a children's book, which became . . . *and Now Miguel,* a Newbery Medal winner in 1954. The book was filmed in 1965 at Universal Studios and may be available as a video.

Teaching the Introduction

A boy and a lamb, the cover of Joseph Krumgold's book, and mountains are shown on page 161.

1. Read the unit introduction with students, and ask someone to tell what a documentary film is. Give students a little of the preceding information about the author, and tell them that this novel takes place in the southwestern United States and involves Miguel, whose family members make their living by raising sheep.

2. If you have students who have helped to raise and shear sheep or who have watched the birth of a lamb, ask them to tell about the experiences.

3. In the first excerpt, Miguel asks his younger brother, ". . . suppose you could have anything you want. Is there anything you want?" Ask students to answer this question for themselves. Although Pedro reveals what he wants, Miguel does not say what he wants in so many words. After reading the second excerpt, students can make some inferences about Miguel's wants.

Opening Activity

At this point in the *Sourcebook,* students have read about a great many different types of people in very different situations. Ask them to recall their favorite character so far and to write two or three sentences explaining their choice.

STUDENT PAGES 162-169

Skills and Strategies Overview

THEME	Joseph Krumgold
READING LEVEL	easy
VOCABULARY	◆simple ◆trout ◆beneath ◆commotion ◆spoiled
PREREADING	one minute quickwrite
RESPONSE	visualize
COMPREHENSION	story frame
PREWRITING	storyboard
WRITING	narrative paragraph / commas
ASSESSMENT	style

BACKGROUND

. . . and now Miguel is Joseph Krumgold's moving novel about a family of New Mexican sheepherders whose lives at the base of the Sangre de Cristo Mountains are a series of impossible struggles and exhilarating joys. The narrator of the story is a boy named Miguel, who is determined to prove to everyone that he is finally a man.

"I Am Miguel" is an excerpt from Krumgold's award-winning novel. In this short selection, Miguel introduces himself and explains to his brother (and himself) how it feels to long for something that is just out of reach.

UNIT THEME Joseph Krumgold explores the theme of growing up in this short piece about a boy named Miguel.

GRAPHIC ORGANIZER A Venn diagram such as this one can help students compare two characters in a story.

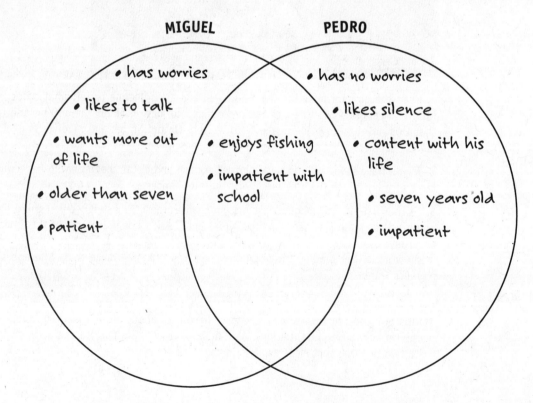

MIGUEL

PEDRO

- has worries
- likes to talk
- wants more out of life
- older than seven
- patient

- enjoys fishing
- impatient with school

- has no worries
- likes silence
- content with his life
- seven years old
- impatient

BEFORE YOU READ

Ask a student to read aloud the introduction to the lesson. Offer background information on Joseph Krumgold and the novel . . . *and now Miguel* if you have not actually done so. Then assign the prereading strategy, a **one-minute quickwrite**. (Refer to the **Strategy Handbook** on page 40 for more help.)

Motivation Strategy

Explain that in this story, the narrator is alternately annoyed with his brother and envious of him. Ask students to think of a family member they would enjoy writing about. Have them jot down the person's name in the margin of the text and then make a brief note about why this person would be interesting to describe.

MOTIVATING STUDENTS Borrow a copy of . . . *and now Miguel* or *Onion John* and read aloud a few passages to students as a warm-up to Krumgold's style. Look for parts that are funny or that offer clues about Krumgold's stylistic technique.

Vocabulary Building

Help students use **context clues** as they read to figure out the meanings of challenging words, especially the key vocabulary for this lesson: *simple, trout, beneath, commotion,* and *spoiled.* (Only *commotion* is footnoted.) Remind students that defining in context allows the reader to continue reading without interruption. The reader's goal is to find one or two clues about the unfamiliar word—just enough so that he or she doesn't have to stop and check a dictionary. Later, the reader can look up the word in a dictionary if a more complete definition is needed. Have students circle the vocabulary words as they come to them in their reading. For additional practice with these words, see page 210.

STRATEGY LESSON: HETERONYMS Explain to students that a heteronym is a word that has the same spelling as another word but a different origin, meaning, and pronunciation. For example, *lead* (to conduct) and *lead* (a type of metal). Show students two more heteronyms: *close* (near; shut) and *tear* (teardrop; to pull into pieces). Then have them think of a few more heteronyms. Students might suggest *content, refuse, sewer, read,* and *wind.*

For additional practice on this strategy, see the **Vocabulary** blackline master on page 210.

Prereading Strategies

The purpose of a **quickwrite** is to get students writing almost before they know it. To make the strategy meaningful, always ask students to quickwrite with a particular topic in mind. In this case, students should read the introductory paragraph at the top of page 162 and then write about what they want and need. When they've finished, have students circle words or phrases in their quickwrite that they like and may want to use in future writing.

Spanish-speaking Students

Un joven lucha entender a sí mismo en "Yo soy Miguel." Una charla con su hermano, Pedro le hace pensar mucho en su vida y en lo que quiere. Está celoso de Pedro porque se alegra fácilmente y está satisfecho. Pero Miguel sabe que es un individuo totalmente diferente y que tiene que llevar su propia vida siendo la persona que es.

READ

*As a response strategy, encourage students to **visualize** the scene on the river bank. Before they begin reading, tell students to watch for descriptive words that help them "see" the two boys and what they are doing. Ask them to draw at least two sketches in the **Response Notes**. Remind students that good readers automatically visualize as they read. Making sketches can help them remember what they saw.*

Response Strategy

QUESTION As an alternate response strategy, have students note any during-reading questions that occur to them. Remind the class that any question they want to ask is valid, no matter how trivial it might seem. Sometimes trivial questions can "piggyback" one upon the other, to the point that the reader finds himself or herself asking a question that gets at the central meaning of the selection.

Comprehension Strategies

Students are asked to fill in **story frames** as they are reading "I Am Miguel." Story frames can help students understand the sequence of events and can prod the reader into thinking carefully about character, setting, plot, and theme.

RETELLING As an alternate prereading strategy, ask students to retell different parts of "I Am Miguel." A whole-class retelling can benefit everyone, not just those in need of extra help. When a reader listens to a retelling, he or she is likely to hear words or phrases that provoke new ideas about the selection. If you like, encourage students to take notes during the retelling just as they do when they are listening to a story read aloud.

For more help, see the **Comprehension** blackline master on page 211.

Discussion Questions

COMPREHENSION 1. Who is the narrator of "I Am Miguel"? *(Miguel)*

2. What are Miguel and Pedro doing? *(fishing)*

3. Why does Pedro have such difficulty catching a fish? *(He makes a big commotion in the water.)*

4. What does Miguel want his brother to talk about? *(He wants Pedro to name something he really wants. He's frustrated because he can't get a sensible answer out of the boy.)*

CRITICAL THINKING 5. What inferences can you make about Miguel? *(Answers will vary. Students might infer that Miguel is troubled by something. He says in an envious way that Pedro has no worries and likes things the way they are. Miguel implies that he himself has plenty.)*

Literary Skill

NARRATOR To introduce a literary skill with this lesson, you might explain the function of the narrator in a piece of writing. Remind students that the narrator is the person who tells the story. In other words, the narrator is like the reader's tour guide. He or she wants to take the reader on a tour through a series of events. Along the way, the narrator usually drops clues about himself or herself, other characters, and the events of the story. Ask students to say what clues Miguel gives the reader about himself. What inferences can students make about his likes and dislikes? Have students make notes in the **Response Notes**. Then explain that students will need to keep these inferences in mind as they read "Sangre de Cristo Mountains," another excerpt from . . . *and now Miguel.*

III. GATHER YOUR THOUGHTS

The prewriting activities on page 167 will prepare students to do some narrative writing of their own. To begin, students will think about a time they wanted something but couldn't have it. Then they'll tell about that time on a **storyboard**. Remind the class that on a storyboard, students both write and draw. Have them tell about the event in chronological order. Next students will write a **topic sentence** for their narrative paragraph.

Prewriting Strategies

WORD BANK If you feel students would benefit from an additional prewriting activity, you might have them create a word bank of sensory words that they can use in their paragraphs. Ask them to think of three or more words that appeal to the five senses and relate to the experience or event they are describing. See the **Prewriting** blackline master on page 212 for a word bank exercise.

IV. WRITE

The directions at the top of page 168 ask students to write a **narrative paragraph** about a time they wanted something but couldn't have it. Tell them that they should feel free to model their writing style on Krumgold's.

WRITING RUBRIC You might want to show students this writing rubric so that they have what you expect to see in their narrative paragraphs.

Do the students' narrative paragraphs

- tell about a time they wanted something but couldn't have it?
- show a clear progression—a beginning, a middle, and an end?
- include adequate details describing the event or experience?
- contain sensory language that helps the reader "see," "hear," and "feel" the event described?

Grammar, Usage, and Mechanics

When students are ready to proofread their work, refer them to the **Writers' Checklist.** At this point, you might want to teach a brief lesson on commas in compound sentences. Remind students that the two parts (independent clauses) of a compound sentence are joined with a comma and a conjunction, such as *and, or, nor, but, so,* and *yet.* For example:

Incorrect: Pedro fished, Miguel watched.

Correct: Pedro fished, and Miguel watched.

V. WRAP-UP

Ask students to reflect on Krumgold's **style** and encourage them to read and respond to the questions on the **Readers' Checklist.** Explain that even if they don't like a writer's style, they should still try to understand its characteristics. Have a volunteer say what he or she liked best and least about the writing. Ask the class to respond to the volunteer's opinion.

Assessment

To test students' comprehension, use the **Assessment** blackline master on page 213.

Name _____

VOCABULARY

Words from the Selection

DIRECTIONS Use the vocabulary words in the box in a paragraph about Miguel or Pedro. Write the paragraph on the following lines.

◇simple ◇trout ◇commotion ◇spoiled ◇beneath

_____

_____

_____

_____

_____

Strategy Lesson: Heteronyms

A **heteronym** is a word that has the same spelling as another word but a different origin, meaning, and pronunciation. For example, *tear* can mean "a drop of liquid," as in a teardrop, or "pull apart."

DIRECTIONS Use the clues in each sentence to tell you the meaning of the underlined word. Circle the correct definition in parentheses.

6. Pedro is <u>content</u> with playing inside or out. (satisfied / all things inside)

7. I walked <u>close</u> to the river so that I could see the trout. (shut / near)

8. I <u>refuse</u> to take the dog for a walk when it is raining outside. (trash / say "no")

9. Our ball fell in the <u>sewer</u> and now it smells terrible. (one who sews / underground pipe for waste)

10. The <u>wind</u> blew the branch that the bird was sitting on. (air in motion / to wrap or be wrapped around something)

Name _____

COMPREHENSION
Graphic Organizer

DIRECTIONS Use this storyboard to tell what happens in "I Am Miguel." Refer to your story frame notes as needed.

Name _____

PREWRITING

Using Sensory Language

Keep in mind that good writers use words that appeal to the five senses to make their writing more vivid and interesting.

DIRECTIONS Think of sensory words that you can use in your paragraph about a time you wanted something but couldn't have it.

1. Try to come up with three words for each of the five senses.

2. Write the words on the chart.

sight words	sound words	smell words	touch words	taste words

Sketch

DIRECTIONS In the frame below, make a sketch of what you wanted but couldn't have. Be as detailed as possible.

Name _____

ASSESSMENT

Multiple-Choice Test

DIRECTIONS On the blanks provided, write the letter of the item that best answers each question or completes each statement.

_____ 1. Who narrates this story?
   A. Pedro
   B. Miguel
   C. Miguel's father
   D. Miguel's teacher

_____ 2. How are Pedro and Miguel related?
   A. They are cousins.
   B. They are father and son.
   C. They are brothers.
   D. They aren't related.

_____ 3. According to Miguel, Pedro has no . . .
   A. worries.
   B. money.
   C. loyalty.
   D. fun.

_____ 4. Pedro wants to spend less time . . .
   A. fishing.
   B. in school.
   C. in the house.
   D. being with Miguel.

_____ 5. Why is Pedro unable to catch a fish?
   A. He moves too much.
   B. He is looking in the wrong place.
   C. He doesn't have a pole.
   D. The fish are too tiny.

_____ 6. What does Pedro want?
   A. a big rock
   B. a baseball glove
   C. some coins
   D. a big fish

_____ 7. What does Miguel do well?
   A. He can see the bright side of things.
   B. He can read lots of books.
   C. He can catch fish.
   D. He can paint.

_____ 8. What activities does Pedro enjoy doing?
   A. swimming
   B. coloring
   C. playing ball
   D. all of the above

_____ 9. How old is Pedro?
   A. nine
   B. seven
   C. five
   D. three

_____ 10. How does Miguel feel about Pedro?
   A. He's a little envious of him.
   B. He's mad at him.
   C. He's a little sad for him.
   D. He's happy for him.

Short-Essay Test

Is Miguel happy with himself? Use examples from the story to support your answer.

STUDENT PAGES 170–180

Skills and Strategies Overview

THEME	Joseph Krumgold
READING LEVEL	easy
VOCABULARY	◇ mesa ◇ flock ◇ fetch ◇ ewe ◇ burlap
PREREADING	anticipation guide
RESPONSE	predict
COMPREHENSION	reciprocal reading
PREWRITING	brainstorm
WRITING	autobiographical paragraph / usage
ASSESSMENT	depth

BACKGROUND

In this selection from . . . *and now Miguel,* Miguel describes the hustle and bustle of lambing time at his family's ranch. It is a time when the entire family must pitch in to help, sometimes working around the clock to ensure the safety of the lambs.

Even at his busiest moments, however, Miguel never stops wondering and worrying about his identity. He is tired of being a child like Pedro and longs to be thought of as a man. The Sangre de Cristo Mountains beckon to him, and he is determined to heed their call. First, however, he must prove himself to his father and uncles.

UNIT THEME Krumgold explores themes of growing up and personal identity in his award-winning novel.

GRAPHIC ORGANIZER Students might create a story star after they finish reading "Sangre de Cristo Mountains." Later, they'll make a star for their own autobiographical stories.

WHO WAS THERE? Miguel, his parents, his uncles, his siblings

WHAT HAPPENED? The family works feverishly during lambing time. Miguel wants his father to notice him.

WHERE? The family ranch at the base of the Sangre de Cristo Mountains

TITLE: "Sangre de Cristo Mountains"

HOW DID IT END? The lambs are safe, but Miguel is frustrated by his father's lack of attention.

WHEN? springtime

BIBLIOGRAPHY Students might also enjoy one of these Newbery Award–winning books: *Dear Mr. Henshaw* by Beverly Cleary (average, 1983); *Sarah, Plain and Tall* by Patricia MacLachlan (easy, 1985); *Joyful Noise: Poems for Two Voices* by Paul Fleischman (easy, 1988); *Number the Stars* by Lois Lowry (average, 1989); *Shiloh* by Phyllis Reynolds Naylor (average, 1991).

BEFORE YOU READ

To get things started, ask a student to summarize "I Am Miguel." Then explain that students are about to read a second excerpt from . . . *and now Miguel.* Tell them the Sangre de Cristo Mountains are in south-central Colorado and north-central New Mexico. The highest peak is more than 14,000 feet high. Have students complete the prereading activity, an **anticipation guide.** (Refer to the **Strategy Handbook** on page 40 for more help.)

Motivation Strategy

Borrow a copy of the audiocassette of . . . *and now Miguel* and have students listen to the first part of the book. This will allow them to "hear" Miguel's voice and may make it easier for them to visualize the action of the story when they are reading.

ENGAGING STUDENTS Explain that "Sangre de Cristo Mountains" is about a boy's search for an identity. Ask students to complete this statement: "I think identity is _____." The question will help them begin thinking about one of Krumgold's themes.

Vocabulary Building

Draw attention to the key vocabulary words for this lesson: *mesa, flock, fetch, ewe,* and *burlap.* Have students circle these words in the text. Ask students to volunteer definitions for the words. Also have them use the words in sentences of their own. A series of quick vocabulary exercises can help students become more comfortable with any words that are new to them. For more practice work, have students complete the **Vocabulary** blackline master on page 218.

STRATEGY LESSON: MEXICAN SPANISH Tell students that many English words come from the Spanish language or Mexican Spanish. *Fiesta* and *mesa* (page 172), as well as the name of the mountains, are all from Spanish. Give students a list of words to define and pronounce. Words on your list might include *canyon* (a deep valley with steep walls on both sides), *pueblo* (village of stone and adobe buildings, built by Native Americans in the southwestern United States), *burrito* (a tortilla rolled around a seasoned filling, usually beef, chicken, or beans), *sombrero,* and *siesta.*

For additional practice on this strategy, see the **Vocabulary** blackline master on page 218.

Prereading Strategies

Use the **anticipation guide** on page 170 as a warm-up to Krumgold's story. An anticipation guide asks students to activate prior knowledge about a topic or idea and then apply that knowledge to a set of statements about the story. Usually an anticipation guide will help arouse students' interest in the selection. Have your students revisit the anticipation guide as they are reading and later, when the reading is completed. Students can observe how their responses changed or stayed the same as a result of their reading of "Sangre de Cristo Mountains."

PICTURE WALK As an alternate prereading strategy, ask students to do a picture walk of the selection. Based on what they've seen, what do they predict "Sangre de Cristo Mountains" will be about? When they have finished reading, they might return to the art and explain the connections they see between the art and the story.

Spanish-speaking Students

"Las montañas de Sangre de Cristo" continua el cuento de la selección anterior. Miguel describe una de las tradiciones más importantes de su familia—la excursión a las montañas para cuidar a las ovejas. Quiere mostrar a todos que está preparado para el viaje, y que es bastante maduro para ayudar. Es evidente, sin embargo, que todavía tiene mucho que aprender.

II. READ

Explain to students that **predicting** as they read can make reading all the more interesting and entertaining. Have them get into the habit of making predictions about characters and outcomes automatically (many of your students may do this already). Each time they make a prediction, they should note it in the **Response Notes**. When they've finished reading, have them return to their notes to see which of their predictions came true.

Response Strategy

CLARIFY It is important that students keep clear in their minds the many hurdles Miguel must overcome before he can accompany the men on their trip to the Sangre de Cristo Mountains. Each time Miguel mentions a problem or a concern, students should clarify the difficulty by making a comment in the **Response Notes**. Later, when students need to think critically about the character of Miguel, they'll be able to return to their notes.

Comprehension Strategies

In a **reciprocal reading**, readers share the process of decoding and responding to a text. This can make the reading process easier and more enjoyable for students, help refine their cooperative group skills. Ask students to work together in a group to read the Krumgold selection. Have them switch readers every page or so. Each time a reader comes to an interrupter question, he or she should direct the question to the group and lead the others in brainstorming a response. In some cases (with the predict question, for example), the group may come up with several different answers. These can be noted in the book and shared with the rest of the class later.

STORY FRAME As alternate comprehension strategy, ask students to complete a story frame as they are reading. Write these words on the board: "*First, Next, Then, Later,* and *Finally.*" Ask students to plot the sequence of events in the story using these words as sentence starters.

For more help, see the **Comprehension** blackline master on page 219.

Discussion Questions

COMPREHENSION 1. What time of year does the story take place? *(springtime)*

2. Why does Miguel ask his father a series of questions that he doesn't really need to ask? *(He wants his father to notice him.)*

3. What does Miguel want most in his life? *(to be able to go to the Sangre de Cristo Mountains with the men)*

CRITICAL THINKING 4. What sort of relationship would you say Miguel has with his father? *(Answers will vary. Possible: His father seems distant or perhaps too preoccupied to pay attention to Miguel.)*

5. What advice would you like to give Miguel? Why? *(Answers will vary.)*

Literary Skill

STYLE *Style* is the way in which a writer uses words and sentences to suit his or her ideas. Help students think about Krumgold's writing style. Ask: "What is the tone and mood of the two selections? What imagery (sensory language) can you find?" (Tone, mood, and language all affect an author's style.) Have students pay particular attention to the informal, conversational feel of Krumgold's writing. Notice how Miguel speaks directly to the reader at times, almost as if the reader is his close friend: "But about the Sangre de Cristo Mountains I know for sure. If you are ready and the time comes, then that's all. You will go." Point out that Krumgold's simple, unadorned style matches the simple, uncomplicated lives of Miguel and his family.

III. GATHER YOUR THOUGHTS

Prewriting Strategies

The prewriting activities on pages 177 and 178 are meant to help students reflect on what they have read and then build a bridge between the reading and their own lives. Students will begin by thinking about the events of the story Miguel tells. Then they'll **brainstorm** about a time something important happened to them and their family and make notes about the event on the web at the top of page 177.

After they finish their webs, students will **narrow the focus** of their topic. (Remind the class how important it is to think of a topic that is not too broad. Topics that are broad are impossible to cover in just one paragraph.)

As a final prewriting activity, students will make a story star that organizes the story they want to tell. The star on page 178 asks them to comment on who, what, where, when, and how.

Have students use the **Prewriting** blackline master on page 220.

IV. WRITE

Remind students that their assignment is to write an **autobiographical paragraph** about an event in their lives that was important. Students should begin with a topic sentence and then tell about the event using chronological order.

WRITING RUBRIC Use this writing rubric to help students focus on the assignment requirements and for assistance with a quick assessment of their writing.

Do students' autobiographical paragraphs

- open with a sentence that names the event to be described?

- include descriptive details about time and place?

- stay focused on this one event throughout?

Grammar, Usage, and Mechanics

After students have written a first draft, have them read it carefully to be sure that it makes sense and that it is ordered properly. Then have them proofread their writing, looking carefully for grammatical, mechanical, and usage errors. Draw their attention to the **Writers' Checklist** if they haven't noticed it already. At this point, you might want to teach a brief lesson on problems with *to/too/two* and *affect/effect*. For practice, ask students to correct errors in this sentence:

Her decision too go too the movies effected us all.

V. WRAP-UP

Take a moment at the end of the lesson for students to self-assess the **depth** of their understanding of Krumgold's writing. Have them read the questions on the **Readers' Checklist** and then explain what the two Krumgold selections made them think about.

Assessment

To test students' comprehension, use the **Assessment** blackline master on page 221.

Name _____

VOCABULARY

Words from the Selection

DIRECTIONS To build vocabulary, answer these questions about five words from the selection.

1. Is a <u>mesa</u> flat on top or pointed? _____

2. Is a <u>flock</u> a single animal or a group of animals? _____

3. If you are asked to <u>fetch</u> something, do you hide it or go get it?

   _____

4. Is a <u>ewe</u> a male or a female sheep? _____

5. Would you use <u>burlap</u> to make a sturdy bag or a fancy napkin?

   _____

Strategy Lesson: Mexican Spanish

DIRECTIONS Use context clues to help you decide which words belong in the paragraph. Write the words on the blanks. You will not use one word.

(6) The _____ was busy working in the field collecting the fruits and vegetables for the harvest. (7) He decided to work through the _____, though everyone else took a rest. (8) He was thankful he was wearing his _____ on his head because the sun beat down on him. (9) Finally he was finished, and everyone went to a _____ to celebrate. They all brought food and drinks to the celebration. During the party, the farmer turned on the radio to hear the final score. (10) He was a real _____ of baseball.

fiesta
siesta
sombrero
burrito
campesino
aficionado

Name _____

COMPREHENSION
Group Discussion

DIRECTIONS Get together in a small group and discuss "Sangre de Cristo Mountains." Use the discussion questions below to get your discussion started and to keep things moving.

Discussion Question #1

What three words would you use to describe Miguel?

Explain your choices.

_____
_____
_____
_____

Discussion Question #2

What theme (central idea) does Krumgold explore in "Sangre de Cristo Mountains"?

_____
_____
_____
_____

Discussion Question #3

Do you predict Miguel will ever be able to get his father's attention? Say what you think will happen.

_____
_____
_____
_____

Discussion Question #4

Which character in the story reminds you most of yourself? Why?

_____
_____
_____
_____

Name _____

PREWRITING

Writing a Topic Sentence and Details

Every paragraph you write must have a topic sentence. A topic sentence tells the subject of the paragraph and how you feel about the subject. You can use this formula to help you write a topic sentence:

(A specific topic) + (a specific feeling) = a good topic sentence.

DIRECTIONS Write your topic sentence and supporting details for your autobiographical paragraph on the organizer below. Finish by writing a concluding sentence.

My topic: _____

MY TOPIC SENTENCE		
DETAIL #1	DETAIL #2	DETAIL #3
MY CONCLUDING SENTENCE		

Name _____

ASSESSMENT

Multiple-Choice Test

DIRECTIONS On the blanks provided, write the letter of the item that best answers each question or completes each statement.

_____ 1. What is Miguel's opinion of the Sangre de Cristo Mountains?
A. He thinks they are wonderful.   C. He thinks they are ugly.
B. He thinks they are dark and spooky. D. He thinks they are small.

_____ 2. What animals does a shepherd take care of?
A. cows   C. sheep
B. pigs   D. fish

_____ 3. Miguel says that in order to go to the mountains, one must be able to . . .
A. catch fish.   C. shoot a gun.
B. ride a horse.   D. all of the above

_____ 4. How does Miguel feel about going to the mountains?
A. He wants to prove that he   C. He doesn't really care.
   is ready to go.
B. He's afraid and doesn't want to go. D. none of the above

_____ 5. What do the children in Miguel's family do when they are asked to bring water?
A. They complain about the job.   C. They take turns.
B. They do it, no questions asked.   D. none of the above

_____ 6. How does Miguel's mother help out during the birth of the lambs?
A. She gets the water with the   C. She is always cooking.
   children.
B. She cares for the lambs.   D. She milks the cows.

_____ 7. Why are all the uncles and cousins staying at Miguel's house?
A. to help harvest the fruit   C. to help pick the corn
B. to help with the birth   D. to help milk the cows
   of the lambs

_____ 8. Why doesn't Miguel's dad look at him when giving him directions?
A. He is angry at Miguel.   C. He is too busy working.
B. He is blind and cannot see.   D. none of the above

_____ 9. How does Miguel try to get his father to notice him?
A. He asks his father a few questions. C. He pretends he is hurt.
B. He refuses to do what   D. He sings a song.
   he's asked to do.

_____ 10. In the story, Miguel feels . . .
A. ashamed.   C. silly.
B. loved.   D. unnoticed.

Short-Essay Test

What do you think Miguel means when he says it's hard to be himself?

Finding An Identity

Unit Background   **FINDING AN IDENTITY** (pages 181–200)

Two novel excepts, the first by Louis Sachar from *There's a Boy in the Girls' Bathroom* and the second by Jean Craighead George from *On the Far Side of the Mountain,* make up this unit.

Louis Sachar's first book was *Sideways Stories from Wayside School* (1978, 1985), which was followed, at the request of enthusiastic readers, by *Wayside School Is Falling Down* (1989). His other books include *The Boy Who Lost His Face* (1989) and *Holes* (1998). Sachar was born in 1954 in East Meadow, New York, and moved with his family to Tustin, California, when he was nine. He has a law degree from the University of San Francisco, and a family, and has adapted to writing mornings and practicing law afternoons.

Sam Gribley, the main character in *On the Far Side of the Mountain,* first appeared in *My Side of the Mountain.* The first book was a Newbery Honor Book and an American Library Association Notable Book in 1979. Sam, who ran away to live off the land, is still living on his own in the excerpt that appears in this **Sourcebook** but now he has new problems.

Jean Craighead George was born in 1919 in Washington, D.C., and now lives in Chappaqua, New York. Her many books for young readers, both fiction and nonfiction, include the Newbery Medal-winner *Julie of the Wolves* (1972), *The Talking Earth* (1983), and *Missing 'Gator of Gumbo Limbo: An Ecological Mystery* (1992).

Teaching the Introduction

A falcon, a piano player, and several young people are pictured on page 181.

1. Ask someone to find the word *identity* in a dictionary and read the definition to the class. Ask what it means to find an identity. Is it easy or hard? Do people find an identity at a certain age or do people search for an identity all their lives?

2. Have students talk about whether one can find one's identity alone or whether other people are needed to help.

3. Someone has said that one's identity is shaped by the choices one makes. Ask students to discuss this statement.

Opening Activity

Ask students to draw a picture of themselves labeled "This Is Me" but not to sign it. After drawings are posted, ask whether others in the class can figure out the subject of the drawing.

Bradley Chalkers

Skills and Strategies Overview

THEME	Finding an Identity
READING LEVEL	easy
VOCABULARY	◇mumbled ◇bulging ◇scribbled ◇gobs ◇distorted
PREREADING	word web
RESPONSE	react and connect
COMPREHENSION	retell
PREWRITING	support an opinion
WRITING	persuasive paragraph / contractions
ASSESSMENT	meaning

BACKGROUND

In Louis Sachar's enormously popular novel *There's a Boy in the Girls' Bathroom* (1987), fifth-grader Bradley Chalkers, whom everyone seems to despise, finds his way to the door of the school counselor, who eventually is able to show him how to help himself.

The excerpt, "Bradley Chalkers," will appeal to any student who knows how it feels to be the underdog. The lesson Bradley must learn—that he can like himself—is a lesson worth teaching to any fifth- or sixth-grade child.

UNIT THEME A new kid tries to befriend a boy that everyone ignores.

GRAPHIC ORGANIZER A plot line can help students see the essential elements of a plot: exposition, rising action, climax, falling action, and resolution.

CLIMAX:
Jeff catches up to Bradley on the playground and makes another attempt at friendship.

RISING ACTION:
Bradley is a problem student. Jeff smiles at him, but Bradley refuses to smile back.

FALLING ACTION:
Bradley considers what Jeff has said for a moment.

EXPOSITION:
Jeff Fishkin is introduced to the class and is seated next to Bradley.

RESOLUTION:
Bradley threatens to spit at Jeff.

BIBLIOGRAPHY Students might also enjoy these books by Louis Sachar: *Marvin Redpost: Kidnapped at Birth?* (easy, 1992); *Sixth Grade Secrets* (average, 1998); *Holes* (advanced, 1998).

BEFORE YOU READ

Read through the introduction to the lesson (page 182) with students. The purpose of this opening paragraph is to introduce the theme and motivate students to begin reading. When you feel the class is ready, ask them to begin work on the prereading activity, a **word web**. (Refer to the **Strategy Handbook** on page 40 for more help.)

Motivation Strategy

In "Bradley Chalkers," a new boy tries to befriend a boy whom everyone avoids. Ask students to think about a time they tried to make friends with someone who seemed lonely or unhappy. What happened? Were they successful, or wasn't the person interested? Why? A brief discussion on this topic will serve as an excellent warm-up to the theme of Sachar's story.

ENGAGING STUDENTS Read aloud a passage or two from one of Sachar's novels. (You might choose to read from another section of *There's a Boy in the Girls' Bathroom* or borrow another book from your library. See the bibliography section on the previous page.) Help students get to know Sachar's style.

Vocabulary Building

Have students use **context clues** as they read to figure out the meanings of difficult words, especially the key vocabulary words for this lesson: *mumbled, bulging, scribbled, gobs,* and *distorted.* Have students circle the words in the text. Although the footnotes define these words, students will want to continue practicing searching for clues as they are reading. Remind them that this is faster and easier than checking a footnote or a dictionary definition. For additional practice with these words, see page 228.

STRATEGY LESSON: WORD FAMILIES The word *scribble* and many other words all come from the Latin word *scribere,* "to write." Common English spellings derived from scribere are *–scrib–* and *–script–.* Ask students to suggest some other words that come from this root, and then assign the **Vocabulary** blackline master on page 228.

Prereading Strategies

Webs give students the chance to explore abstract words or concepts that are important to a selection. (The web on page 182 asks students to consider the word *friendship.* Other words that relate to this selection and might work just as well for this activity include *loneliness* and *new kid.*) Creating a web can help make an abstraction or a concept more concrete. In a word web, writers list phrases, situations, experiences, and emotions that they associate with the word or words in the center. The items they write on their webs can come from what they've read or seen or from their own ideas and experiences. When they've finished, students will have created their own definitions. They'll understand what the word or concept means to them, which in turn will help them understand how the concept is treated in the situation at hand.

Spanish-speaking Students

Bradley Chalkers es un abusador joven sin amigos. Nadie en su clase de la escuela quiere sentarse cerca de el porque tiene una personalidad muy fea. Cuando un estudiante nuevo, Jeff, se sienta al lado de Bradley, los otros estudiantes están compasivos. Jeff intenta ser el amigo de Bradley, pero aprende rápidamente que Bradley no quiere ser el suyo.

READ

At this point, students should be more than familiar with the **react and connect** strategy. If students need reminding, however, tell them to write their personal reactions to the events and characters the author describes and try to connect the plot or characters of the story to their own lives. Questions that they should ask themselves include: "Has this ever happened to me before?" "Who does this remind me of?" and "How would I react if faced with the same situation?"

Response Strategy

MARK   As an alternate response strategy, ask students to mark or highlight important information about Bradley. Sachar doesn't tell readers everything they need to know about his characters. Instead, readers should make reasonable inferences based on the evidence provided. Each time students make an inference about Bradley, they should note it in the margin. They'll use these inferences later, when it is time to analyze Sachar's story.

Comprehension Strategies

As they read, students are to stop ocasionally in order to **retell** events described. Each time they come to a **stop and retell**, they should write one or two sentences that summarize events up to that point.

For more help, see the **Comprehension** blackline master on page 229.

Discussion Questions

COMPREHENSION   1. What is Mrs. Ebbel's attitude toward Bradley? *(She's clearly disgusted with him.)*

2. How does she treat the new student, Jeff Fishkin? *(She acts interested in him and is reluctant to seat him near Bradley.)*

CRITICAL THINKING   3. What do the kids dislike about Bradley? *(Sachar doesn't say, although he seems disruptive and not someone you would necessarily want to sit next to.)*

4. What, if anything, do you think is wrong with Bradley? *(Answers will vary. Students may guess that he's a bully, or terribly lonely, or a combination of the two. Remind them to support what they say with evidence from the selection.)*

5. In what ways is this a story about finding your identity? *(Answers will vary. Ask students to connect the theme of the unit to Sachar's story. Help students see that Bradley seems confused about how to treat Jeff. He doesn't know whether he wants to be a friend or an enemy.)*

Literary Skill

THEME   One literary term you might introduce with "Bradley Chalkers" is *theme*. Remind the class that theme is the main idea or underlying meaning of a piece. It is what the author wants the reader to remember most about the selection. Some stories contain one theme. Others contain several. Finding one's identity, looking for friendship, experiencing loneliness, or facing hostility are all possible themes of this excerpt.

III. GATHER YOUR THOUGHTS

The prewriting activities on page 187 are designed to show students how to form an opinion and then **support that opinion** with evidence. Before they begin, remind the class of one important point: When writing a **persuasive paragraph** or point-of-view paper, the writer uses his or her own thoughts and ideas to create the opinion statement but supports that opinion with proven facts and details. The strongest, most convincing opinions are supported with evidence from books, magazines, newspapers, or Internet articles—including the selection "Bradley Chalkers"; expert testimony (from someone who knows about the topic); personal experience (I saw this once . . .).

Prewriting Strategies

OPINION STATEMENT At the bottom of page 187, students are asked to write an opinion statement for their paragraphs. Your students may need some help. If this is the case, explain that an opinion statement is similar to a topic sentence. Writers often use this formula when writing an opinion statement:

(A specific topic) + (a specific opinion about that topic) = a good opinion statement.

(Jeff Fishkin) + (should ignore Bradley) = I think Jeff Fishkin should start ignoring Bradley.

For additional practice, have students use the **Prewriting** blackline master on page 230.

IV. WRITE

Read aloud the directions on page 188. Remind the class that a **persuasive paragraph** is one that presents information to support or prove a point. It expresses an opinion and tries to convince the reader that the opinion is correct or valid.

WRITING RUBRIC Use this rubric when you are ready to evaluate students' writing.

In their persuasive paragraphs, do students

- open with a clearly worded opinion statement?
- provide adequate facts and details to support the opinion in the body of the paragraph?
- stay focused on the topic of Jeff and Bradley throughout?

Grammar, Usage, and Mechanics

When students are ready to proofread for grammatical and mechanical errors, refer them to the **Writers' Checklist** and consider teaching a quick lesson on contractions. Review the rules for creating a contraction and then have students edit the following sentence for errors:

Im so sad that theyve said they dont want to stay.

V. WRAP-UP

Take a moment at the end of the lesson for students to think about the **meaning** of Sachar's selection and the theme of the unit. Have them begin by reading and responding to the **Readers' Checklist**.

Assessment

To test students' comprehension, use the **Assessment** blackline master on page 231.

Name _____

VOCABULARY

Words from the Selection

When you come to a difficult word, be sure to look at surrounding words and phrases. You might be able to pick up hints or clues about the word's meaning. This is called using context clues.

DIRECTIONS Read the phrases that follow. Write the word from the box that best fits each description.

> ✦mumbled   ✦bulging   ✦scribbled   ✦gobs   ✦distorted

1. wrote in a messy way _____

2. twisted out of shape _____

3. said unclearly _____

4. large amounts of something _____

5. eyes that are big and sticking out _____

Strategy Lesson: Word Families

The word parts –scrib– and –script– both come from a Latin word meaning "to write." The five words in the box all have something to do with writing.

> ✦manuscript   ✦postscript   ✦script   ✦scribbled   ✦inscribed

DIRECTIONS Choose one of the words from the box to fill in each blank below.

6. Each actor read from her or his copy of the _____v_____.

7. The play was about a valuable fifteenth–century _____ that was stolen.

8. It was _____ to a queen.

9. On the last page, someone had written a _____ and signed it B. J.

10. Someone else had _____ some pictures in the margins.

Name _____

COMPREHENSION
Graphic Organizer

DIRECTIONS Use this character map to show what you know about Bradley Chalkers. Then use this information in your opinion paragraph.

HOW HE ACTS	HOW HE FEELS

Bradley Chalkers

HOW HE ACTS	HOW HE FEELS

Name _____

PREWRITING
Writing an Opinion Paragraph

DIRECTIONS Follow these steps to write an opinion paragraph about the topic of friendship.

STEP 1. **WRITE AN OPINION STATEMENT.** Use this formula to help you write your opinion statement:

MY OPINION STATEMENT: Friendship is

STEP 2. **SUPPORT YOUR OPINION.** Now gather support for your opinion. Use one fact or detail from each of these three sources:

- Louis Sachar's "Bradley Chalkers" or another story

- "an expert" (your teacher, a friend, a family member, or anyone else who knows something about the topic)

- personal observations or experiences (I once had a friend who . . .)

support #1	support #2	support #3

STEP 3. **WRITE.** Write your opinion paragraph.

⇒ Open with your opinion statement.

⇒ Then give your support.

⇒ End with a closing sentence that states your opinion statement in a slightly different way.

MY CLOSING SENTENCE: _____

_____

Name _____

ASSESSMENT
Multiple-Choice Test

DIRECTIONS On the blanks provided, write the letter of the item that best answers each question or completes each statement.

_____ 1. Where does Bradley Chalkers sit in Mrs. Ebbel's classroom?
A. He sits in the front row.　　C. He sits in the closet.
B. He sits next to the teacher's desk.　　D. He sits in the back row.

_____ 2. How do Mrs. Ebbel and the rest of the class feel about Bradley?
A. They appear not to like him.　　C. They like him very much.
B. They appear to think he is funny.　　D. none of the above

_____ 3. Who is Jeff Fishkin?
A. He is the class president.　　C. He is the class clown.
B. He is the principal.　　D. He is the new kid.

_____ 4. Where does Jeff originally come from?
A. Philadelphia　　C. Washington, D.C.
B. New York City　　D. Puerto Rico

_____ 5. How does Jeff act when he is in front of the class?
A. He acts silly.　　C. He acts friendly.
B. He acts shy.　　D. He acts mean.

_____ 6. Some of the students advise Jeff not to . . .
A. sit next to Bradley.　　C. turn in homework late.
B. write with a pen in class.　　D. be late for lunch.

_____ 7. What does Bradley do during Mrs. Ebbel's lesson?
A. He takes a lot of notes.　　C. He tries to talk to Jeff.
B. He scribbles all over the place.　　D. He sleeps.

_____ 8. How does Bradley do on his English test?
A. He gets an A.　　C. He gets a C.
B. He gets a B.　　D. He gets an F.

_____ 9. How does Jeff feel about sitting next to Bradley?
A. He is very upset.　　C. He doesn't mind.
B. He is a little annoyed.　　D. He's very happy about it.

_____ 10. Why do you think Bradley doesn't have any friends?
A. He makes rude remarks to others.　　C. He is teacher's pet.
B. He is a phony.　　D. all of the above

Short-Essay Test

Do you think Bradley and Jeff could ever become friends? Why or why not?

Sam Gribley

STUDENT PAGES 190–200

Skills and Strategies Overview

THEME Finding an Identity

READING LEVEL average

VOCABULARY ✧pheasant ✧demure ✧weed ✧meadow ✧hesitate

PREREADING skim

RESPONSE question

COMPREHENSION graphic organizer

PREWRITING using sensory language

WRITING descriptive paragraph / usage problems

ASSESSMENT understanding

BACKGROUND

"Sam Gribley" is an excerpt from Jean Craighead George's award-winning book, *On the Far Side of the Mountain.* In this novel, a boy named Sam Gribley lives in a hollowed-out tree in the Catskill Mountains. His peaceful existence of hunting game, gathering edible plants, and befriending critters of the mountains is rudely interrupted by a visit from a conservation officer who demands that Sam's peregrine falcon, Frightful, be turned over immediately.

Before they begin reading, students might benefit from some background information on peregrine falcons. Peregrines are usually 15 to 20 inches long, with most females being substantially larger than males. Adult peregrines have blue-gray backs and whitish underbellies. During the mid-twentieth century, the U.S. peregrine population was severely compromised by chemical pesticides such as DDT. These pesticides caused peregrines and many other birds to lay thin-shelled eggs that broke easily. At one point, the peregrine nearly became extinct in North America.

Thanks to a successful captive breeding program and the 1974 North American ban on DDT, peregrine populations have been able to recover. Many now live in urban areas, where they nest on skyscrapers and bridges. In 1999, the peregrine was officially removed from the U.S. Fish and Wildlife Service endangered species list, although it is still against the law to hunt or own a peregrine falcon.

UNIT THEME A boy named Sam Gribley befriends a wild peregrine falcon, whom he calls Frightful.

GRAPHIC ORGANIZER A web such as the one below can help readers keep track of important facts and details.

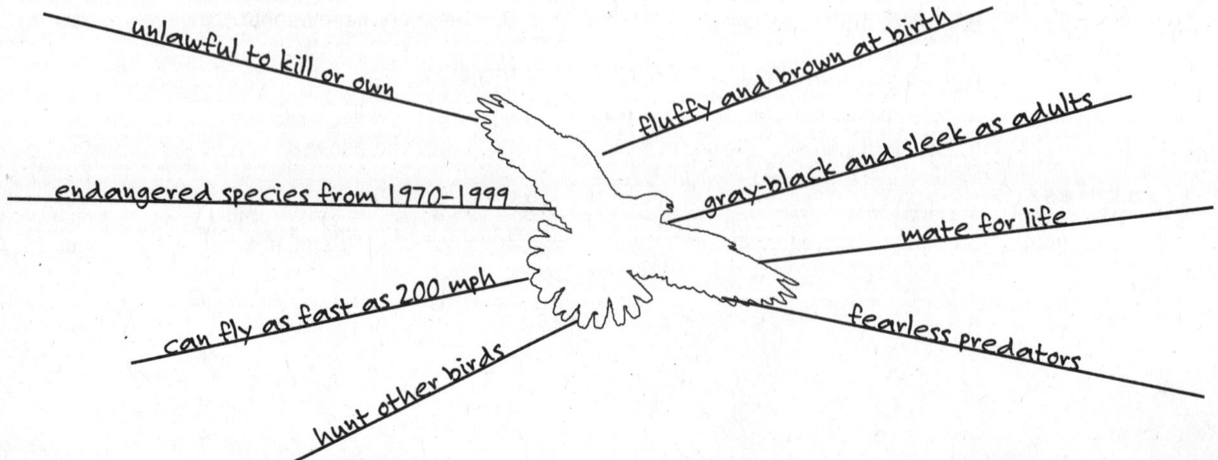

unlawful to kill or own
endangered species from 1970–1999
can fly as fast as 200 mph
hunt other birds
fluffy and brown at birth
gray-black and sleek as adults
mate for life
fearless predators

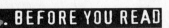

BEFORE YOU READ

Read through the introduction to the lesson with students to help motivate and focus them. Then introduce the prereading activity, a **skim**. (Refer to the **Strategy Handbook** on page 40 for more help.)

Motivation Strategy

Invite one or more students to visit the official Web site for the U.S. Fish and Wildlife Service at www.fws.gov/. Students can find out and then report on recent additions to or deletions from the endangered species list. Ask them to do a search using the keyword *peregrine* so that can tell about recent news regarding this beautiful bird.

ENGAGING STUDENTS Ask students to discuss a time they or a friend tried to tame a wild creature and keep it as a pet. What happened? Were they able to keep their new pet or did they have to let it go? Help students recall a time they had some of the same feelings Sam Gribley has for Frightful.

Vocabulary Building

Draw attention to the key vocabulary words for this lesson: *pheasant, demure, weed, meadow,* and *hesitate.* Have students circle the words in the text, and have them use the words in sentences of their own. A series of quick vocabulary exercises can help students become more comfortable with any words that are new to them. For more practice work, have students complete the **Vocabulary** blackline master on page 236.

STRATEGY LESSON: CONTEXT CLUES Have students pay particular attention to unfamiliar words as they read. Before they check the footnote definitions, however, students should try to define the words in context. They can search surrounding words and sentences for clues about meaning.

For additional practice on this strategy, see the **Vocabulary** blackline master on page 236.

Prereading Strategies

Skimming introduces readers to the selection topic and at the same time alerts them to any problems they might have (such as challenging vocabulary or complex questions) during their close readings. When they skim, students should look quickly at the first sentence of every paragraph. They should pay particular attention to key words and phrases and watch for repeated or unfamiliar words. Be sure students understand that skimming is a strategy that they can use in most of their classes. It can be an invaluable strategy to use with textbooks for subjects such as history and science. Ask the class to keep in mind the questions on page 190 as they skim. They should also watch for ideas that relate to the theme of "Sam Gribley."

Spanish-speaking Students

Sam Gribley es una joven que ha adoptado un falcón como un animal domesticado. Le fascina el falcón y lo cuida atentamente. Sam frecuentemente tiene pesadillas de perder el falcón pero siempre está allí al despertarse en la mañana. Una mañana, sin embargo, un hombre que está encargado de proteger a los especies en peligro quita el falcón de Sam. Sobre todo, está prohibido cuidar a un animal así.

II. READ

Response Strategy

Ask a volunteer to read aloud the short set of directions at the top of page 191. Be sure students understand that any **question** they want to ask about the selection should be considered valid, no matter how trivial it might seem. Point out the example given. The reader asks a question about a relatively insignificant point, but it's something he or she is curious about. Sometimes these little questions can lead to big, important questions about meaning.

Comprehension Strategies

Without a doubt **graphic organizers** can keep students organized and on task as they read. For this selection, students will complete five different organizers that can help them think about and remember the essential elements of the reading: setting, character, conflict, and resolution. Remind them to consider each organizer carefully and jot down as many notes as they like in the boxes. When you conduct an after-reading discussion, students can use their notes from the organizers to help them with their responses.

RECIPROCAL READING As an alternate strategy, have students do a reciprocal reading of the narrative. This will help those who are struggling with the language or themes of the piece. First assign reading partners. Then have students take turns reading aloud, switching every page or so. As they read, students should work together to 1. clarify the problem, characters, and setting; 2. predict outcomes; 3. summarize events; and 4. raise questions about the literature. Have them make notes about anything they and their reading partner can't figure out.

For more help, see the **Comprehension** blackline master on page 237.

Discussion Questions

COMPREHENSION 1. Who is Frightful? *(Sam Gribley's peregrine falcon)*

2. Where does this selection take place? *(in a mountain wilderness near a forest)*

3. What message does the conservation officer have for Sam? *(The officer must confiscate Frightful, since it is illegal for Sam to keep a peregrine falcon.)*

CRITICAL THINKING 4. What are some of the things Sam likes or admires about Frightful? *(Answers will vary. Possible: He admires his freedom and loves the fact that the bird is so devoted. Remind students to support what they say with evidence from the selection.)*

5. How do you think Sam reacts to the news that Frightful will have to be confiscated? Support your answer. *(Ask students to read the final few lines of page 196 before answering this question. Then have them use other parts of the story as support.)*

Literary Skill

SENSORY LANGUAGE To introduce a literary skill with this selection, you might teach a short lesson on imagery, or sensory language. Remind the class that sensory language appeals to the five senses. Notice how heightened Sam's senses are as he plays with Falcon in the clearing. He hears the snap of sticks, smells the musky scent warning from a weasel, and sees how Frightful's feathers are flattened. For practice with this skill, ask the class to skim this scene again. Have them circle words and phrases that appeal to the five senses. Then discuss the effect this imagery has on the text as a whole. Students might suggest that the imagery builds excitement and suspense.

GATHER YOUR THOUGHTS

Prewriting Strategies

One of the goals of the prewriting activities on pages 197–198 is to help students see how **sensory language** can bring vibrancy and add interest to writing.

As a first activity, students will sort a bank of descriptive words into three categories: sight, smell, and touch. Next students will **brainstorm** a list of sensory words that they could use to describe an animal that is special to them.

On page 198, they will write sentences describing their special creature, after choosing five sensory words from their word banks on the previous page. When it is time to write their descriptive paragraphs, students can lift words directly from the chart on page 198.

Have students use the **Prewriting** blackline master on page 238.

IV. WRITE

Read aloud the directions on page 199 to be sure that students understand the assignment. Remind them that their **descriptive paragraphs** should begin with a topic sentence that tells the topic of the paragraph and their thoughts and feelings about the topic. Tell the class that in a descriptive paragraph, the writer might describe something by sharing details of an experience. The best paragraphs pull readers into the story and keep them wondering what will happen next.

WRITING RUBRIC   Use this writing rubric for help with a quick assessment of students' writing.

Do students' paragraphs

- begin with a topic sentence?

- use specific, sensory details that help pull readers into the writing?

- stay focused on just one topic or experience?

Grammar, Usage, and Mechanics

When they are ready to proofread their work, refer students to the **Writers' Checklist.** At this point, you might want to teach a brief lesson on using *good, well, bad,* and *badly.* Remind the class that an adjective such as *good* or *bad* describes or modifies a noun or pronoun. An adverb such as *well* or *badly* modifies a verb, an adjective, or another adverb. Since students often have trouble deciding when to use *good* and *well* and when to use *bad* and *badly,* you might have them practice by correcting these sentences.

Sam felt ~~well~~ good about his decision. He wanted to keep Frightful very ~~bad~~ badly.

V. WRAP-UP

Take a moment at the end of the lesson for students to think about whether they **understood** the reading. Have them begin by reading and responding to the **Readers' Checklist.** Its intent is to help students ask the questions good readers ask of themselves.

Assessment

To test students' comprehension, use the **Assessment** blackline master on page 239.

Name _____

VOCABULARY
Words from the Selection

DIRECTIONS To build vocabulary, answer these questions about five words from the selection.

1. Is a <u>pheasant</u> a large bird or a small rodent? _____

2. If you are <u>demure</u>, are you wild or shy? _____

3. If you <u>weed</u> your garden, are you pulling out or putting in plants?

_____

4. Is a <u>meadow</u> a high hill or a grassy area? _____

5. If your cat <u>hesitates</u> before going out, is she leaving right away or delaying?

_____

Strategy Lesson: Context Clues

DIRECTIONS Use context clues to figure out the meaning of the underlined words. Write your best guess about what you think each word means on the line.

6. Sam <u>hollowed</u> out the old tree to make plenty of room to put his backpack.

hollowed probably means _____

_____

7. I searched under the trees to find some <u>kindling</u> to help us start a fire.

kindling probably means _____

_____

8. Sam was accused of <u>harboring</u> a wild animal instead of letting it go free.

harboring probably means _____

_____

9. The peregrine falcon was an <u>endangered</u> bird. There weren't many of its kind left.

endangered probably means _____

_____

10. I would be very upset to see the officer <u>confiscate</u> the bird. I know Sam would miss her if she were taken away.

confiscate probably means _____

_____

Name _____

COMPREHENSION
Graphic Organizer

DIRECTIONS An important part of reading is making a connection between yourself and the characters or people the author describes. Use this Venn diagram to compare and contrast yourself to Sam Gribley. Check the text if you can't remember specific details about Sam.

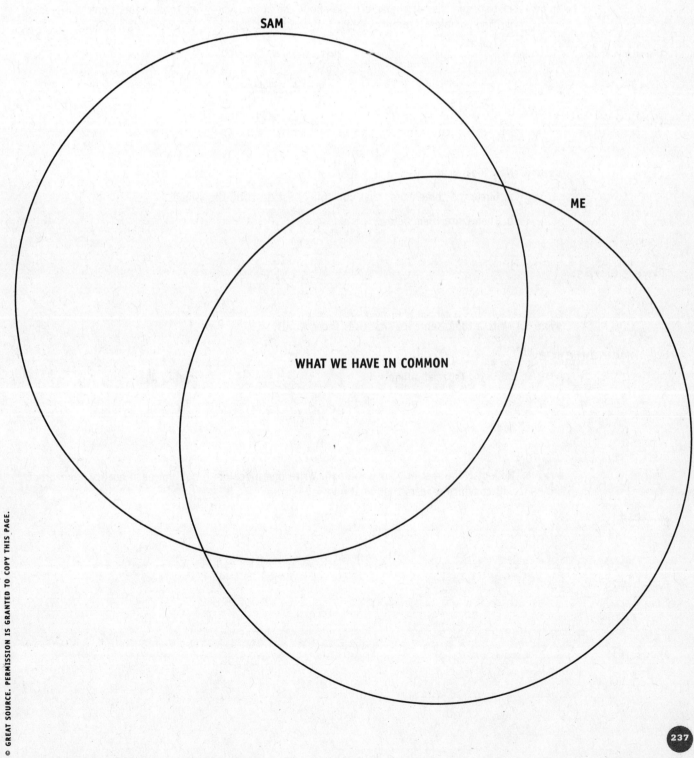

SAM

ME

WHAT WE HAVE IN COMMON

Name _____

PREWRITING

Writing a Descriptive Paragraph

The first sentence of a paragraph should set the stage for what you want to tell readers. The first sentence is your topic sentence.

DIRECTIONS Follow these steps to write a topic sentence and supporting details for your descriptive paragraph.

STEP 1. List six qualities or characteristics about the animal you want to describe. Don't worry about writing complete sentences—just list words that you think describe this creature.

quality #1: _____   quality #2: _____

quality #3 : _____   quality #4: _____

quality #5 : _____   quality #6: _____

STEP 2. Now look at your list.

a. Circle the three words that you think best describe the animal.

b. Then write them below.

Three words: _____   _____   _____

STEP 3. Write a topic sentence that uses these words.

My topic sentence: _____ is _____ ,

(special animal)   quality #1

_____ , and _____ .

quality #2   quality #3

STEP 4. Now plan the rest of your paragraph. Write one piece of "proof" for each quality. Your proof will convince readers that what you say is true.

proof #1: _____

_____

proof #2: _____

_____

proof #3: _____

_____

Name _____

ASSESSMENT
Multiple-Choice Test

DIRECTIONS On the blanks provided, write the letter of the item that best answers each question or completes each statement.

_____ 1. What kind of creature is Frightful?
   A. a black bear
   B. a little mouse
   C. a weasel
   D. a falcon

_____ 2. What happens after Sam kicks up a rabbit or pheasant?
   A. Frightful swoops down and catches it.
   B. Sam catches it and gives it to Frightful.
   C. The rabbit runs away.
   D. Sam gets frightened.

_____ 3. Frightful communicates with Sam by . . .
   A. making screeching sounds.
   B. shaking her feathers.
   C. flattening her feathers.
   D. all of the above

_____ 4. What does Sam have nightmares about?
   A. He worries that she will drown.
   B. He worries that Frightful will leave.
   C. He worries that she will starve.
   D. all of the above

_____ 5. What event makes Sam think Frightful might leave him?
   A. when she disappears for two days
   B. when she joins a male
   C. when she eats his meal
   D. none of the above

_____ 6. What is the setting of this story?
   A. a dark cave
   B. an ocean beach
   C. a hot dessert
   D. a mountain forest

_____ 7. How does Sam know danger is coming?
   A. Frightful lets him know.
   B. He hears gun shots.
   C. The sun goes away.
   D. He smells burning leaves.

_____ 8. What does Leon Longbridge do for a living?
   A. He is a veterinarian.
   B. He is a firefighter.
   C. He is a conservation officer.
   D. He is a school principal.

_____ 9. What is Longbridge's message to Sam?
   A. Sam has to go back to school.
   B. Leon has to take Frightful away.
   C. There is a fire nearby.
   D. Alice is missing.

_____ 10. How does Sam react to Longbridge's message?
   A. Sam thinks it is a good idea.
   B. Sam is confused.
   C. Sam is shocked.
   D. none of the above

Short-Essay Test

Do you think Sam will turn Frightful over to Mr. Longbridge? Explain your answer.

Native Americans

Unit Background   NATIVE AMERICANS (pages 201–222)

An excerpt from Luther Standing Bear's autobiography *My Indian Boyhood* and an excerpt from Sara H. Banks's novel *Remember My Name* are included in this unit.

Ota k'te, or Plenty Kill, (1868?–1939) was sent by his father to the Carlisle Indian School in Carlisle, Pennsylvania, in 1879, where he was given the name Luther Standing Bear. In 1884 he moved back to the Rosebud Reservation and worked as an assistant at the school there. He later worked at the Pine Ridge Reservation. In 1902 he auditioned for and received a part in Buffalo Bill's Wild West Show. He left the show during the second season and worked at various occupations until 1912, when he moved to California and found work as a movie actor in silent and sound films, all Westerns. He wrote four books: *My People, the Sioux* (1928), *My Indian Boyhood* (1931), *Land of the Spotted Eagle* (1933), and *Stories of the Sioux* (1934). He was a strong advocate and speaker for Indian rights.

Sara H. Banks was born in Tuscaloosa, Alabama, in 1940 and raised in Savannah, Georgia, which inspired her interest in the Cherokees. She has written several books for young readers, including *Willowcat and the Chimney Sweep* (1980), *The Way Was Through Woods: The Story of Tomo-Chi-Chi* (1993), *Under the Shadow of Wings* (1997) and *Abraham's Battle: A Novel of Gettysburg* (1999).

Teaching the Introduction

The photos on page 201 show two Native-American women and a child from an early period, a buffalo, and a group of present-day Native-American children

Native Americans

The first white people came to the land we now call America about 500 years ago. Native Americans had already been living here for more than 15,000 years. They had established tribes and ways of life. How much do we really know about the history, culture, and beliefs of Native Americans?

201

1. Tell students that the first excerpt is from the autobiography of Luther Standing Bear, whose Indian name was Ota k'te or Plenty Kill, a Lakota Sioux born in the 1860s. His people depended on the buffalo or bison for food as well as for hides, and a boy's first buffalo hunt was an important event.

2. There is some information on the Cherokee Nation with the lesson plan for "The Sunflower Room." However, you may want to explain that in 1830, The Removal Act forced all Indian nations out of their territories east of the Mississippi River into Western Indian Territory, now Oklahoma. The result was the Cherokee journey that became known as the Trail of Tears.

Opening Activity

In the teacher's guide to her anthology, *Native American Literature,* Lawana Trout presents an exercise to help students detect bias about Native Americans and suggests having students ask ten people at random, "What do you think of when I say 'Indian'? 'Native American'?" Students can then compare surveys, create an "image profile," and determine what the profile says about Native Americans and the people who answered the survey questions.

Alternatively, ask students to recall what they have learned about Native Americans from reading and hearing about them during study of this *Sourcebook.*

Buffalo Hunt

Skills and Strategies Overview

THEME	Native Americans
READING LEVEL	average

VOCABULARY

◇clutched   ◇distinguish   ◇companions   ◇anxious   ◇game

PREREADING	K-W-L
RESPONSE	mark or highlight
COMPREHENSION	directed reading
PREWRITING	storyboard
WRITING	personal narrative / comma splices
ASSESSMENT	depth

BACKGROUND

"Buffalo Hunt" is an excerpt from Luther Standing Bear's autobiography, *My Indian Boyhood*. In this selection, he describes his first buffalo hunt and his pride that he has finally become a man.

The Sioux Indians are an important confederacy of seven Native-American tribes that speak the Siouan language and have lived for hundreds and hundreds of years in the Great Plains area of the United States. The Sioux usually call themselves Lakota or Dakota, meaning "allies." For generations, the basic social unit of the Sioux was the *tiyospe*, or *tiospaye*, an extended family group that traveled together in search of game. The Sioux were considered gifted hunters and ferocious warriors.

Today, approximately 100,000 Sioux live on reservations in Minnesota, North Dakota, South Dakota, Montana, and Nebraska. They retain their language, and much of their culture remains intact. The Sioux are very active in the modern Native-American civil rights movement. Their chief reason for participation is to fight for the return of land that was once theirs. In 1979, the Sioux were awarded reparations of $105 million for injustices that date back hundreds of years.

UNIT THEME Luther Standing Bear, a Sioux Indian, describes one of the proudest moments of his life.

GRAPHIC ORGANIZER A word bank can help writers who can't think of a word or who tend to use the same words over and over again. This is a word bank students might draw from if asked to write about "Buffalo Hunt."

WORD BANK

prancing	running	arrows	herd
Ho-ka-he!	horsemen	fear	exhilaration
	game	wound	

BEFORE YOU READ

Ask a volunteer to read aloud the opening of the lesson (page 202). The purpose of these opening paragraphs is to briefly introduce the skill students will use to make the reading process easier and more meaningful. When you feel students are ready, assign the prereading activity, a **K-W-L**. (Refer to the **Strategy Handbook** on page 40 for more help.)

Motivation Strategy

Ask students to retell a Native-American story they've read or describe a movie or television show they have seen about Native Americans. Have them explain which parts have stayed with them most and why. Allow the class to work together to set the mood for the reading.

ENGAGING STUDENTS Invite students to tell about a time they were able to prove to others that they were capable of doing an adult's job. Later, they can compare their own experiences to the experience Luther Standing Bear describes in "Buffalo Hunt."

Vocabulary Building

Draw attention to the key vocabulary words for this lesson: *clutched, distinguish, companions, anxious,* and *game.* Students should add some new words to their vocabulary each time they read. For additional practice, see the **Vocabulary** blackline master on page 246.

STRATEGY LESSON: HOMOPHONES A homophone is a word that has the same pronunciation as another word but a different spelling and meaning. For example, *pray* and *prey* are homophones. Tell students that the meaning of such words is usually made clear by context, but that their spelling could possibly cause trouble. Sometimes it is helpful to visualize homophones in phrases that give a clue to their meaning: *I pray that I won't be the hunter's choice of prey.*

For additional practice on this strategy, see the **Vocabulary** blackline master on page 246.

Prereading Strategies

The purpose of a **K-W-L** is to activate prior knowledge and allow students to take responsibility for their own learning gaps. In the K column, students will make notes about buffalo and how they were hunted. (Encourage them also to say what they know about the Sioux.) Students should reserve the W column for what they want to learn, or where they will go to do a little research. Later, they will chart what they learned about the topic in the L column. A K-W-L can show students that ultimately they are responsible for their own learning.

SKIM As an alternate prereading strategy, ask students to skim "Buffalo Hunt." (You might tell them to skim for an answer to these questions: "Who is the narrator of the selection?" and "What does he tell about?") Have students make notes about words, phrases, or ideas that pop out at them. Also have them look carefully at the footnoted material and the interrupter questions. A quick skim will make the article seem familiar territory when it comes time for a close reading. This is a particularly valuable strategy to use with longer selections.

Spanish-speaking Students

En esta selección Luther Standing Bear describe su primera caza de búfalo. Para los Indios norte americanos, la caza de búfalo era imprescindible para la supervivencia. Pero era peligroso perseguir a búfalo. Cazadores tenían que ser valientes y talentosos. Standing Bear estaba muy deseoso mostrar al resto del tribu que poseía estas calidades.

READ

Before they begin reading, remind students to **mark** or **highlight** important facts and details that help them answer these questions from the K-W-L chart. Have them make a note of details about place; emotions, ideas, or feelings; and words or phrases that offer information about tone.

If students need to reread the excerpt, have them use a different colored pen to write their second set of notes. This will help them see that doing an additional reading can strengthen their understanding of the author's message.

Response Strategy

REACT AND CONNECT   As an alternate response strategy, ask students to write their reactions and connections to Luther Standing Bear's memoir in the **Response Notes**. Students should note connections between what the narrator describes and an important "growing-up" experience that they themselves had. These kinds of notes can forge a strong connection between reader and text, which in turn can help improve the reader's comprehension.

Comprehension Strategies

You may find that one of the best comprehension strategies to use with nonfiction is a **directed reading**. The reason for this is simple. Many students are intimidated by nonfiction. They worry that it will be too hard or that they will miss important details that they may be tested on later. A directed reading allows you to closely monitor students' reading progress. In addition, it helps you gauge students' understanding of a text. If you feel students will benefit, have them work as a group to answer the interrupter questions that are scattered throughout the text. Or you might review their work as a class after they've finished.

For more help, see the **Comprehension** blackline master on page 247.

Discussion Questions

COMPREHENSION   1. Who was Luther Standing Bear's father? *(the chief)*

2. Why was this buffalo hunt so special to Luther Standing Bear? *(It was his first.)*

3. Why did Luther Standing Bear become overwhelmed halfway through the hunt? *(He finds himself caught up in the middle of the fleeing herd.)*

CRITICAL THINKING   4. Explain Luther Standing Bear's feelings when he shot the buffalo calf. *(Answers will vary. He was exhilarated and proud but a little disappointed that no one was there to see him do it.)*

5. How did Luther Standing Bear change as a result of the hunt? *(Answers will vary. Possible: He was now a man and was eligible to hunt with the other men of the tribe. He was no longer the nervous boy who sat with his father at the campfire listening to some last-minute instructions.)*

Literary Skill

CLIMAX   To introduce a literary skill with this lesson, explain that the most intense part or the turning point of a narrative is called the *climax*. Have students skim "Buffalo Hunt" again. Where does the climax occur? (Most students will suggest that the climax occurs when Luther Standing Bear finally kills the buffalo calf.)

III. GATHER YOUR THOUGHTS

Use the prewriting activities on page 210 to help students plan a **personal narrative** about a time they succeeded at something they had not done before. As a first activity, students will think of a topic for their writing and then plan details on a **web**.

Next, students will fill out a **storyboard** that shows the beginning, middle, and end of the event. (Students should use chronological order to tell about this experience.) Since there are only three cells on the storyboard, students will have to decide beforehand which details are most important.

Prewriting Strategies

TOPIC SENTENCE If you feel students need an additional prewriting strategy, you might have them write the topic sentence for their paragraphs. Remind the class that their topic sentences should name the event or experience to be described and at the same time say how the event or experience helped them prove themselves.

For additional practice, assign the **Prewriting** blackline master on page 248.

IV. WRITE

The directions at the top of page 211 ask students to write a **personal narrative**. Remind the class to use sensory language in their writing.

WRITING RUBRIC Do students' narrative paragraphs

- tell about a time they proved themselves?
- show a clear progression—a beginning, a middle, and an end?
- include adequate details describing the event or experience?
- contain sensory language?

Grammar, Usage, and Mechanics

When they are ready to proofread their work, refer students to the **Writers' Checklist.** At this point, you might want to teach a brief lesson on comma splices. Explain that a comma is not strong enough to join two simple sentences (independent clauses). To fix a comma splice, the writer either adds a conjunction and a comma, inserts a semicolon, or divides the two clauses into two separate sentences. For example:

Incorrect: The buffalo hunt was scary it was fun too.

Correct: The buffalo hunt was scary, but it was fun too.

Correct: The buffalo hunt was scary. It was fun too.

V. WRAP-UP

Take a moment at the end of the lesson for students to reflect on the **depth** of their understanding using the **Readers' Checklist.** Help them express what this autobiographical article made them think about or reminded them of in their own lives.

Assessment

To test students' comprehension, use the **Assessment** blackline master on page 249.

Name _____

VOCABULARY

Words from the Selection

DIRECTIONS Substitute a synonym from the word box for the underlined word or words.

◇clutched ◇distinguish ◇companions ◇anxious ◇game

1. The guide told us where we could see the wild animals. _____

2. I wasn't able to identify the object in the distance. _____

3. I asked Papa to make the horses go faster because I was uneasy about getting to town.
_____

4. I went to town in a wagon filled with my friends. _____

5. When I noticed the horse was going too fast, I held tightly to the reins and
pulled._____

Strategy Lesson: Homophones

DIRECTIONS A **homophone** is a word that has the same pronunciation as another word but a different spelling and meaning. For example, *ate* and *eight* are homophones. Choose the word in parentheses that correctly completes each sentence, and write it on the blank.

6. The buffalo gathered on the (plain / plane) to eat grass during the day.
_____

7. The hawk spied its (pray / prey) on the field and got ready to attack.
_____

8. We (road / rode) all the way to town on our horses. _____

9. The tribe followed the trail of the buffalo for a (week / weak) before they spotted them.
_____

10. Luther Standing Bear was afraid when he was in the middle of the (heard / herd).
_____

Name _____

COMPREHENSION
Retell

Directions Retell what happened on Luther Standing Bear's buffalo hunt.

1. Use your own words, not the author's words.

2. Be sure to include all important details.

Beginning _____

_____

_____

_____

_____

Middle _____

_____

_____

_____

_____

_____

End _____

_____

_____

_____

_____

Name _____

PREWRITING

DIRECTIONS Use this story frame to tell about a time you proved yourself.

The incident took place _____

_____ (where)

_____

_____ (when) _____

_____

_____ was there when it happened.

_____ was also there.

_____ (who)

I was _____

_____

_____ while the incident was taking place.

_____ (what)

The main problem was _____

_____

_____

Another problem was _____

_____

_____

The problems were solved when _____

_____

_____

When the whole thing was over, I felt _____

_____

_____

Name _____

ASSESSMENT
Multiple-Choice Test

DIRECTIONS On the blanks provided, write the letter of the item that best answers each question or completes each statement.

_____ 1. Luther Standing Bear was . . .
- A. bitter.
- B. determined and independent.
- C. lazy.
- D. none of the above

_____ 2. What did the hunters use as weapons?
- A. bows and arrows
- B. horses
- C. guns
- D. A. and C.

_____ 3. Why does Luther Standing Bear feel the horses are anxious for the hunt?
- A. Their tails were waving in the air.
- B. Their ears were straight up.
- C. They were prancing about.
- D. all of the above

_____ 4. What do "pack animals" do?
- A. They chase after the buffalo.
- B. They carry extra weapons and blankets.
- C. They carry the women.
- D. none of the above

_____ 5. What position did Luther Standing Bear's father hold?
- A. He was a scout.
- B. He was a planter.
- C. He was the chief.
- D. He was a doctor.

_____ 6. What did it mean when one of the leaders shouted "Ho-ka-he"?
- A. "Run for your life!"
- B. "Stop what you are doing now!"
- C. "Ready, go!"
- D. "Leave that buffalo for me!"

_____ 7. How did Luther Standing Bear feel when he was in the middle of the buffalo herd?
- A. scared
- B. tired
- C. confused
- D. sick

_____ 8. What kind of buffalo did Luther Standing Bear decide to hunt?
- A. an old buffalo
- B. a sick buffalo
- C. a young calf
- D. none of the above

_____ 9. How many arrows did it take for Luther Standing Bear to get his buffalo?
- A. one
- B. five
- C. twenty
- D. He didn't get the buffalo.

_____ 10. Why was Luther Standing Bear disappointed at the end of the hunt?
- A. He wasn't able to get a buffalo.
- B. No one saw him get a buffalo.
- C. It rained too much.
- D. He got hurt in the raid.

Short-Essay Test

Explain how Luther Standing Bear's feelings changed from the beginning of the hunt to the end.

LESSON 22

The Sunflower Room

STUDENT PAGES 213–222

Skills and Strategies Overview

THEME Native Americans

READING LEVEL easy

VOCABULARY ✧glossy ✧gripped ✧features ✧faint ✧broad

PREREADING picture walk

RESPONSE clarify

COMPREHENSION reciprocal reading

PREWRITING narrow the topic

WRITING reflective paragraph / subject-verb agreement

ASSESSMENT meaning

BACKGROUND

Sara H. Banks's novel *Remember My Name* is the story of Annie Rising Fawn Stuart, a young Cherokee girl who lives in Georgia in 1838 and is forced to undertake a dangerous journey to escape the brutal Indian Removal of 1838 (also known as the Trail of Tears).

In "The Sunflower Room," an excerpt from Banks's novel, Annie prepares to go to live with her uncle, a rich plantation owner in Georgia. Later, Annie and a young slave girl make a pact to help each other during the forced Indian removal.

To offer context for the time period, explain a little about the Indian Removal of 1838 to students. For centuries, the Cherokee people lived and farmed successfully in the southeastern United States. In 1827, they established themselves as the Cherokee Nation and ratified their own constitution. Shortly thereafter, gold was discovered on their land, and the government forced the tribe to move West to land in what is now Oklahoma. The Cherokee exodus was led by Chief John Ross, who watched helplessly as thousands of his people died along the way. For this reason, the Cherokee people call this journey the Trail of Tears.

UNIT THEME A young Cherokee girl is forced to take a new name and leave her home for the "white world" in Georgia.

GRAPHIC ORGANIZER A circular story map can help students see the structure of a plot that begins and ends in the same place.

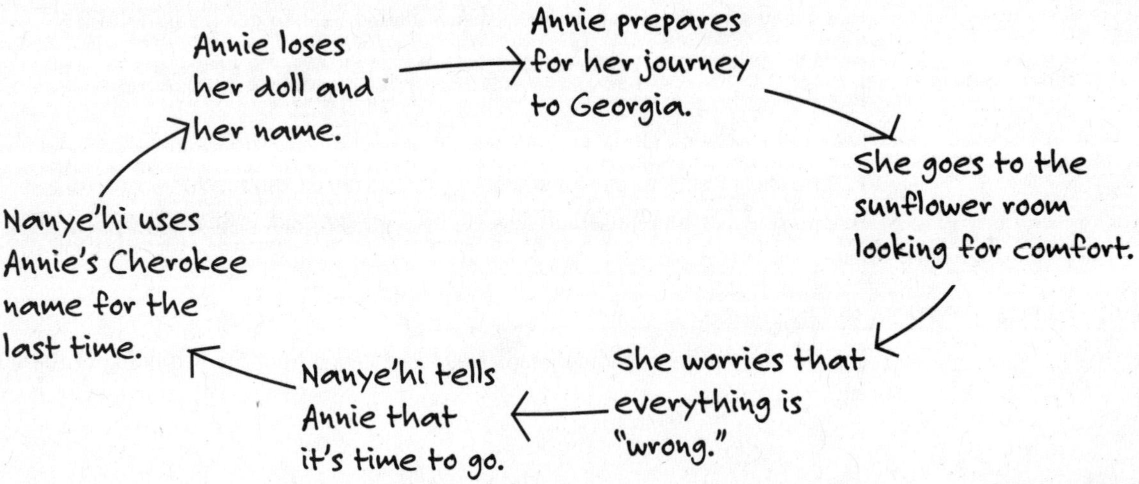

Annie loses her doll and her name.
Annie prepares for her journey to Georgia.
She goes to the sunflower room looking for comfort.
She worries that everything is "wrong."
Nanye'hi tells Annie that it's time to go.
Nanye'hi uses Annie's Cherokee name for the last time.

BEFORE YOU READ

Remind students of the theme of the unit (Native Americans) and read the introduction to "The Sunflower Room." Then assign the **picture walk**. (Refer to the **Strategy Handbook** on page 40 for more help.)

Motivation Strategy

Have students discuss the importance of family first or middle names and names that have been passed down through generations. Explain that in the past, slave owners or his or her government officials would simply rename an immigrant or Native American if their name was "too hard" to pronounce. A quick discussion on the topic of names will be a warm-up to one of the themes of Banks's story.

Vocabulary Building

Help students use **context clues** as they read to figure out the meanings of difficult words, especially the key vocabulary for this lesson: *glossy, gripped, features, faint,* and *broad.* Model using context and then checking your ideas against the footnote. For additional practice with these words, see page 254.

STRATEGY LESSON: SUFFIXES Word games can improve students' vocabulary and make them feel more confident about their language skills. Show how easy it is to attach suffixes to words. Give students a group of common suffixes such as *–ous* and *–ness*. Have them think of words that use the suffixes. Make a list on the board of the words and then ask for volunteers to define each one. You might incorporate these words from the selection: *blackness* and *fierceness.*

For additional practice on this strategy, see the **Vocabulary** blackline master on page 254.

Prereading Strategies

For their prereading activity, students will do a **picture walk** of "The Sunflower Room." Have them tell you which pictures capture their attention and why. What do the pictures reveal about the topic (Native Americans) and mood (one of sadness?) of the selection? Have them pay particular attention to the photo of the little girl on page 215. How does this picture make them feel? Also be sure that students read the captions for the art. What questions do they have about the captions? Students can make notes about the art and their predictions on page 213.

READ-ALOUD As an alternate or additional prereading strategy, work with students on a read-aloud of the first few paragraphs of the story. A read-aloud can help those who are reluctant to begin and pique the interest of those who don't "feel like reading." Ask a volunteer to read aloud page 214 (the last paragraph carries over to page 215). Then have students answer these questions: Who are the character(s)? Where does the story take place? What do you think it will be about? What do you predict a major conflict will be?

A read-aloud and brief discussion beforehand can make the selection seem familiar when it comes time for students to read on their own.

Spanish-speaking Students

"La sala de girasoles" viene de la novela *Remember My Name*, escrito por Sara H. Banks. En esta selección, una chica Cherokee se despide de su pasado y prepara para el futuro. Ha llevado toda su vida viviendo con su abuela, y ahora tiene que abandonar todo lo que conoce para vivir con su tío. Antes de irse, entierra una muñeca especial y su nombre Cherokee en su sitio favorito.

READ

Students work in pairs on this reading. One student can read aloud while the other takes notes. The note-taker should be sure to make notes that **clarify** the characters, action, and conflict of the reading. Have students switch readers at the bottom of every page.

Response Strategy

PREDICT As an additional response strategy, have students make predictions as they are reading. Each time they switch readers, they should stop and make a quick prediction about Annie and the action of the story. Have them note their predictions in the **Response Notes**. Making predictions can help keep readers engaged and encourage them to keep reading until the end.

Comprehension Strategies

In a **reciprocal reading**, readers share the process of reading and responding to a text. This simple strategy can make the reading process easier and more enjoyable for students. If you like, divide the class up into small groups, and ask the groups to read the selection cooperatively. Each time students come to an interrupter question, they should first note their own answer in the book and then discuss what they've written with the rest of the group. (This technique will also work well with pairs.) Remind the class that it is not important to reach consensus on an answer. Part of the fun of interpreting and discussing a story is listening to other people's ideas about the same character, event, theme, and so on.

For more help, see the **Comprehension** blackline master on page 255.

Discussion Questions

COMPREHENSION 1. What is the setting of "The Sunflower Room"? *(September of 1838. The story takes place on Star Mountain.)*

2. Who is Nanye'hi, and what is her relationship to Annie? *(She is Annie's grandmother.)*

3. Why is Annie leaving Star Mountain? *(Banks doesn't say exactly, although she implies that Annie will go to Georgia in order to be educated.)*

4. How does Annie feel about leaving? *(Answers will vary. Point out to students that Annie experiences several different emotions, from fear to distrust to a type of calm acceptance.)*

CRITICAL THINKING 5. Explain the significance of Annie burying her doll in the sunflower room. *(Answers will vary. Help students see that this action shows that Annie is in some ways resigned to what is about to happen to her. She is going to leave her doll—and her childhood—behind, in order to venture out into the "white" world with her new name.)*

Literary Skill

FLASHBACK "The Sunflower Room" provides an excellent opportunity to review the characteristics of— and purpose for—a flashback. Explain that a *flashback* is an interruption in the narrative to show an episode that happened before the interrupted point in the story. Writers use flashbacks, to shed light on the story they are telling. Banks's flashback, which begins on page 217, helps explain why the sunflower room is so important to her. The reader understands that it is a place that reminds her of her life before her parents died. As such, it is a "safe" place that Annie does not want to leave behind.

III. GATHER YOUR THOUGHTS

Prewriting Strategies

The prewriting activities on page 220 are intended to prepare students to write a **reflective paragraph** about one of these four topics: My Family; School Days; Growing Up; or Friends. To begin, students will think carefully about the topic that appeals to them most. Then they'll **narrow the focus of their topic** so that their writing is as specific and meaningful as possible. Point out the example on the left side of the page and have students use this as a model for their work.

Next students will reflect on their chosen topic. To help, they'll answer four questions that will encourage them to decide how the topic makes them feel.

Have students use the **Prewriting** blackline master on page 256.

IV. WRITE

Set aside plenty of time for students to write their **reflective paragraphs.** Remind the class that reflective writing is writing that examines or comments upon some part of the writer's experience. This type of writing is a form of "self-study" in which the writer ponders different aspects of life to better understand what they mean and why they might be important. Reflective writing often begins with a question, such as: How is this friend important to me? How did this experience make me feel more grown up? In what ways did this experience change my feelings about school?

WRITING RUBRIC Use the writing rubric to help students focus on the assignment requirements and for assistance with a quick assessment of their writing.

Do students' reflective paragraphs

- begin with a topic sentence that names the topic and how the writer feels about it?

- contain details that help illuminate the feelings expressed in the topic sentence?

- end with a concluding sentence that restates the topic sentence and ties up any loose ends?

Grammar, Usage, and Mechanics

When they are ready to proofread their work, refer students to the **Writers' Checklist.** At this point, you might want to introduce a mini-lesson on subject-verb agreement. Remind the class that the subject and verb of a sentence have to work together, or "agree." A singular subject needs a singular verb. A plural subject needs a plural verb. For example:

Incorrect: My grandmother and grandfather loves me and wants me to be successful.

Correct: My grandmother and grandfather love me and want me to be successful.

V. WRAP-UP

Take a moment at the end of the lesson for students to explain what "The Sunflower Room" **meant** to them personally. Have them use the **Readers' Checklist** as a starting point for discussion. Explain that it is important to stop and think about what a reading made you think about. Good readers do this automatically whenever they finish a selection.

Assessment

To test students' comprehension, use the **Assessment** blackline master on page 257.

Name _____

VOCABULARY

Words from the Selection

DIRECTIONS Write the word from the box that best replaces the underlined word or words in each sentence.

◇ glossy   ◇ gripped   ◇ features   ◇ faint   ◇ broad

1. I am told I have a <u>wide</u> smile. _____

2. People say that <u>parts of my face</u> are similar to my mom's.

   _____

3. She <u>took hold of</u> the rope and pulled. _____

4. I glanced at the <u>shiny</u> leaves. _____

5. My friends in the meadow were <u>hard to see</u> in the distance.

   _____

Strategy Lesson: Suffixes

DIRECTIONS The suffix *-ness* means "state or quality of." Write the word from the box at the right that best completes each sentence.

6. The _____ in the hunter's

   eyes showed he would stop at nothing to catch the

   buffalo.

7. Annie remembers the _____

   that filled her heart when her parents were alive.

8. The neighbors showed many acts of

   _____ as they helped

   Annie get through the tough times.

9. At night, Annie was filled with

   _____ as she thought of

   how things used to be.

10. The _____ of the sky led

    us to believe it was time to go to sleep.

kindness
loneliness
darkness
happiness
fierceness

Name _____

COMPREHENSION
Storyboard

DIRECTIONS Use this storyboard to show the events of "The Sunflower Room."

1. Draw sketches in the four boxes.

2. Write a description of what happens on the lines.

Name _____

PREWRITING
Writing a Reflective Paragraph

DIRECTIONS Follow these steps to write a reflective paragraph about one of these topics:

(circle one)   My Family   School Days   Growing Up   Friends

My narrowed topic (copy from page 220): _____

STEP 1. ASK A QUESTION. Reflective writing almost always begins with a question. (For example: "How did this experience make me feel more grown up?")

My question: _____

STEP 2. ANSWER THE QUESTION. Give three or four different answers to your question.

answer #1: _____

_____

answer #2: _____

_____

answer #3: _____

_____

answer #4: _____

_____

STEP 3. WRITE A TOPIC SENTENCE. Write a topic sentence that tells your narrowed topic and how you feel about it. You can use the answers you listed above for the body of the paragraph.

My topic sentence: _____

Name _____

ASSESSMENT

Multiple-Choice Test

DIRECTIONS On the blanks provided, write the letter of the item that best answers each question or completes each statement.

_____ 1. Annie feels _____ because she knows it's time to leave.
  A. happiness
  B. sadness
  C. enthusiasm
  D. scared

_____ 2. Whom is Annie waiting for?
  A. her parents
  B. her grandmother
  C. her cousin
  D. her uncle

_____ 3. Where does Annie live?
  A. Star Mountain
  B. New Echota
  C. The Cherokee Capital
  D. none of the above

_____ 4. Where are Annie's parents?
  A. They are in New Echota with her uncle.
  B. They are out hunting.
  C. They are dead.
  D. none of the above

_____ 5. Nanye'hi is . . .
  A. Annie's grandmother.
  B. Annie's Cherokee name.
  C. Annie's mother.
  D. Annie's doll.

_____ 6. What creature tells Nanye'hi that Uncle William is coming soon?
  A. a fish
  B. a mockingbird
  C. a coyote
  D. an eagle

_____ 7. Annie's favorite place to be alone is . . .
  A. on top of Star Mountain.
  B. by the shores of Big Lake.
  C. underneath the sunflowers.
  D. in her tipi.

_____ 8. How old is Annie when she discovers her secret place?
  A. two
  B. six
  C. twelve
  D. sixteen

_____ 9. What does Annie take to the sunflower room?
  A. a book
  B. a bird
  C. a letter
  D. a doll

_____ 10. When she buries her doll in the sunflower room, Annie shows she is ready to . . .
  A. leave her name and culture behind.
  B. say good-bye to nature.
  C. buy a new doll.
  D. none of the above

Short-Essay Test

Why is the sunflower room so special to Annie? Use details from the story to support your answer.

Norton Juster

Unit Background   NORTON JUSTER (pages 223–238)

Two excerpts from the first part of Norton Juster's celebrated book *The Phantom Tollbooth* appear in this unit.

Born in 1929 in Brooklyn, New York, Juster has been a successful architect, professor of design, and writer. He has received a Fulbright fellowship, a Ford Foundation grant, and a Guggenheim fellowship during his distinguished career. He became emeritus professor of design at Hampshire College in Amherst, Massachusetts, in 1992. His books for young people include *The Dot and the Line: A Romance in Lower Mathematics* (1963, 2001), *Alberic the Wise* (1965, 1992), *Otter Nonsense* (1982, 1994), and *As: A Surfeit of Similes* (1989).

Teaching the Introduction

The cover of Norton Juster's book, a Jules Feiffer illustration from the book, and a collection of the many objects that might appear in Milo's room are shown on the opening page. Although the dog on the cover does not appear in these excerpts, you might tell students that he is a watchdog (could students have guessed?), that his name is Tock, and that he has a brother named Tick.

1. Ask someone to suggest or find a definition of *phantom (something seen or sensed but having no physical reality)*. What might this definition say about the tollbooth?

2. Ask students to speculate about what a tollbooth might indicate about the plot of this novel. *(The main character will be traveling.)*

3. Tell students that this novel is so popular that if, when they finish reading the two excerpts in the **Sourcebook** they wish to continue reading, they can probably find the book in their school or local library.

Opening Activity

Take a survey of the class, and ask students to rank their three favorite reading topics. Give them these categories (add to the categories if you wish), compile the list, and post it on the bulletin board: sports, mysteries, science fiction, fantasy, animals, historical fiction, nonfiction about ancient civilizations, fiction about people your age.

Milo

STUDENT PAGES 224–230

Skills and Strategies Overview

THEME Norton Juster

READING LEVEL average

VOCABULARY ✧dejectedly ✧seeking ✧dashed ✧grumbled ✧puzzled

PREREADING web

RESPONSE predict

COMPREHENSION double-entry journal

PREWRITING forming an opinion

WRITING paragraph of opinion / adjectives

ASSESSMENT enjoyment

BACKGROUND

"Milo," an excerpt from Norton Juster's beloved classic *The Phantom Tollbooth,* is the story of a boy named Milo who complains "that almost everything is a waste of time." Milo is surprised one day to find that a tollbooth has mysteriously arrived in his bedroom. Having nothing better to do, Milo jumps into his small electric car, drives through the tollbooth, and enters the incredible Kingdom of Wisdom.

Juster uses wit and irony to tell this *Alice in Wonderland*-style adventure. Milo and his chronic complaining are as memorable as Alice's never-ending questions. Over the course of the journey, Milo learns that to be bored is to be boring, and that to be boring is one of the worst things in the world that you can be.

UNIT THEME A bored boy is surprised one day to find a large box, addressed to him, in the middle of his bedroom.

GRAPHIC ORGANIZER The webs students create on page 229 may look something like this:

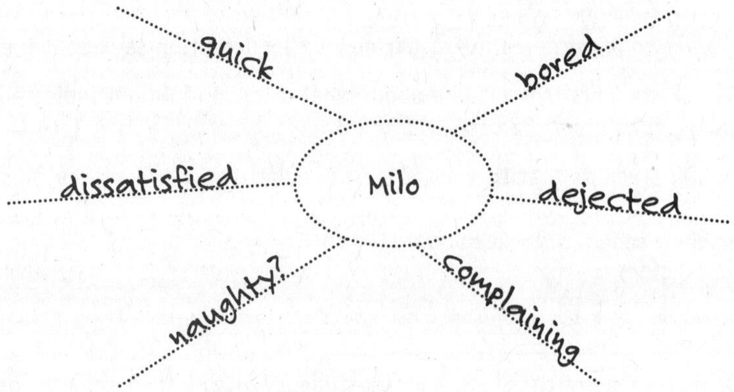
Milo
quick
bored
dissatisfied
dejected
naughty?
complaining

BEFORE YOU READ

Read aloud the introduction to the lesson with students. Offer background information on Norton Juster or *The Phantom Tollbooth* as a way of introducing the selection students are about to read. Then have the class complete the **word web** on page 224. (Refer to the **Strategy Handbook** on page 40 for more help.)

Motivation Strategy

Ask students to say whether they agree or disagree with this statement: "Bored people are boring." Have them explain their answers. What is it like to be with a person who is always complaining that there's nothing to do? Have students ever said this? If so, how did the people around them react?

ENGAGING STUDENTS Ask volunteers to tell what a fantasy is (a work that takes place in an unreal world and often contains supernatural events). Then ask them to tell what movies or books they have seen or read that are fantasies. Borrow a copy of the film version of *The Phantom Tollbooth* (1969), which combines live action with animation, and tell students that you are going to show the first part of it after they read the selections in the *Sourcebook*. Then invite students to view the rest of the film on their own time.

Vocabulary Building

Help students use **context clues** to figure out the meaning of unfamiliar words, especially the key vocabulary for this lesson: *dejectedly, seeking, dashed, grumbled,* and *puzzled.* (Note that *puzzled* is used as a verb in "Milo.") Have students circle these words in the text. Since a few challenging words are not footnoted (for example: *regarded* on page 225 and *enormous* on page 227), you might have students try defining these using context clues. For more practice with context clues, see page 264.

STRATEGY LESSON: Negative Prefixes Tell students that the prefixes *un-, non-, ir-,* and *dis-* are negative prefixes. As such, they can change the meaning of a word. Ask students to build lists of words that contain these prefixes. (Students might suggest: *unhappy, unmotivated, unfair, unnatural, unbutton, nontaxable, nontoxic, nonexistent, nonsense, irregular, irrational, disjointed,* and *dissatisfied.*) For additional practice with negative prefixes, see the **Vocabulary** blackline master on page 264.

Prereading Strategies

The purpose of a **word web** is to help students brainstorm and make a connection to a key concept in the selection, before they begin reading. Word webs can be done independently or as a whole-group activity. Begin the webbing activity on page 224 by having students read the first three paragraphs of "Milo" on page 225. Then ask them to brainstorm words, phrases, or impressions that relate to the word *boredom.* These ideas should come from both the text and students' own lives. Word webs can develop students, conceptual knowledge and help them make connections between what they know already and what they will learn from the reading.

Spanish-speaking Students

"Milo" viene de la novela *The Phantom Tollbooth,* escrito por Norton Juster. Esta selección describe Milo, un chico muy infeliz y pesimista. A él no le gusta estudiar ni jugar con sus compañeros de clase. Le aburre todo y se queja mucho. Está confuso y curioso, sin embargo, al describir un regalo misterioso en su cuarto. Decide abrirlo, por si acaso haya algo interesante adentro.

READ

Before students begin the selection, remind them that they should keep track of the **predictions** they make as they are reading. When they finish, have them make a few more predictions about what they think will happen next. (They may find out by reading the continuation that some of their predictions do in fact come true.) Each time they make a prediction, they should make a note of it in the **Response Notes**.

Response Strategy

QUESTION   As an alternate or additional response strategy, encourage students to list questions as they read. Model this for students, suggesting such questions as: *What kind of kid is Milo? Why is he so bored? What's in the big box?* Use students' questions as the basis for a whole-class discussion after the reading.

Comprehension Strategies

By now, students should be familiar with the process of using a **double-entry journal**. A double-entry journal gives students the chance to record their ideas about parts of a reading that are interesting, puzzling, or thematically important. On the left side of each double-entry journal box there is a quotation from the story. Students should read the quotation carefully and then explain their thoughts and feelings in the right-hand box. You might expand on this activity by having students choose one or two quotations to respond to on their own.

For more help, see the **Comprehension** blackline master on page 265.

Discussion Questions

COMPREHENSION   1. How does Milo feel about school? *(He doesn't see the point of learning and thinks seeking knowledge is a complete waste of time.)*

2. Why does Milo "hurry" when he walks? *(Although he's never anxious to be where he is going, he likes "to get there as quickly as possible.")*

3. What is Milo's reaction when he sees the big box? *(He is curious and excited. He thinks about it for a little bit and then decides to open the box "just to be polite.")*

CRITICAL THINKING   4. What would you say is Milo's biggest problem? *(Answers will vary. Students might say that his problem is that he doesn't know what to do with himself, that he's spoiled, that he has no imagination, and so on. Remind them to support what they say with evidence from the text.)*

5. What is the most important piece of advice that you could give to Milo? *(Ask students to state their advice and then explain their choice.)*

Literary Skill

FORESHADOWING   *Foreshadowing* is the technique of providing the reader with hints or clues about the future action of a story or novel. Ask students what Milo's glum mood might foreshadow about what is going to happen to him. What hints or clues foreshadow what might be in the enormous package?

III. GATHER YOUR THOUGHTS

Prewriting Strategies

The prewriting activities on page 229 will help students think about the character of Milo—the traits and characteristics that make him unique. To begin, students will create a **web** about his character. Encourage them to return to the selection to look for particular words or phrases that describe him. Also remind them that they may want to make their own inferences (reasonable guesses) about his character.

Next students will prepare to write a **paragraph of opinion** about Milo. Using the notes they have made on their webs, students will list four important character traits. (Some of these might be lifted directly from the web.) Then they will write a topic sentence (or opinion statement) that tells how they feel about this character. Remind the class to support their opinions with specific facts and details from the selection. Encourage them to use direct quotations whenever possible.

Have students use the **Prewriting and Writing** blackline master on page 266.

IV. WRITE

The writing assignment on page 266 is to write a **paragraph of opinion** about Milo. They should open their paragraphs with a topic sentence (opinion statement), support that sentence in the body of the paragraph, and finish by writing a concluding sentence.

Students might give their opinion paragraphs to a writing partner for review. Writing partners should check to be sure that the opinion statement is supported with at least three strong facts or details from the text. Use the questions below in the writing rubric to help with a quick assessment of students' work.

WRITING RUBRIC Do students' opinion paragraphs

- begin with a clear opinion statement?

- include three or more facts from the selection that support the opinion statement?

- stay focused on the topic of Milo and what he's like?

Grammar, Usage, and Mechanics

When they are ready to proofread their work, refer students to the **Writers' Checklist.** Inexperienced writers or students who speak English as a second language occasionally have trouble creating the superlative form of adjectives such as *best* and *worst*. For practice, ask students to correct these sentences:

This was the bestest book I've ever read. It's about the mostest bored boy in the world.

V. WRAP-UP

Ask students to reflect on their **enjoyment** of "Milo." (Determining students' comfort level with and enjoyment of the story will be particularly important, since they will read a continuation of the story in the next lesson.) Ask the class to read and answer the questions on the **Readers' Checklist.**

Assessment

To test students' comprehension, use the **Assessment** blackline master on page 267.

Name _____

VOCABULARY

Words from the Selection

DIRECTIONS Choose the word from the box that best completes each sentence.

> ◆dejectedly   ◆seeking   ◆dashed   ◆grumbled   ◆puzzled

1. Milo was _____ something interesting to do.

2. He kicked at a stone _____ because there was nothing going on.

3. Milo _____ into his room and failed to notice the strange box at first.

4. Milo _____ to himself, "I'm sure there isn't anything exciting in this box."

5. He _____ over the writing on the envelope.

Strategy Lesson: Negative Prefixes

DIRECTIONS The prefixes *ir–, non–,* and *dis–* all mean "not." Underline the prefixes in the words below. Then use each word in a sentence of your own.

6. nonsense

_____

7. irresponsible

_____

8. disrespect

_____

9. disloyal

_____

10. nonfiction

_____

Name _____

COMPREHENSION

Reader Response

DIRECTIONS On the lines below, write a brief journal entry about Milo. Choose one of these three phrases as the opening for your entry:

I know the feeling . . . _____

I can't really understand . . . _____

If I were . . . _____

_____

_____

_____

_____

_____

_____

_____

Reader Response

DIRECTIONS Work with a partner or a small group to answer these questions about the story "Milo." Be ready to share your answers with the rest of the class.

What is the tone of Juster's story? _____

_____

_____

Is Milo a likable or unlikable character? Why? _____

_____

_____

_____

Name _____

PREWRITING AND WRITING
Writing an Opinion Paragraph

DIRECTIONS Follow these steps to write an opinion paragraph.

STEP 1. WRITE AN OPINION STATEMENT. An opinion statement is the same as a topic sentence. Use it as the first sentence of your paragraph.

(A specific topic) + (a specific opinion) = a good opinion statement.

("Milo") + (how I feel about him) = your opinion statement.

I think Milo is _____.

WRITING TIP

Opinion statements must be clear and brief. Avoid using strong words such as *all, best, every, never,* or *worst* because they are usually hard to prove, no matter how good your facts are.

STEP 2. SUPPORT YOUR OPINION. An opinion must be supported by facts. Find three facts from "Milo" that support your opinion.

fact #1: _____

_____

fact #2: _____

_____

fact #3: _____

_____

STEP 3. WRITE. Write your opinion paragraph here. Begin with your opinion statement. Then offer your facts. Close with a sentence that ties everything together.

_____

_____

_____

_____

_____

_____

Name _____

ASSESSMENT

Multiple-Choice Test

DIRECTIONS On the blanks provided, write the letter of the item that best answers each question or completes each statement.

_____ 1. What is Milo's main problem?
  A. He can't stop reading books.
  B. Nothing interests him at all.
  C. He loves to be at school.
  D. Everything interests him.

_____ 2. What does Milo think about school?
  A. He sees it as a waste of time.
  B. No one remembers his name.
  C. It's too hard.
  D. He loves it.

_____ 3. What word best describes Milo?
  A. suspicious
  B. angry
  C. happy
  D. bored

_____ 4. Where does Milo live?
  A. on a farm
  B. in an apartment
  C. in a big house
  D. on the streets

_____ 5. What does Milo own that he doesn't play with?
  A. games
  B. an electric automobile
  C. bats and balls
  D. all of the above

_____ 6. What happens when Milo enters his room?
  A. He finds a note from his parents.
  B. He finds a big package.
  C. He notices his puppy is gone.
  D. He sees that all his games are missing.

_____ 7. What does the note say?
  A. "For Milo, who has plenty of time."
  B. "To Milo, open this very carefully."
  C. "From your secret admirer."
  D. "Happy Birthday!"

_____ 8. How does Milo feel about the package?
  A. He is angry and curious.
  B. He is sad and mad.
  C. He is puzzled and excited.
  D. He doesn't care at all.

_____ 9. Milo receives the package because . . .
  A. he has been very good.
  B. it is his birthday.
  C. Christmas is coming soon.
  D. none of the above

_____ 10. What is Norton Juster's purpose in *The Phantom Tollbooth*?
  A. to inform
  B. to entertain
  C. to persuade
  D. all of the above

Short-Essay Test

Whom does Milo remind you of in your own life and why?

Milo, continued

Skills and Strategies Overview

THEME	Norton Juster
READING LEVEL	average
VOCABULARY	◇erected ◇regulations ◇fare ◇concluded ◇wistfully
PREREADING	anticipation guide
RESPONSE	react and connect
COMPREHENSION	predict
PREWRITING	supporting an opinion
WRITING	letter / end punctuation
ASSESSMENT	ease

BACKGROUND

In the second excerpt from *The Phantom Tollbooth*, Milo decides he has no other choice but to open the big box sitting in his bedroom. Inside he finds a tollbooth, directions for assembling it, signs, coins, a map, and a book of rules. Although he is not exactly an enthusiastic child, Milo decides to assemble the tollbooth and choose a destination; he then drives up to the entrance of the tollbooth.

Juster uses word play, imagery, and parallel structure to make his writing style accessible and interesting. Phrases such as "three precautionary signs to be used in a precautionary fashion" add a kind of humor and silliness that matches exactly the humorous and silly events that unfold in the story. If students seem to enjoy Juster's plot and style, encourage them to finish reading *The Phantom Tollbooth* or have them choose another Juster book.

UNIT THEME A young boy can't resist the allure of a mysterious tollbooth.

GRAPHIC ORGANIZER This sequence organizer shows the chain of events that occur in both parts of "Milo."

> Milo walks home from school feeling dejected.

> He scurries into his apartment building and dashes to his bedroom.

> He notices a box that he's never seen before.

> He reads the envelope attached to the box. It says: "For Milo, who has plenty of time."

> He decides to open the envelope. Inside are directions for assembling a tollbooth.

> Milo follows the instructions and builds the tollbooth.

> He examines the map and decides on a destination at random.

> Milo dusts off his car, hops in, and drives slowly up to the tollbooth.

BEFORE YOU READ

Before you begin the lesson, ask a student to remind everyone of what happened the first part of "Milo." How did that selection end? Then introduce the prereading activity, an **anticipation guide**. (Refer to the **Strategy Handbook** on page 40 for more help.)

Motivation Strategy

Borrow a copy of *The Phantom Tollbooth* from your library and give students the chance to look at the whimsical line drawings by illustrator Jules Feiffer. Three of these drawings are reprinted in the *Sourcebook,* and there are many more in the original.

ENGAGING STUDENTS Ask students to tell you where they would choose to go if they were allowed to pick any place they wanted. Have them name the place, explain why they want to go there, and say what they would expect to see.

Vocabulary Building

Draw attention to key vocabulary words for this lesson: *erected, regulations, fare, concluded,* and *wistfully.* Some of these will be familiar to students, although they may be a little uncertain about definitions and pronunciations. Ask students to circle the words in the text. For practice work, turn to the **Vocabulary** blackline master on page 272.

STRATEGY LESSON: PREFIXES Knowing the prefix of a word can help students figure out the word's meaning. Show this list of words from the selection: *precautionary, impractical,* and *refunded.* Offer definitions for the three prefixes, and then ask students to think of other words that use these same prefixes.

pre- = before	*prewar, preview, prepay, predict, precook*
im- = not	*imperfect, impure, impatient, impersonal*
re- = back, again	*return, reclaim, revive, reappear, refold, repaint*

For additional practice on this strategy, see the **Vocabulary** blackline master on page 272.

Prereading Strategies

An **anticipation guide** is an excellent prereading strategy to use when you're asking students to read a continuation of a selection. Most students will be ready and willing to make some interesting predictions. Point out the guide on page 231. After they finish reading the continuation, they can return to their answers and see which were correct. Anticipation guides can heighten interest in a reading as well as activate prior knowledge about a character, plot, or theme.

THINK-PAIR-AND-SHARE As an alternate prereading strategy, ask students to work with a partner to put three sentences from the second part in order. Choose sentences from the text that you think will pique students' interest. Then ask:. "Which sentence comes first? Which comes next? What clues can you find?"

Spanish-speaking Students

En la continuación del cuento, Milo abre el regalo misterioso y descubre una garita de peaje. Las instrucciones indican cómo operarla y a cuáles lugares ajenos se puede visitar. Milo piensa que el regalo es raro, pero decide usar la garita de peaje e ir a un sitio llamado Dictionopolis. Como el pesimista que es, sin embargo, duda que se vaya a divertir.

READ

> Be sure students write their **reactions** to Juster's story in the **Response Notes**. Point out the example given on page 232 and remind students that all readers have these kinds of reactions without even thinking about it. Ask them to make a note each time they catch themselves reacting in some way to the literature.

Response Strategy

VISUALIZE As an alternate or additional response strategy, ask students to make quick sketches of the people and items they visualize. Each time students "see" something new, they should make a note of it in the margin. Many students will enjoy sketching the purple tollbooth. Their sketches may come in handy later, when they are asked to write their response to "Milo."

Comprehension Strategies

At several different points in the story, students will **stop and predict** what they think will happen next. In addition to helping maintain interest, making predictions can forge a connection between text and reader, so that the reader feels more directly involved in the action and outcome. Predictions also encourage readers to make inferential responses to a text. If you like, post an organizer on the board that students can make notes on as they are reading "Milo." Your organizer might be as simple as this chart:

I predict . . .	What really happens . . .
Milo will	
the tollbooth will	
the ending will be	

For more help, see the **Comprehension** blackline master on page 273.

Discussion Questions

COMPREHENSION 1. What is inside the box in Milo's bedroom? *(a tollbooth, three precautionary signs, coins for paying tolls, a map, and a rule book)*

2. How does Milo choose his destination on the map? *(He closes his eyes and points.)*

CRITICAL THINKING 3. Why do you think Milo decides to go ahead and drive through the tollbooth? *(Answers will vary. Have students use the inferences they've made about Milo to help them answer this question.)*

4. What do you think the phrase "lands beyond" means? *(Answers will vary. Encourage students to use prior knowledge to answer this question. Where have they heard this phrase or a phrase that sounds similar? What did it mean in that context?)*

5. What would you do if you found a tollbooth in your bedroom? *(Answers will vary. Help students make a connection between the literature and their own lives.)*

Literary Skill

STYLE *Style* is the way in which a writer uses language to suit his or her ideas. The way in which an author uses words and sentences affects the tone and mood of the writing. Help students think about Juster's writing style. Ask: "What is the tone and mood of 'Milo'? What sensory language can you find?" Have students pay particular attention to the informal feel of Juster's writing. In what ways is the informal phrasing in keeping with the topic of the selection?

Ⅲ. GATHER YOUR THOUGHTS

Prewriting Strategies

The prewriting activities on page 236 are meant to help students gather what they've learned from reading Juster's story and then use that information to develop a **paragraph** that **supports an opinion.** First students will decide how the writing made them feel. Remind them that they'll be required to give three or more reasons for their opinions.

Next students will make notes about the connections they've made to Juster's story. (Remind them to refer to their during-reading notes for ideas.)

Students will finish by stating an opinion of the selection and then choosing three reasons that support that opinion. In their concluding sentence, they are to say whether or not they'd like to read more of Juster's writing.

Have students use the **Prewriting** blackline master on page 274.

Ⅳ. WRITE

The directions on page 237 ask students to write a **letter** to the author. Explain that a key part of their letter will be an explanation of their connections to the reading.

WRITING RUBRIC Use this rubric to help students focus on the assignment requirements and for assistance with a quick assessment of their writing.

Do students' letters

• open with a sentence that states their opinion of Juster's writing?

• contain three or more reasons in support of this opinion?

• include a discussion of the connections they were able to make to the reading?

• end with a statement of whether or not they'd like to read more of Juster's writing?

Grammar, Usage, and Mechanics

When students are ready to revise, have them consult the **Writers' Checklist** for punctuation problems. Remind the class to capitalize the first word in every sentence and to end all sentences with the correct end punctuation. In addition, they should check to be sure that every sentence expresses a complete thought. For practice, ask students to correct capitalization and punctuation problems in this sentence:

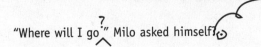

"Where will I go," Milo asked himself.

Ⅴ. WRAP-UP

Ask students to reflect on whether they found Juster's writing **easy** or difficult to read. Have them use the **Readers' Checklist** as a starting point for their comments. Ask students, "What reading strategies could you use to make a story like this one easier to read and understand?"

Assessment

To test students' comprehension, use the **Assessment** blackline master on page 275.

Name _____

VOCABULARY
Words from the Selection

DIRECTIONS To build vocabulary, answer these questions about five words from the selection.

1. If a building was <u>erected</u> in your neighborhood, was it built or destroyed?
_____

2. Are <u>regulations</u> questions or rules? _____

3. If you are asked to pay a <u>fare</u>, do you give money or trade objects?
_____

4. If I <u>concluded</u> we shouldn't have school today because of the snow outside, did I reach a decision or make a promise? _____

5. If you say something <u>wistfully</u>, are you making a wish or complaining in a loud voice?
_____

Strategy Lesson: Prefixes

DIRECTIONS The prefix *im-* means "not" and the prefix *pre-* means "before." Write the word from the list at the right that correctly completes each sentence.

6. Milo saw three _____ signs warning that the tollbooth was coming up soon.

7. Milo felt it was _____ to have a tollbooth without a highway.

8. At times, Milo acts in an _____ manner.

9. A person who doesn't like a group of people without even meeting them may be _____.

10. I thought it was _____ to take a real trip in a toy car, but I was wrong.

impractical
impossible
prejudiced
immature
precautionary

Name _____

COMPREHENSION
Evaluate

DIRECTIONS Use these scales to rate "Milo." Then answer three questions about the literature.

The plot is . . .

1	2	3	4	5	6	7	8	9	10

not at all   sort of   very
interesting   interesting   interesting

The characters are . . .

1	2	3	4	5	6	7	8	9	10

not easy to   somewhat easy   easy to
relate to   to relate to   relate to

The setting is . . .

1	2	3	4	5	6	7	8	9	10

not easy to   sort of easy   easy to
understand   to understand   understand

What is your favorite part of "Milo"? Why? _____

_____

What is your least favorite part? _____

_____

What would you say is the theme (or main idea) of this story? _____

_____

Name _____

PREWRITING
Writing About Literature

....

DIRECTIONS Prepare to write a paragraph about Norton Juster and his story.

STEP 1. First do a one-minute quickwrite about the topic. Write everything you can think of about the author and "Milo."

One-Minute Quickwrite

_____

_____

_____

_____

_____

_____

_____

_____

_____

STEP 2. Now read what you wrote. Highlight words, phrases, and ideas that you think are interesting and would like to use in your letter to the author.

STEP 3. Finish by writing an opinion statement for your letter to Juster. Use this formula:

(A specific statement) + (a specific opinion) = a good opinion statement.

_____

(Juster's writing and "Milo")   +   (how I feel about them)

_____

= my opinion statement.

Name _____

ASSESSMENT

Multiple-Choice Test

DIRECTIONS On the blanks provided, write the letter of the item that best answers each question or completes each statement.

_____ 1. What is in the package that Milo receives?
- A. a radio
- B. a magic bottle
- C. a truck
- D. a tollbooth

_____ 2. What else does the package contain?
- A. three signs
- B. a map
- C. a book
- D. all of the above

_____ 3. What will be refunded if Milo is not "perfectly satisfied" with the package?
- A. his money
- B. his wasted time
- C. his effort
- D. all of the above

_____ 4. This tollbooth is different from any other tollbooth Milo has seen because . . .
- A. it is bigger and striped.
- B. it is invisible.
- C. it is smaller and purple.
- D. it talks to Milo.

_____ 5. What does Milo feel is lacking with the tollbooth?
- A. It is missing a highway.
- B. It is missing signs.
- C. It is missing instructions.
- D. all of the above

_____ 6. What do the precautionary signs say?
- A. "Slow down; approaching tollbooth."
- B. "Please have your fare ready."
- C. "Have your destination in mind."
- D. all of the above

_____ 7. According to Milo, what is wrong with the map?
- A. It is hard to read.
- B. There are places he has never heard of.
- C. You can see through it.
- D. Nothing is wrong.

_____ 8. How does Milo choose where to go?
- A. He closes his eyes and points.
- B. He finds a familiar place.
- C. He decides to go north.
- D. He picks somewhere close.

_____ 9. Where is Milo going?
- A. to Pencilvania
- B. to Schoolville
- C. to Dictionopolis
- D. to New Chalk City

_____ 10. Milo worries that his adventure will be . . .
- A. exciting.
- B. scary.
- C. boring.
- D. entertaining.

Short-Essay Test

What three words would you use to describe Milo? Why?

Answer Key

FATHER

II. Read

(Students' answers will vary.)

What are they doing?
(They are watering the ground and preparing it for a new lawn.)

What big change suddenly occurred?
(Father was hurt at work and died.)

How does the narrator feel about the death of his father?
(He is confused and shocked.)

Sequence Organizer:

1. The narrator and his father are working on the ground, preparing it so they can plant a new lawn.

2. Father and Mother sit and flirt happily together and watch the narrator water the lawn. The narrator is working hard because he wants to please Father.

3. Father is hurt at work and dies two days later.

4. The narrator goes to the hospital and then to the funeral, feeling emotionally numb about his father's death.

5. The narrator is playing marbles with his brother and sister to distract himself from the sadness brought by his father's death.

Vocabulary

1 Students should circle "spotted," the definition for *flecked*.
2 Students might circle "held up" and "pointed to it" as context for *imply*, meaning "suggest."
3 Students should circle "wound the hose in a spiral" as context for *coiled*.
4 Students might circle "wasn't happy" and "but neither" as context for *sorrow*.
5 Students might circle "big smile" and "teeth" as context for *gleamed*, meaning "shone."
6 unfurnished
7 depressed
8 recall
9 uncertain
10 return

Assessment

1	D	6	D
2	D	7	A
3	B	8	B
4	A	9	D
5	C	10	C

MOTHER

I. Before You Read

Vocabulary

(Students' answers will vary.)

What do you think "Mother" is about?
(It is about the way the author's family lived when she grew up, and about the values and beliefs her mother instilled.)

How does the author feel about her mother?
(She respects her for how she raised the family. Despite their being poor, the children have led good, happy lives.)

When and where is this story set?
(It is not clear exactly when and where the story is set. It seems to have been a few decades ago, as now the girl in the story is an adult looking back on her childhood.)

Vocabulary

1 with a husband
2 stiff
3 before
4 too much
5 he gave some to another person
6 job
7 enough
8 angry
9 poor
10 produce

II. Read

Assessment

What does Freddie's mother say about keeping clean?
(She says that one should make sure to keep everything he or she has clean. If things are well maintained, no one will know how few things the family actually possesses.)

How does Freddie feel about her mother?
(She admires her mother because she always put food on the table and taught the children valuable life lessons.)

What is the author trying to express to readers?
(The author is trying to express that money is not the most important part of life. Happiness is based on strong, loving relationships.)

1	D	6	A
2	B	7	C
3	C	8	B
4	B	9	D
5	A	10	C

THE GREAT WHALES

II. Read

(Students' answers will vary.)

Is a whale a fish or a mammal? Explain how you know.
(A whale is a mammal. The selection says that whales, like people, are warm-blooded mammals.)

How does the humpback whale breathe?
(A humpback whale breathes through two blowholes at the top of its head and must surface to inhale fresh oxygen.)

What does a whale use its tail for?
(Whales move their tails up and down to push themselves through the water.)

Vocabulary

1 leaping
2 rise to the top of the water
3 breathe in
4 straight up and down
5 backbone
6 extract
7 subtract
8 tractor
9 attract
10 traction

Assessment

1	B	6	D
2	C	7	B
3	A	8	A
4	C	9	C
5	A	10	D

THE KILLER WHALES

I. Before You Read

(Students' answers will vary.)

This selection is fiction/nonfiction because:
(The selection is nonfiction because it gives facts and information about the killer whale.)

What is the topic of the first paragraph?
(Killer whales can be found all over the world but are most common near land.)

What is the last paragraph about?
(The last paragraph is about the ways that whales can survive deep dives under water without breathing.)

Vocabulary

1 children
2 travel around
3 show it
4 firmly express it
5 annoy them
6 plume
7 exhale
8 poles
9 pod
10 dominance

II. Read

Key term	What is it?	What is it for?
pod	a group of killer whales	hunting and traveling together
clan	groups of related pods	occasional meetings
resident pod	group that stays in a general location	large groups, mainly fish eaters
transient pod	group that travels widely	smaller groups, eat seals and other whales
breaching	leaping out of the water	communicate, knock off parasites, for fun
mammal	animal that breathes air	N/A
spout	misty column of air	condensation formed when whales exhale
blowhole	opening on top of whale's head	breathing

Assessment

1	C	6	C
2	A	7	D
3	D	8	D
4	B	9	D
5	A	10	B

III. Gather Your Thoughts

(Students' answers will vary.)

A. IDENTIFY THE MAIN IDEA
The main idea of "Killer Whales" is (that killer whales are unique and fascinating animals):

B. PLAN A SUMMARY

Main Idea:
(Killer whales are unique and fascinating animals.)

Detail #1: (Killer whales live in groups, called pods, which vary in size and in habits.)

Detail #2: (Killer whales exhibit social behavior and assert their strength and dominance in order to determine the social order.)

Detail #3: (Killer whales breach for many reasons, including communicating and knocking parasites off of their bodies.)

Detail #4: (Killer whales are mammals that breathe air through blowholes on the top of their heads.)

Closing Sentence
(Killer whales have many interesting habits and behaviors and are well adapted to their place in the ecosystem.)

JOSHUA

I. Before You Read

(Students' answers will vary.)

5. "Mr. Muhlen called us all together in the afternoon. He said that it was important to him that the drive be successful."

2. "'Mr. Muhlen wants you to go up north on the trail,' Mama said."

4. "You went up the trail you were a man."

3. "I did not look too excited, because I could see Mama was not too keen on the idea of me going on the trail."

1. "I told him I was Joshua Loper and I was sixteen."

II. Read

(Students' answers will vary.)

What was the time?
(It was April 30, 1871.)

What was the place?
(It is not made clear in the selection, but it seems as if the story is set in Texas.)

Who are the main characters?
(The main characters are Joshua Loper, Mama, the Captain, and Mr. Muhlen.)

What is the problem or challenge in the story?
(The problem is that Mr. Muhlen has asked Joshua to help drive the cattle to Kansas, but Captain doesn't want to take any African Americans on the drive.)

Which character will face this challenge or problem?
(Joshua Loper will face this challenge.)

Story Frame:

1. (Joshua talks about an encounter he had with the Captain and how he didn't see any use for African Americans.)

2. (Mama tells Joshua that Mr. Muhlen wants him to go north on the trail, but she doesn't sound happy about this.)

3. (Mr. Muhlen and Captain argue. Captain says that he doesn't want to take African Americans on the drive. Mr. Muhlen says that Joshua is a good boy.)

4. (Joshua talks to Timmy O'Hara about the drive. Joshua seems excited about the opportunity to participate.)

III. Gather Your Thoughts

(Students' answers will vary.)

A. DESCRIBE A CHARACTER

How he feels:	How he looks:
(nervous, excited, curious, proud, uncertain)	(grinning, proud, determined)

What he says:	How he acts:
(quiet, keeps his feelings to himself, doesn't say much)	(reserved, excited, patient)

B. DEVELOP A TOPIC SENTENCE

Joshua Loper is both (uncertain) and (quiet).

uncertain:

Detail #1:
(He doesn't know what to make of the Captain when he first meets him. Captain asks him his name and age and then walks away.)

Detail #2:
(He doesn't know if he's really going on the cattle drive because he hears Mr. Muhlen and the Captain argue about African Americans participating.)

quiet:

Detail #1:
(He doesn't say much in his conversation with Mr. Muhlen; as he prefers to listen and quietly evaluate others' opinions.)

Detail #2:
(Even though he and Timmy O'Hara are talking about the drive, Joshua doesn't say anything about the Captain not wanting to take African Americans.)

Vocabulary

1 land
2 enthusiastic
3 in a group
4 a group of cattle
5 disagree
6 D
7 A
8 E
9 C
10 F
11 B
12 Sentences will vary.

Assessment

1	B	6	A
2	B	7	C
3	D	8	A
4	C	9	C
5	C	10	B

THE MAN

(For all sections, students' answers will vary.)

Vocabulary

1 shining brightly
2 inside a building
3 giving you permission
4 only part
5 dented
6 E
7 A
8 B
9 G
10 F

Assessment

1	B	6	A
2	A	7	D
3	C	8	D
4	D	9	A
5	D	10	C

WHAT HAPPENED DURING THE ICE STORM

III. Gather Your Thoughts

(Students' answers will vary.)

A. REFLECT

Think about the story. Why do the boys help the pheasants? What prompted their kindness?

The boys feel sorry for the pheasants because they are vulnerable and have no way of sensing the danger and flying away. The boys probably think it is unfair to capture defenseless birds.)

Vocabulary

1 huddled
2 livestock
3 pheasants
4 crouching
5 glazed
6 pounce
7 gelatin
8 glistened
9 harvest
10 pheasants

Assessment

1	A	6	C
2	C	7	D
3	C	8	A
4	B	9	D
5	A	10	B

CHEATING

II. Read

(Students' answers will vary.)

This story takes place (in both a school, where the narrator has cheated on a math test, and in his room, where he is lying on the floor thinking that he's a bad person.) (The narrator, a school-age boy) **is telling the story.**

A problem happens when (cheating on a math test makes him wonder if he is a bad person.)

After the problem develops, what happens next is (the narrator stays in his room all day after school and tells his parents he has a stomachache. He eventually tells his father that he cheated on the test.)

The incident ends when (the narrator calls his teacher and tells him what he has done. The teacher tells him to come in on Saturday for another test.)

What is the author's main idea or message in the story? (The author shows that cheating or doing something that one knows is wrong can inspire guilty feelings. The only way to get rid of those feelings is to be honest and do the right thing.)

Vocabulary

1 decent
2 core
3 clinch
4 absolutely
5 hedge
6 law-abiding person
7 confident
8 hide
9 eager
10 good

Assessment

1	D	6	B
2	A	7	B
3	D	8	A
4	A	9	D
5	C	10	B

EGYPTIAN MUMMIES

I. Before You Read (Students' answers will vary.)

What is the selection about?
(The selection is about the ancient Egyptians and how they treated their dead, especially kings.)

What is the time period?
(The time of the ancient Egyptians, from about 4,500 to about 2,000 years ago.)

II. Read

How long ago did the Egyptians start making mummies?
(The oldest mummies date from before 2,500 B.C., or more than 4,500 years ago.)

Why did the Egyptians bury pottery and jewelry along with their dead?
(They believed in life after death. The pottery and jewelry were for the dead to use in the next life.)

What were tombs and pyramids used for?
(Egyptians believed that the spirits of the dead needed houses. The tombs and pyramids served as such houses.)

Vocabulary

1	b	10	became
2	d	11	did
3	a	12	grew
4	a	13	thought
5	c	14	built
6	had	15	drank
7	was		
8	wrote		
9	found		

III. Gather Your Thoughts

Why were they made?
(The ancient Egyptians believed in life after death. For a spirit to continue to live, however, it needed a body in which to rest on earth. The bodies were preserved so the spirits would recognize them in their transition to the spirit world.)

How were they made?
(They embalmed the bodies, using a substance that prevented rotting. Some of the oldest mummies that were not embalmed were wrapped and buried in the sand, which then dried and prevented decay.)

Egyptian Mummies

When were they made?
(They were made more than 2,000 years ago.)

Assessment

1	B	6	C
2	D	7	C
3	B	8	D
4	D	9	A
5	A	10	B

MUMMIES

II. Read

He was a South American copper miner.

The tunnel in which he was working collapsed and killed him.

He was an Indian, found in a Kentucky cave.

The salts from the cave and the movement of dry air mummified the body.

Copper Man

The mummy formed naturally because of the dry air and salt in the mine.

He was named Copper Man because the copper salts and oxygen in the mine turned his body a dull green.

He was originally called Little Alice until careful examination proved that he was a male.

Little Al

He was mummified about 2,000 years ago.

They lived in the American Southwest between A.D. 100 and 700.

They left various items, such as beads and weapons, with the bodies.

Basket Makers

They placed bodies in caves to preserve them.

They only put some bodies in the caves to become mummies, while other dead people were simply buried in pits.

Vocabulary

1	providing
2	multiply
3	rapid
4	prying
5	trade
6	wheels
7	again
8	circle
9	like (or alike)
10	like

Assessment

1	C	6	B
2	A	7	D
3	A	8	A
4	D	9	C
5	A	10	B

III. Gather Your Thoughts (Students' answers will vary.)

A. ORGANIZE DETAILS
Egyptian Mummies:
(Thought that dead pharaohs turned into kings of the dead; made tombs and pyramids for pharaohs; learned how to embalm bodies very early)
Other Mummies:

(Sometimes many mummies were buried together; often buried and preserved because mines and caves collapsed.)
Both:
(Often formed naturally because their rapid drying prevented bacteria from growing; scientists now test to determine

the age of mummies; sometimes other things, were preserved with the mummies.)
B. WRITE A TOPIC SENTENCE
(Although there are differences between mummies from different cultures and time periods, they are all formed because the bodies dried and because bacteria was not able to penetrate them.)

SUMMER BERRIES

II. Read

1. List details you have learned so far:
Pretty Girl:
1. (Her parents will not say whom they have chosen for her to marry.)
2. (She has cared for Shy-Bear for two summers.)
3. (She is worried she will have to marry an old man.)
4. (Her mother told her she should start sewing a new pair of moccasins suitable for a bride.)

Sweetgrass:
1. (She is excited that Pretty-Girl is getting married.)
2. (She is 15 and wants her parents to announce her marriage.)
3. (She is happy to be in nature, picking berries.)
4. (She thinks that some details of Pretty-Girl's story sound odd.)

2. Add new details you have learned about Pretty-Girl and Sweetgrass.
Pretty-Girl:
(Her mother said she would make her a good, new dress.)
(She seems depressed about the marriage.)
(She has big eyes and beautiful hair.)

Sweetgrass:
(She is very interested in the wedding plans.)
(She thinks that Pretty-Girl is beautiful.)
(She wishes that she looked like Pretty-Girl.)

3. Add any new details you have learned.
Pretty-Girl:

1. (As her family is poor, she thinks that her father will force her to marry an older man in order to get more horses.)
2. (She is scared that her chosen husband will already have other wives and will make her do hard work all day.)
3. (She cries because of her situation.)
4. (She doesn't care about the dress her mother is making, only whom she is going to marry.)

Sweetgrass:
1. (She thinks that Pretty-Girl should talk to her parents about her fears.)
2. (She says that no Blackfoot girl should cry about the happy event of marriage.)
3. (She thinks that Pretty-Girl is lucky because her mother is making her a new wedding dress.)
4. (She wonders what kind of decorations Pretty-Girl's mother will put on the dress.)

Add any new details you have learned.
Pretty-Girl
1. (She says that Shy-Bear will not be able to bring back enough horses from the horse raid to convince her father he is a worthy husband.)
2. (She doesn't believe she will be treated like a new wife.)
3. (She says that her new husband won't give her beautiful things, and that her life is not a story.)
4. (She thinks that Sweetgrass is spoiled.)
Sweetgrass:

Vocabulary
1 daintily
2 shame
3 sorrow
4 sacrificed
5 plucking
6 quality of being happy
7 full of care
8 like thunder
9 condition of being round
10 full of beauty

Assessment
1	A	6	C
2	B	7	A
3	D	8	D
4	B	9	A
5	C	10	D

1. (She tells Pretty-Girl that she's as beautiful as a girl in an old story and that her new husband will treat her well.)
2. (She feels strange because Pretty-Girl is sad.)
3. (Many young children have died in her tipi, and she has only one sibling, a younger brother.)
4. (Her mother died when she was young, and her mother's sister, called Almost-Mother, now takes care of her.)

SUMMER BERRIES continued

II. Read (Students' answers will vary.)

What do Pretty-Girl and Sweetgrass want most out of life?
Pretty-Girl: (She wants to be able to control her own life and to marry the man she wants.)
Sweetgrass: (She wants to marry and have a baby soon.)
What words would you use to describe each of the girls?
Pretty-Girl: (shy, sad, curious, unsure, pretty)
Sweetgrass: (hopeful, comforting, spoiled, confident)
What does each girl want the result of the horse raid to be?
Pretty-Girl: (She wants Shy-Bear, the boy she loves, to have captured enough horses to please her father and allow their marriage.)
Sweetgrass: (She wants Eagle-Sun to return and brighten her days. She also hopes that her younger brother, Otter, is safe and successful on his first horse raid.)

Vocabulary
1 tie it
2 your mind is spinning
3 scared
4 rough
5 spread out
6 spring
7 graceful
8 victory
9 sweetheart
10 reassurances

Assessment
1	C	6	A
2	B	7	D
3	B	8	C
4	D	9	B
5	C	10	D

A BETTER LIFE

I. Before You Read (Students' answers will vary.)

Selection Title: **Author:**
("A Better Life")   (Bill Gutman)

What is Sammy Sosa like?
(He is a talented baseball player. According to this article, he rose to greatness from very humble beginnings in the Dominican Republic.)

What is this selection about?
(The selection is about Sammy Sosa's childhood in the Dominican Republic.)

II. Read (Students' answers will vary.)

What was Sammy's childhood like?
(He was born into a large family who lived in the Dominican Republic. As a young child, he played with other kids in the fields and streets but didn't know anything about baseball.)

Why did Sammy's mother go to work?
(Sammy's father died when he was seven and the family had to support itself without him. Sammy's mother worked in order to earn money so that the family could eat and pay the bills.)

How did Sammy spend his time when he was young?
(He shined shoes, sold oranges, and washed cars to earn money for the family. Like his siblings, he worked every day in order to ensure that the family could survive.)

What happened when Sammy first started playing baseball?
(It was clear that Sammy had a natural talent and feel for the game.)

What did Sammy think when he started playing baseball?
(He knew that there were many major league players from the Dominican Republic who lived very well. He knew that baseball was an opportunity to help his family live better lives.)

Vocabulary

1 doing everything they could
2 about the same size as a one-bedroom apartment
3 build up
4 many troubles
5 messy
6 E
7 A
8 D
9 B
10 C

Assessment

1	B	6	D
2	C	7	A
3	B	8	C
4	B	9	B
5	D	10	A

JACKIE ROBINSON'S FIRST GAME

I. Before You Read (Students' answers may vary:)

What's special about Jackie Robinson?
(He was a great baseball player and the first African-American player to play in the major leagues.)

When and where do the events take place?
(The events take place in the mid-1940s. Jackie's first game is on April 18, 1946. The training camp takes place in two cities in Florida, Jacksonville and Daytona. His first game takes place in Jersey City, New Jersey.)

II. Read

Sequence Organizer:
1. (Baseball season begins in Florida.)
2. (The Florida newspapers make it clear that Jackie is not welcome in the segregated South.)
3. (The Royals' first game in Jacksonville is canceled because whites and blacks are not allowed to compete against each other on city-owned playgrounds.)
4. (The president of the Royals says that either Jackie Robinson will play with the team, or the Royals will not play.)
5. (Jackie struggles to concentrate on baseball. He is nervous about making the team, and as far as baseball playing is concerned, Robinson is just one of the guys.)
6. (Jackie is switched to first base, a position he has never played, for his first game of spring training.)
7. (The exhibition season ends without Jackie proving his ability.)
8. (Thirty-five thousand fans are in Jersey City to watch Jackie play his first game in the major leagues.)
9. (In the third inning, Jackie hits a three-run home run.)
10. (Jackie scores two more runs in the game and demonstrates he is a daring base runner.)

Vocabulary

1 a place to stay
2 focused
3 her first
4 different every time
5 likely to trust you
6 tense
7 tension
8 tendency
9 tendon
10 intend

Assessment

1	B	6	A
2	C	7	C
3	D	8	A
4	A	9	D
5	B	10	A

III. Gather Your Thoughts

A. DESCRIBE

Quality: (focused)
Example: (Though many were upset that Jackie was playing baseball with white people, he still concentrated.)

Quality: (hard working)
Example: (He wanted to perform well in spring training, but ended up trying too hard and hurting his arm.)

Quality: (talented)
Example: (He demonstrated why he was good enough to play in the Majors in his first professional game.)

Quality: (honorable)
Example: (Even though so many people spoke out against him because of his race, he didn't respond to them or get caught in their debates. He simply played baseball and let his actions speak for him.)

B. FORM A TOPIC SENTENCE
The two finest qualities of Jackie Robinson are (his focus) and (his talent.)

THE STRANGERS ARRIVE

III. Gather Your Thoughts

(For all sections, students' answers will vary.)

Vocabulary

1 shimmering
2 combat
3 terror
4 momentous
5 serpents
6 headdress
7 plunged
8 unnatural
9 turquoise
10 reclaim

Assessment

1	D	6	B
2	B	7	A
3	A	8	C
4	D	9	B
5	C	10	A

THE GREAT MOCTEZUMA

I. Before You Read (Students' answers will vary.)

2. "Moctezuma was almost crazy with worry and indecision."
1. "Moctezuma knew that this year was one of the times in the cycle of years that legend said Quetzalcoatl, the Plumed Serpent, might return to earth to rule his people."
4. "After one week in Tenochtitlán, Hernán Cortés took Moctezuma and his family prisoners and made Moctezuma announce to all of the people that Cortés was now in charge."
3. "When the Spanish finally arrived at the crest of the hill above Tenochtitlán in November, they could hardly believe their eyes."
5. "The city and all of its treasures now belonged to the Spanish."

Vocabulary

1 fiction
2 pray
3 stone
4 killed them
5 They were sad.
6 indecision
7 mission
8 omens
9 bribed
10 chaos

II. Read (Students' answers will vary.)

Why does Moctezuma believe that Cortés is Quetzalcoatl?
(The year was one in which Quetzalcoatl was supposed to return to earth and rule his people. The legend said that Quetzalcoatl had white skin and a beard. In addition to being white-skinned and bearded himself, Cortés destroyed temples that disrespected Quetzalcoatl.)

What do you think Cortés wants?
(Some students may guess that he is not going to be a friendly visitor.)

What did Cortés do with the Aztec treasures? Why?
(Cortés either kept the treasures for himself or sent them to Spain. He believed that he was on a mission from God to save the Indians' souls. The gold he acquired was God's reward.)

How did Cortés treat Moctezuma and his people?
(Cortés killed many of the Aztec people, possibly including Moctezuma.)

III. Gather Your Thoughts

A. ORDER EVENTS
1. Moctezuma hears that strangers are making their way toward Tenochtitlán.
2. (Moctezuma believes that these strangers are representatives of Quetzalcoatl, whom he thinks is returning to rule his people.)
3. (Cortés and his party arrive at Tenochtitlán and are amazed by the beautiful city.)
4. (Moctezuma welcomes Cortés and his party to Tenochtitlán with a celebration and gives them many valuable gifts. He soon realizes that the men are not representatives of Quetzalcoatl.)
5. (After one week, Cortés forces Moctezuma to relinquish power to the Spaniards.)
6. (Cortés takes gold jewelry and treasures, melts them, and then sends them to Spain.)
7. (Spanish soldiers kill many unarmed Aztecs on a holy day. In the chaos that follows, Moctezuma is killed.)

Assessment

1	C	6	C
2	B	7	A
3	D	8	C
4	C	9	C
5	D	10	B

I AM MIGUEL

II. Read (Students' answers will vary.)

What's the setting?
(The setting is on a farm by the Rio Pueblo.)

Who are the main characters?
(The main characters are Pedro and Miguel.)

What did you learn about Pedro and Miguel from the story about the trout?
(Some students may think that the story is a lesson about the value of patience and persistence, and that unlike Miguel, Pedro is impatient.)

What problem or conflict do you think Miguel faces?
(Miguel faces the problem of finding his identity and being content in life. He is envious of Pedro, who is so easily pleased. Miguel is much more worried and introspective.)

Vocabulary

1–5 Paragraphs will vary.
6 satisfied
7 near
8 say "no"
9 underground pipe for waste
10 air in motion

Assessment

1	B	6	D
2	C	7	C
3	A	8	D
4	B	9	B
5	A	10	A

SANGRE DE CRISTO MOUNTAINS

I. Read (Students' answers will vary.)

Why is Miguel so eager to be a helper?
(Miguel is eager to help because he wants to contribute to his family, be responsible, and prove to others that he can make the journey to the mountains.)

What does Miguel want his father to notice?
(He wants his father to notice that he is helping out a lot and is, in fact, ready to help with the lambs in the mountains.)

What does Miguel want people to understand?
(He wants to be recognized as both an adult and as a hard worker. He feels his father will respect him more when he sees his motivation and drive to succeed.)

Vocabulary

1 flat on top
2 a group of animals
3 go get it
4 female
5 a sturdy bag
6 campesino
7 siesta
8 sombrero
9 fiesta
10 aficionado

Assessment

1	A	6	C
2	C	7	B
3	D	8	C
4	A	9	A
5	B	10	D

BRADLEY CHALKERS

II. Read (Students' answers will vary.)

What have you learned about Bradley so far?
(He sits alone and feels separate from the rest of the class. He wishes he could hide even more.)

What do Bradley's classmates think of him?
(Nobody wants to be near him.)

What have you learned about Bradley?
(Bradley is unpopular and reacts smugly to people's insults. He doesn't do well in school, spending his time scribbling on paper. He repels potential friends.)

Vocabulary

1 scribbled
2 distorted
3 mumbled
4 gobs
5 bulging
6 script
7 manuscript
8 inscribed
9 postscript
10 scribbled

Assessment

1	D	6	A
2	A	7	B
3	D	8	D
4	C	9	C
5	B	10	A

SAM GRIBLEY

I. Before You Read

(Students' answers will vary.)

Who's Frightful?
(A peregrine falcon)

What's this story about?
(A boy named Sam and his pet falcon)

How would you describe her?
(He is a young boy who loves animals.)

II. Read (Students' answers will vary.)

What have you learned about the two characters? (Students' answers will vary.)
Sam: He cares about his pet. He even invents his own language to talk to her.
Frightful: Even though she is a wild bird that can kill a lot of animals, she is kind to Sam. He likes to work with her to catch things.)

What 2 things have happened in the story so far?
1. Sam watches Frightful hunt.
2. Sam does his chores.

What are 2 things you have learned about Sam Gribley?
1. He feels very comfortable with animals, as if they are human.
2. He knows a lot of things about the outdoors, such as how to hear footsteps from far away.

Who has arrived? What do you think will happen?
1. Some kind of man in a uniform, maybe a ranger.
2 (Students' answers will vary.)

What problem does Sam face? How do you think Sam will solve it?
1. The conservation officer wants to take Frightful away.
2. (Students' answers will vary.)

Vocabulary

1 a large bird
2 shy
3 pulling out
4 a grassy area
5 delaying
6 cleared out to leave a hole
7 wood used to start a fire
8 sheltering
9 threatened; nearly extinct
10 take away

Assessment

1	D	6	D
2	A	7	A
3	D	8	C
4	B	9	B
5	B	10	C

III. Gather Your Thoughts (Students' answers will vary.)

A. ANALYZE SENSORY WORDS

Appearance	Behavior	Traits
tawny	wild	endangered
gorgeous	tense	musky
white	flesh-ripping	flattened
soft	demure	high-pitched
heavy	high [flying]	hot
cozy		

BUFFALO HUNT

II. Read (Students' answers will vary.)

What scene or setting has Standing Bear described?
(He has described how the men of his tribe ride their horses out to the buffalo herd before a hunt.)

How does Standing Bear feel as the hunt begins?
(At first, he likes the feeling of riding toward the herd with the adults. When he enters a cloud of dust, however, he gets scared because he cannot see anything.)

Why does Standing Bear feel less afraid now?
(He can start to see and hear things other than the buffalo again, and he realizes that he is safe.)

Why do you think Standing Bear makes a point to say "I was on the plain alone"?
(Although Standing Bear accomplishes his goal, he now has a new problem. He is so far away from everyone else that no one has seen his triumph. Also, he has no idea where his father is.)

Vocabulary
1 game
2 distinguish
3 anxious
4 companions
5 clutched
6 plain
7 prey
8 rode
9 week
10 herd

Assessment
1	B	6	C
2	D	7	A
3	D	8	C
4	B	9	B
5	C	10	B

THE SUNFLOWER ROOM

II. Read
(Students' answers will vary.)

Why is Annie unhappy about leaving?
(She misses her parents and worries that her uncle may have changed since she saw him last. She is happy living with her grandmother.)

How would you describe Annie's secret place?
(It is similar to a private room with sunflowers growing in a square. They are taller than she is, so they give her shade from the sun.)

What does it mean that Annie buried her doll and her name?
(She feels that since she is leaving her home and grandmother and starting a new life. She feels that by putting those things behind her it will be easier to leave.)

Go back over the story. Retell the main events in the boxes below.

1. Annie sits on the cabin steps waiting for her uncle to arrive. → 2. Annie remembers her parents and misses them. → 3. Annie's grandmother tells her to get ready and uses her Cherokee name.

4. Annie returns to her private place. → 5. She buries her doll in the ground and decides to "bury" her name too. → 6. She decides that everything is going to be different when she leaves.

Vocabulary
1 broad
2 features
3 gripped
4 glossy
5 faint
6 fierceness
7 happiness
8 kindness
9 loneliness
10 darkness

Assessment
1	B	6	B
2	D	7	C
3	A	8	B
4	C	9	D
5	A	10	A

MILO

II. Read (Students' answers will vary.)

Read this quote from the story. Then write how it makes you feel:
"And worst of all...there's nothing for me to do, nowhere I'd care to go, and hardly anything worth seeing."
(Milo is bored and needs to notice the fun things in the world to be happy.)

Read this quote from the story. Then write your thoughts about it:
"He looked glumly at all the things he owned."
(Milo is not grateful for his things.)

Read and respond to the quote below:
"Most probably I won't like it anyway, but since I don't know where it came from, I can't possibly send it back."
(Milo may be saying something bad about the package to hide his curiosity and hope that he will like what is inside.)

Vocabulary

1 seeking
2 dejectedly
3 dashed
4 grumbled
5 puzzled
6–10 Sentences will vary.

III. Gather Your Thoughts

A. UNDERSTAND A CHARACTER

unsatisfied, unhappy, bored, shallow, Milo, cynical, pessimistic

B. DESCRIBE AN OPINION

1. **Milo is like** a hermit because he keeps to himself.
2. **He is also like** a robot because he does not appreciate things or feel their value.
3. **Milo is not like** the other kids in his class.
4. **Milo is also not like** laid-back people who find happiness easily.

Assessment

1 B 6 B
2 A 7 A
3 D 8 C
4 B 9 D
5 D 10 B

MILO continued

II. Read

What do you think Milo will do with the tollbooth?
(Students' answers may vary.)

What will Milo do with his map and tollbooth?
(Students' answers may vary.)

What do you think will happen to Milo in Dictionopolis?
(Students' answers will vary.)

Vocabulary

1 built
2 rules
3 give money
4 reach a decision
5 making a wish
6 precautionary
7 impractical
8 immature
9 prejudiced
10 impossible

III. Gather Your Thoughts

(All answers will vary)

Assessment

1 D 6 D
2 D 7 B
3 B 8 A
4 C 9 C
5 A 10 C

Index

PE signals a pupil's edition page number.
TG signals a pupil's edition page number.

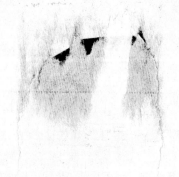